Comments on High ... *from readers*

'...readable and comprehensive ... pressure...'

Dr Sylvia McLauchlan MB, ChB, MSc, FFPHM
Director General, The Stroke Association

'it is very readable, I think pitched at just the right level'

Professor Godfrey Fowler,
Emeritus Professor of General Practice, University of Oxford

'I have thoroughly enjoyed reading this book, it has covered all the questions that I and most people especially those with high blood pressure would like to ask.'

Evelyn Thomas SRN, Glyncorrwg

'This book answers the questions you always wanted to ask about high blood pressure, plus many you haven't even thought of.'

Gwen Hall RMN, RGN, BSc, Hindhead

'...a clear and comprehensive review of hypertension, its causes, clinical picture and treatment. A must for the bookshelf of all those interested in, or suffering from, high blood pressure.'

H. Rees, Killay

'I have always been health conscious and a believer in taking control of my own health. When I was told by my GP that I had high blood pressure, I wanted to find out everything I could about it before starting any treatment. This book has not disappointed me – it has answered all my questions, and I now feel more confident about arranging a suitable treatment plan with my GP.'

Andrea Bagg, Tunbridge Wells

'As someone who has had high blood pressure for 29 years I still found this book enlightening and was impressed by the fact that I felt because of the way the author had written the book that it was really speaking to me, and as a result I didn't find it wearisome reading like some information books.'

Babs Walters, Port Talbot

'The language is pitched at just the right level so that the reader feels he has been taken into partnership with the doctor in understanding his condition.'

Dr A G Donald, Edinburgh

'This is a really excellent book and a very valuable addition to the series.'
Professor Paul Wallace, Royal Free Hospital School of Medicine

'Exactly the right style for dealing with the sort of problems that patients regularly have. It is not only educational but extremely enjoyable.'
Professor John Swales, Professor of Medicine, University of Leicester

Reviews of **High blood pressure at your fingertips**

'This well written book is capable of informing health professionals ... The question and answer format of the book gives comprehensive coverage.' *Adrienne Willcox, Practice Nurse*

'Dr Julian Tudor Hart has produced an excellent book ... with a comprehensive question and answer format which will solve any query.'
Dr Donald McKendrick, Saga Magazine

High blood pressure at your fingertips

THE COMPREHENSIVE AND MEDICALLY ACCURATE MANUAL ON HOW TO MANAGE YOUR HIGH BLOOD PRESSURE

SECOND EDITION

Julian Tudor Hart MB, BChir, DCH, FRCP, FRCGP
Honorary Research Fellow at Welsh Institute for Health and Social Care, University of Glamorgan, Pontypridd

assisted by
Tom Fahey MSc, MD, MFPHM, MRCGP
Senior Lecturer in General Practice, University of Bristol; General Practitioner at Bradgate Surgery, Bristol

with a chapter on high blood pressure in pregnancy by
Wendy Savage FRCOG
Senior Lecturer and Honorary Consultant in Obstetrics and Gynaecology, London Hospital Medical College and Royal Hospitals Trust; Visiting Professor, Middlesex University

HEALTH HARMONY

> **NOTE FROM THE PUBLISHERS**
> Any information given in this book is not intended to be taken as a replacement for medical advice. Any person with a condition requiring medical attention should consult a qualified practitioner or therapist.

High blood pressure at your fingertips

FIRST INDIAN EDITION, 2000

Reprint edition 2002

Reprinted by Special Arrangement with Class Publishing, Barb House, Barb Mews, London to sell within Indian sub-continent
© Copyright Julian Tudor Hart 1996

All rights are reserved. No part of this publication may be reproduced, stored in a retrieval system or transmitted, in any form or by any means, mechanical, photocopying, recording or otherwise, without prior written permission of the publishers.

Price: Rs. 150.00

Printed & Published by

KULDEEP JAIN

for

HEALTH 🌿 HARMONY
an imprint of
B. Jain Publishers (P) Ltd.
1921, Chuna Mandi, St. 10th Paharganj,
New Delhi-110 055
Ph: 7770430, 7770572, 7536418,
Fax: 011-3610471 & 7536420
Website: www.bjainindia.com, Email: bjain@vsnl.com

Printed in India by:
Unisons Techno Financial Consultants (P) Ltd.
522, FIE, Patpar Ganj, Delhi- 110 092.

ISBN : 81-7021-957-4
BOOK CODE : BH 5428

Contents

Acknowledgements viii
Foreword by Dr Ian Baird ix
About this book x

INTRODUCTION
What you most need to know in nine pages   1

CHAPTER 1 *Blood pressure and high blood pressure*
About blood pressure in general   10
Low blood pressure   17
High blood pressure explained   18
Types of high blood pressure   21
The scale of the problem   25

CHAPTER 2 *Symptoms, causes and diagnosis*
Symptoms   31
Causes   35
Diagnosis and initial investigations   46

CHAPTER 3 *Measuring BP*
Sphygmomanometers   52
Accuracy and reliability   59
Measurements by doctors and nurses   64
Measuring blood pressure at home   66

CHAPTER 4 Managing high blood pressure

Aims of treatment	79
Treatment without drugs	82
BP-lowering drugs	84
Treatment with BP-lowering drugs	92
Treatment for young adults	99
Treatment for elderly people	103
Practical aspects of drug treatment	106
Monitoring treatment and follow-up	113

CHAPTER 5 How to help yourself

Weight control	120
Healthy eating	131
Fats and oils	138
Sodium and salt	142
Exercise	148
Stopping smoking	152
Complementary therapies	155

CHAPTER 6 High blood pressure plus ...

Other problems in general	162
High blood cholesterol	164
Heart and circulation problems	177
Pain, particularly joint pain and arthritis	181
Asthma and other breathing problems	188
Diabetes	192
Digestive system problems	195
Kidneys and prostate problems	197
Psychological problems	198

CHAPTER 7 Living with high BP

Work	202
Insurance and mortgages	207
Travel and holidays	209
Sports	213
Sex	214
Contraception	218
The menopause	222
Miscellaneous	224

Contents

CHAPTER 8 *Pregnancy*
High blood pressure in pregnancy   228
Pre-eclampsia and eclampsia   234
Diagnosing and treating PE   240

CHAPTER 9 *Long-term consequences and complications*
What can go wrong   246
Heart attacks   253
Angina   257
Heart failure   263
Stroke   264

CHAPTER 10 *Research and the future*
Drug testing and clinical trials   268
The future   276

GLOSSARY   279

APPENDIX 1
BP-lowering drugs   288

APPENDIX 2
Useful addresses   319

APPENDIX 3
Useful publications   326

INDEX   330

Acknowledgements

We should like to thank the following people for their generous help in giving up their time for critical reading of early drafts, to ensure that the final text was accurate, useful, and comprehensible to readers without specialised knowledge:

Betty Ackery, Aarti Dattani BSc DipHNut, Dr Godfrey Fowler, Gwen Hall RMN RGN BSc, Mona Harris, Janet Jones SEN, Margaret Jones SRN, Mary Law, Dr George T. Lewith, Dr Caroline Miller-Sykes, Julie Nedin BSc SRD, Billy Peck, Professor John Swales, Evelyn Thomas SRN, Babs Walters, Ted Willis and Bill Williams.

Any errors are our own.

Foreword

by Dr IAN BAIRD MD, FRCP

Trustee, HOPE Project (High Blood Pressure Open Public Education) and former Medical Spokesman, British Heart Foundation

High blood pressure is one of the most important risk factors in causing both heart attacks and angina and is a major factor predisposing to stroke. Judging by the large number of patient enquiries we received regularly during my time at the British Heart Foundation there is a real need for Dr Julian Tudor Hart's book. The format of the book using questions and answers is designed to inform the reader about a wide range of subjects, including how high blood pressure affects the patient in daily life. It is clear and understandable without complex medical terms. The section on treatment is topical and gives current medications which could be of value to both patients and some health professionals. There are aspects of high blood pressure, such as its association with pregnancy, and occurrence in children and the elderly, that are difficult to find in standard texts.

The Foundation has always stressed the importance of early diagnosis and adequate management of high blood pressure which affects at least 10% of the adult population in the UK.

Many are unaware of having high blood pressure, and some fail to continue medication. The knowledge in this book provides a means of improving the diagnosis and management of high blood pressure which complements the research endeavours of the British Heart Foundation.

Ian Baird

About this book

Most of you reading this will have been told that either you, or someone in your family, has raised blood pressure. The questions in this book are those asked by people like you every day; the answers are intended to help you be as informed as possible about your own care so that your treatment will be more successful and you will feel more in control. Remember that no one involved in this subject (including doctors and nurses) ever stops learning more about it. In fact, a few of you may read this book not because of your own health problems, but because in your work you are concerned with the health problems of other people.

Because different people have different requirements for information about high blood pressure, this book has been designed in a way that means you do not have to read it from cover to cover unless you wish to do so. The questions are arranged into chapters and sections, so you may care to dip into it in sections at a time, or look for the answer to a particular question by using the contents table and the index. Cross-references in the text will lead you to more detailed information where this might be helpful, and essential information is repeated wherever it seems to be necessary. Having said all this, the book begins with a brief general outline of high blood pressure – **What you most need to know in nine pages**. However much you dip into and skip through the rest of the book, may we ask you please to read these few pages thoroughly?

Not everyone will agree with every answer we have given, but future editions of this book can only be improved if you let us

About this book

know where you disagree, or have found the advice to be unhelpful, or if you have any questions which you think we have not covered. Please write to us c/o Class Publishing, Barb House, Barb Mews, London W6 7PA.

Updates in this latest edition have been made by Dr Tom Fahey, a practising GP with a research interest in the management of high blood pressure in the community.

And finally, what are giraffes doing in this book? Obviously more pressure is needed to push blood up than to push it down. The animals which have to cope with the biggest changes in blood pressure are therefore giraffes, whose brain capillary blood pressure has to be kept constant whether their heads are six feet or so below their hearts (as when they drink) or six feet above them (when they eat leaves off trees). For this reason, a giraffe graces each chapter of this book, in an effort to reassure you that it is not unreadable.

Introduction
What you most need to know in nine pages

High blood pressure is the most common continuing medical condition seen by family doctors. At just what measurement 'normal' blood pressure becomes 'high' blood pressure that justifies action being taken to reduce it is still a subject for professional argument among doctors (although most now agree on a pressure of somewhere around 160/90 mmHg). Whatever the definition, the numbers of people needing some sort of treatment for high blood pressure include at least 10% of any large group of adults, up to 33% of poorer city adults, and about 50% of all people over 65 years of age - a lot of people.

If you are one of this 10-50%, and you need medication for your high blood pressure, you will probably go on needing it for the rest of your life. If you read, understand, and remember the following few pages, you will be well on the way to understanding the nature of your high blood pressure, what can and what can't be done about it, and both the benefits and risks of treatment. If not, your alternative is to let doctors take decisions about your life, without your help or informed consent. Most doctors today understand how dangerous it is for the people they treat to be so uninformed and uncritical. Safe doctoring depends on the co-operative work of two sets of experts: expert professionals who know a lot about how the human body works but little about the personal lives of the people they are treating; and the people being treated, who are experts on their own lives but know rather less about how their bodies work. Just as doctors can't look after you properly if they are completely ignorant of your life, so you can't interpret their advice safely if you are completely ignorant of human biology.

Even if you remember only these few pages, you will know more about the practical management of high blood pressure than many health professionals, who usually have to cover a much wider range of medical conditions and cannot concentrate only on this one. With or without this knowledge, you, not your doctors, will be responsible for actually using the treatments they recommend. Many different drugs are used to treat high blood pressure, but they all have one thing in common: they don't work if you don't take them. Yet many (if not most) people treated for high blood pressure don't take their tablets regularly. They take them if they feel as though their blood pressure is high, but miss them if they feel well, or plan to have a few drinks, or need to take other tablets for something else and are afraid of mixing them, or if they're afraid of side-effects and even more afraid of admitting this to their doctor. Unless you are in hospital you have to take your own treatment decisions – there are no nurses' rounds to see that you follow orders. To medicate yourself safely you need far more information than any doctor or nurse can impart in the few minutes usually available for a consultation, and one purpose of this book is to provide you with that information.

What high blood pressure is and what it is not

Everybody's blood is under pressure, otherwise it wouldn't circulate around the body. If blood pressure is too high it damages the walls of your arteries. After many years, this damage increases your risks of coronary heart disease, heart failure, stroke, bleeding or detachment of the retina (the back of the eye), and kidney failure. High blood pressure itself is not a disease, but a treatable cause of these serious diseases, which are thereby partly preventable. All these risks are greatly increased if you also smoke or have diabetes.

What you most need to know... 3

Unless it has already caused damage, high BP seldom makes you feel unwell. It can be very high without causing headaches, breathlessness, palpitations, faintness, giddiness, or any of the symptoms which were once thought to be typical of high BP. You may have any or all of these symptoms without having high BP, and you may have dangerously high BP with none of them.

The only way to know if you have high blood pressure (and how high it is) is to measure it with an instrument called a sphygmomanometer while you are sitting quietly. Because BP varies so much from hour to hour and from day to day, this should be done at least three times (preferably on separate days) to work out a true average figure before taking big decisions like starting or stopping treatment.

Mechanisms

Your level of BP depends on how hard your heart pumps blood into your arteries, on the volume of blood in your circulation, and on how tight your arteries are. The smaller arteries are sheathed by a strand of muscle which spirals around them: if this muscle tightens and shortens, it narrows the artery. In this way smaller arteries can be varied in diameter according to varying needs of different organs in different activities. In people with high BP something goes wrong with this mechanism, so that all the arteries are too tight. The heart then has to beat harder to push blood through them. This tightening-up may be caused by signals sent by the brain through the nervous system, or by chemical signals (hormones) released by other organs in the body (such as the kidneys).

Causes

The causes of short-term rises in blood pressure which last only seconds or minutes are well understood, but these are not what we normally mean by high blood pressure. High blood pressure is important only when it is maintained for months or years – it is a high average pressure which is significant, not occasional high peaks. The causes of a long-term rise in average pressure are not fully known, but we do know that it runs in families. This inherited tendency seems to account for about half the differences between people; the rest seems to depend on how they live and what they eat (not just in adult life, but what they ate in infancy and childhood and how well-nourished they were before they were born). We don't know enough about this to be able to prevent most cases.

One cause we do know about is overweight (particularly in young people) and weight reduction is a sensible first step in treatment. Weight loss depends mainly on using up more energy (measured in calories) by taking more exercise, and reducing energy input (the number of calories eaten in food). In practice the most healthy way to do this is by reducing the amount of fats, oils, meat, sugar and alcohol in the diet, and instead eating more fruit, vegetables, cereal foods and fish (some of these foods have other good effects as well as helping weight loss). Eating less fat and oil is by far the most important of these changes. Another benefit from these changes in diet is that they help lower blood cholesterol levels and so reduce the risk of developing coronary heart disease.

Another known cause is excessive alcohol (which means MORE THAN 4 units of alcohol A DAY for a man or 3 units A DAY for a woman – a unit of alcohol is one glass of wine OR one single measure of spirits OR half a pint of average strength beer or lager). Again, the biggest effect is in young people. Limiting alcohol intake often brings high BP back to normal without any other treatment.

Stress

If you are anxious, angry, have been hurrying, have a full bladder or if you are cold then your BP will rise for a few minutes or even a few hours (so BP measured at such times is not reliable) – but none of these things seem to be causes of permanently raised blood pressure. High blood pressure seems to be just as common in peaceable, even-tempered people without worries as it is in excitable people with short fuses. However, feeling pushed at work or at home may be an important cause in some people, if not for everyone.

The word 'hypertension' is used in medical jargon with exactly the same meaning as 'high blood pressure'. This does not mean that feeling tense necessarily raises blood pressure, nor does it mean that most people with high blood pressure feel tense. Blood pressure falls considerably during normal sleep, both in people with normal blood pressure and in those whose BP is high. Training in relaxation certainly lowers blood pressure for a while, and may have a useful long-term effect on high BP in people who learn how to 'switch off' often during the day, but there is no evidence that treatment by relaxation alone is an effective or safe alternative to drug treatment for people with severe high blood pressure.

Salt and sodium

Table salt is sodium chloride: it is the sodium which is important for your blood pressure, not the chloride. High BP is unknown among those peoples of the world whose normal diet contains about 20 times less sodium than a normal Western diet, and even very high BP can be controlled by reducing sodium intake to this low level. The diet required for this consists entirely of rice, fruit and vegetables and would be intolerable to most people in this country.

The usual British diet contains much more salt than anyone needs. It certainly does no harm to reduce sodium intake by not adding salt to cooked meals, and by reducing or avoiding high-sodium processed foods (crisps, sausages, sauces, tinned meats and beans, and 'convenience' foods generally), Chinese take-aways (which contain huge quantities of sodium glutamate) and strong cheeses. Salt can be found in the most unexpected foods – for example, both milk and bread contain salt in amounts which would surprise most people.

There is no convincing evidence that the roughly one-third reduction in sodium intake you can achieve by these dietary changes is an effective alternative to drug treatment for severe high blood pressure. Reducing fat in your diet by about a quarter reduces the potential complications of high BP much more effectively than reducing your salt intake by about half. Most people find it difficult to reduce fat and salt at the same time, and fat reduction deserves a higher priority (especially as cutting down on fats will help you lose weight). However, people whose blood pressure is high enough for them to need to take drugs for it may manage on lower doses of their tablets if they reduce their sodium intake, and very heavy salt-eaters should try to cut down.

Smoking

Smoking is not a cause of high blood pressure, but it enormously increases the risks associated with it. If you have high BP already, then if you also smoke you are three times more likely to have a heart attack than non-smokers if you are under 50 years old, and twice as likely to have one if you are over 50. Heart attacks in people under 45, and in women at all ages, happen much more frequently in smokers.

Smoking is a powerful risk factor in its own right, not only for coronary heart disease and stroke, but also for cancer of the mouth, nose, throat, lung, bladder and pancreas, and for asthma and other lung diseases. Unlike all other risk factors, it also affects your colleagues, family and friends (through passive smoking and the example you set to your children) and it costs a lot of money you could spend better in other ways.

When to have drug treatment

You will probably be advised to have drug treatment for your high blood pressure if there is already evidence of damage to your arteries, brain, heart, eyes or kidneys, or if you also have diabetes. As a very rough guide, drug treatment is otherwise rarely justified unless your average BP (averaged from at least three readings on separate days) is at least 160/100 mmHg. While you don't need to know exactly what these figures mean, you should know what they are in your own case, just as you know your own height and weight.

This threshold figure (plus or minus 5 mmHg either way) is based on evidence from large controlled trials in Britain, Australia, Scandinavia and the USA, which have shown worthwhile saving of life in many thousands of people. The benefits of drug treatment are greatest in the people with the highest pressures, or those who already have evidence of organ damage. Most of the benefit has been in reducing strokes, heart failure, and kidney damage; the effects on coronary heart attacks have been much smaller (more important ways to prevent heart attacks are to stop smoking, maintain regular exercise, and stick to a diet low in saturated fats).

BP-lowering drugs

When severe high blood pressure is reduced by drugs, people live longer than if they are left untreated. Their treatment will not affect how they feel – it seldom makes people feel better, and they may sometimes even feel worse. The aim of all present treatments for high blood pressure is not to cure it, but to prevent its consequences by keeping pressure down to a safer level (whatever the underlying causes of high BP are, they seem almost always to be permanent and are not affected by any of the treatments now available). Treatment must therefore nearly always continue for life – if you stop taking your tablets, your BP will probably rise again, although this may take several months.

Unfortunately, all the drugs used for high BP can cause unpleasant side-effects in some people, although the newer BP-lowering drugs are generally easier to live with than the older ones. If you think your drugs are upsetting you, then say so, as there are alternatives. With so many BP-lowering drugs now available your doctor should be able to tailor an individual treatment for you that minimises side-effects or even eliminates them altogether. Included among the side-effects of BP-lowering drugs are tiredness, depression, and failure of erection: if any of these happen to you, then tell your doctor or nurse, as if they really are caused by your drugs, they will clear up soon after your medication is changed.

If you have any wheezing or asthma, then some BP-lowering drugs can be very dangerous, so make sure your doctor knows about this. Some drugs used for back and joint pains can interfere with the effect of drugs given for high blood pressure, and you should ask your doctor about these if you take them. (Don't try to alter your medication yourself.) The contraceptive pill occasionally raises blood pressure very seriously, so women with high blood pressure should discuss other methods of birth control.

Remembering to take tablets is difficult for many people. Take them at set times, and ask your partner or a friend to help you learn the habit of regular medication. Don't stop taking your tablets just because you're going out for a drink – all BP-lowering drugs can be taken with moderate amounts of alcohol.

Follow-up

Always bring all your tablets (not just those for your high BP) with you in their original containers when you see your doctor or nurse for follow-up, so that they know exactly what you are taking. If your blood pressure doesn't fall despite apparently adequate medication, think about your weight or your alcohol intake. Follow-up visits should be frequent at first, perhaps once a week until your blood pressure is controlled to under 160/90 mmHg. After that most doctors will want to check your blood pressure every three months or so; never go longer than six months without a check.

What you most need to know... 9

The end of the beginning

All this (and I mean all) is the least you need to know to take an intelligent share in responsibility for your future health, not just as a passive consumer of medical care, but as an active producer of better health (as everyone should be). However, I hope by now you are interested enough to want to know more than this. The rest of this book will tell you a lot more both of what we do know about high blood pressure and - just as important - what we don't know.

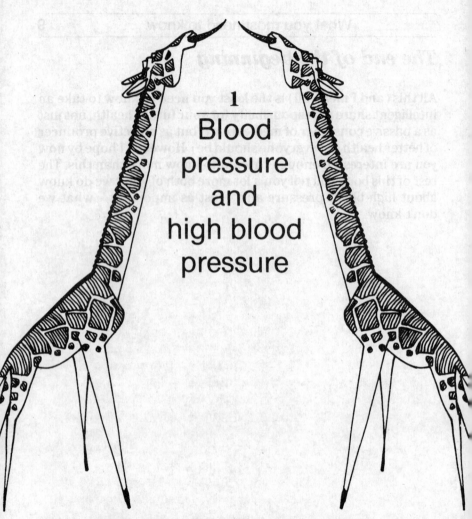

1
Blood pressure and high blood pressure

About blood pressure in general

I don't think I'd ever thought about blood being under pressure before I was told I had high blood pressure. Why should blood be under pressure?

The function of the blood is to transport materials around the body, mainly to take oxygen and food substances (nutrients) to body cells to keep them alive and well, and to remove their waste

Blood pressure and high blood pressure

products such as carbon dioxide. If your blood were not under some pressure (being pumped around your body by your heart) it would just stay where it is, stagnant, neither nourishing nor cleansing the cells of your body, so that within a few seconds first they and then you would die.

How does blood move around the body?

Your circulatory system consists of two circular systems of tubes, the circulation through your lungs (called the pulmonary circulation) and the circulation through all the rest of your body (the systemic circulation). The tubes are your blood vessels – the arteries, veins and capillaries.

Blood is moved through these two systems by two pumps, the right and left sides of your heart. Although these right and left pumps beat together, the blood in each side is entirely separate, and the two pumps can and do to some extent function independently. Because pushing blood through your lungs is much easier than pushing it through every other part of your body, the left side of your heart is bigger, more muscular, and carries a much heavier workload than the right.

Obviously your blood is under pressure at all points throughout both systems, in arteries, capillaries and veins, otherwise it would not circulate. Pressure in your capillaries (the smallest type of blood vessel) is not only extremely small, but has to be kept constant, so that the conditions for the transfer of oxygen and nutrients in and carbon dioxide and waste products out of your body's cells and tissues remain unchanged, despite huge differences in what the rest of your body may be doing. In fact the main reason for the variability of your arterial blood pressure is the need to keep your capillary blood pressure the same.

Pressure is generally much higher in your arteries than in your veins. When doctors talk about 'blood pressure' they normally mean arterial pressure. It is important to understand this. If you cough, sneeze, or push your car out of a ditch, you go red in the face and you can feel your head filling up with blood. This is caused by raised blood pressure in your veins (venous pressure), not in your arteries (arterial pressure). Many people imagine that high blood pressure causes similar symptoms, but this is completely wrong.

Arterial pressure is highest close to your heart and falls as blood moves further out along the arterial tree. Arterial pressure is readily measured in your arm just above your elbow (the artery there is called the brachial artery), and this has long been the international standard way of measuring blood pressure.

What sort of things affect blood pressure?

Blood is a fluid, and blood vessels are basically tubes. The pressure of any fluid flowing in any tube depends on several variables, of which the most important are:

A the rate at which fluid enters the tube;
B the diameter (width) of the tube;
C the friction from the walls of the tube; and
D the viscosity (stickiness and elasticity) and volume of the fluid.

It is easy to imagine how these variables work, just by thinking about water flowing through a hosepipe. For example, when the tap is on full, the water comes out under greater pressure. If you swap a wide hosepipe for a narrower one, then once again the water is under greater pressure. What happens in your body is very similar.

A Rate: your heart pumps blood into your arteries at a variable rate, depending both on what you are doing and what you are thinking.
B Diameter: your smaller arteries are of variable diameter, depending on tension in the strands of muscle which spiral around them. This tension in turn depends mainly on signals from the brain and from various circulating chemicals (hormones) released from other organs in the body.
C Friction: friction along artery walls increases as they get older, rougher, and furred up with waxy plaques made of a mixture of clotted blood and cholesterol. This process of roughening raises blood pressure by increasing resistance to

Blood pressure and high blood pressure

blood flow, and is itself speeded up by raised pressure, a vicious circle.

D Viscosity and volume: both the viscosity and the volume of your blood vary, depending mainly on your salt intake, the efficiency of your kidneys, and the size and shape of your red blood cells, which may be much altered by low levels of iron in your blood, or high levels of blood alcohol.

Blood pressure seems to be written down as a fraction, for example 150/85. What do these figures represent, and what do they mean?

Blood pressure is normally recorded as systolic pressure, diastolic pressure, for example 105/54 mmHg (an unusually low pressure); 125/70 mmHg (an average-ish pressure); 164/95 mmHg (a high-ish pressure); 182/106 mmHg (a definitely high pressure); or 235/140 mmHg (a dangerously high pressure – an emergency).

Blood pressure is measured with a sphygmomanometer (a manometer is an instrument for measuring the pressure of fluids; 'sphygmos' is the Greek word for pulse). Because the earliest sphygmomanometers used columns of mercury calibrated against millimetre scales, the units in which blood pressure is recorded are millimetres of mercury, usually abbreviated to mmHg ('mm' is, of course, the standard abbreviation for millimetres, and 'Hg' is the chemical symbol for mercury). So, strictly speaking, we should write your example as 150/85 mmHg.

The pressure required to stop pumping sounds from the heart is used as an indirect way of measuring the pressure inside the artery. If you put an ear (or, more conveniently, a stethoscope) over the large artery in the crook of your elbow, you will hear nothing; but if you squeeze the artery with an inflatable cuff until it is completely blocked above the listening point, and then very slowly release it, you will first hear clear, regular tapping sounds. The level of pressure at which these sounds are first heard is the systolic pressure, the pressure at which blood is pushed out of the heart into the arteries when the heart muscle is squeezing. (Systolic pressure is the first figure of the 'fraction', so the person in your example has a systolic pressure of 150 mmHg.)

If you keep listening while slowly dropping the pressure in the cuff, the tapping disappears. Then, at a pressure about 50-100 mmHg lower, you will hear regular but much softer whooshing sounds, which will also disappear after a further fall of 5-10 mmHg. The point at which these soft sounds disappear is the diastolic pressure, the pressure of blood in the arteries between heart beats, when the heart muscle is relaxing between squeezes. (This is the second figure of the 'fraction', so the person in your example has a diastolic pressure of 85 mmHg.) At one time doctors disagreed about whether to define diastolic pressure as appearance or disappearance of the whooshing sound, but there is now international agreement to accept it as disappearance.

You will find more information about sphygmomanometers and the practicalities of measuring blood pressure in Chapter 3.

Should I know what my own figures are?

In my opinion, yes, and I think that you should know them as actual figures, not just as general statements such as 'high', 'normal' or 'low'. Doctors will ask you about your blood pressure, and without some figures, your answers will be as meaningless to them as to you.

Does blood pressure vary during the day or does it always stay much the same?

Indeed it does vary, and quite considerably. Figure 1 shows the pattern of blood pressure readings measured every five minutes throughout 24 hours in a doctor (aged 31, and with completely normal blood pressure) who took part in a research project in 1967. Measurements were made very accurately through a polythene catheter (a very fine tube) pushed into an artery in his arm, using a local anaesthetic to ensure a painless procedure which would not itself affect his blood pressure.

As you can see, his blood pressure varied throughout the day, with a sustained fall during sleep, a marked rise when somebody pushed a pin into his skin (marked P on the chart), another

Blood pressure and high blood pressure

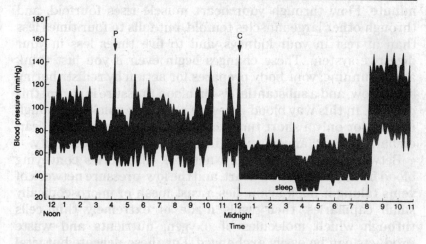

Figure 1: Variations in blood pressure during 24 hours in a person with normal blood pressure. Systolic pressures are shown at the top of the shaded area, and diastolic pressures at the bottom.

when he made love (marked C), and another sustained rise during the first half of the morning. This pattern of rises and falls is typical not only of people with normal blood pressure, but also of those with high blood pressure.

Why does blood pressure vary so much?

Everyone, whether their blood pressure is high or low, has mechanisms for distributing varying amounts of blood to different parts of the body, depending on what they are doing. For example, if you are thinking hard, your brain needs a larger blood flow than when you are asleep; after a large meal you need a much larger blood flow to your digestive system; and if you are running, blood flow to all your large muscles is enormously increased.

In a normal man or woman, total blood flow at rest is about 6 litres a minute, with about 13% going to your brain, 24% to your gut, 21% to your large muscles, 19% to your kidneys, and 4% to your heart muscle. If you run as hard as you can, blood flow to your brain remains exactly the same, but total flow through your body as a whole rises more than fourfold to 25 litres a minute. Flow through your heart muscle rises fourfold, and through other large muscles tenfold, but falls to four times less than at rest in your kidneys, and to five times less in your digestive system. These changes begin even if you just think about running; your body prepares for action by redistributing blood flow, and a substantial rise in blood pressure is part of this process. In this way blood pressure responds quickly, although usually for only a short time, to emotional states such as fear, embarrassment, anger, sexual interest, and simple curiosity.

Between this high-pressure network of arteries conveying blood from the lungs and heart, and the low-pressure network of veins taking it back again, lies a vast mesh of microscopically small capillaries, their walls made of extremely thin cells through which molecules of oxygen, nutrients and waste products can be easily exchanged. For these delicate but vital transactions to take place, pressure within the capillaries must remain constant, within very narrow limits. Given these huge shifts in blood flow between organs, this constancy can be maintained only by precise control of flow through your arteries and arterioles (the very smallest arteries). In fact the main reason for the variability of your arterial blood pressure is the need to keep your capillary blood pressure the same. The control is mainly exerted through changes in tension in the spiral muscles surrounding the smallest arteries (arterioles), which result in big changes in arterial blood pressure.

Does blood pressure vary more in people with high than with normal blood pressure?

No, not really. Figure 2 shows measurements made every five minutes throughout 24 hours for a woman with untreated high blood pressure in a hospital ward. Her fall in blood pressure during sleep was almost as great as in the doctor with normal blood pressure, as shown in Figure 1. However, at the extremely high pressures commonly found in malignant hypertension (there is a question about this in the section on *Types of high blood pressure* later in this chapter), very high pressure is maintained throughout sleep, and with little change during the day.

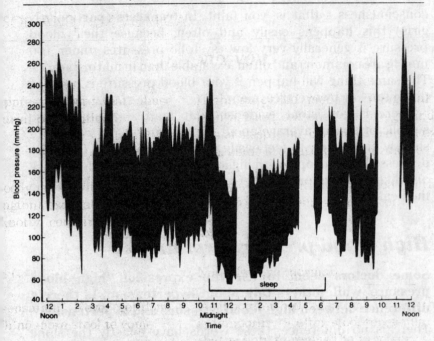

Figure 2: Variations in blood pressure during 24 hours in a person with untreated high blood pressure. Systolic pressures are shown at the top of the shaded area, and diastolic pressures at the bottom.

Low blood pressure

Presumably if there are people with high blood pressure then there can also be people with low blood pressure. Does low blood pressure cause symptoms?

You are right, there are people around with low blood pressure. While most of the people in any typical large group of adults will have 'average' blood pressure, there will be a few who have high blood pressure and a few who have low blood pressure.

The only thing we could really call a 'symptom' of low blood pressure is fainting. If the blood pressure in your neck arteries is not high enough to supply enough oxygen and glucose (a form of sugar) to support the full function of your brain cells, you lose consciousness – that is, you faint. In teenagers (particularly girls) this happens easily and often, because their blood pressure is generally very low (systolic pressures under 100 mmHg are common) and often less stable than in mature adults. The same thing will happen if your blood pressure is brought down too low by overtreatment.

There is consistent evidence that mature adults whose systolic pressures average about 95-105 mmHg (very low) are slightly more likely to feel easily tired, less energetic, or mildly depressed than people with higher pressures, although they are also likely to live longer. There is no evidence that this needs medication.

High blood pressure explained

Some doctors seem to use the expression 'high blood pressure' while others talk about hypertension. Is there a difference between high blood pressure and hypertension?

There is no difference: these words have exactly the same meaning, and are used interchangeably by doctors. 'Hypertension' sounds more technical, that's all.

But 'hypertension' seems to imply a main cause (too much stress or tension) and therefore conveys more meaning than just saying 'high blood pressure'. Is it not therefore a better name?

No. The word 'hypertension' comes from translating the French phrase 'tension arterielle'. This originally referred not to tension in the mind (stress), but to tension (stretching) in the walls of the arteries. Tension in the mind is a possible cause of high blood pressure in some people, but is certainly not the main cause in everybody.

My husband has high blood pressure, but he seems to be just as well as everyone else in our family. So is high blood pressure really an illness?

With the exception of malignant high blood pressure (there is a question about this in the section on *Types of high blood pressure* later in this chapter), high blood pressure is not an illness which you either do or do not have, but a variable and reversible risk factor for other illnesses such as stroke, heart attacks and other problems affecting the circulatory system. Many people (like your husband) have high blood pressure without showing any symptoms, and you will find more information about this in the section on *Symptoms* in Chapter 2. However, not having symptoms does not imply that he is not at risk of any of the potential harmful consequences of having high blood pressure. Most of these consequences can be avoided by treatment, but this treatment is successful only to the extent that blood pressure is brought down and kept down.

What is the dividing line between normal and high blood pressure?

Doctors currently agree that the borderline between 'normal' and 'high' blood pressure lies somewhere around 160 mmHg systolic pressure and 90 mmHg diastolic pressure. They arrived at these figures by reviewing all the research work which has been done on high blood pressure and its treatment. This borderline represents the point at which the **advantages of active treatment are greater than the disadvantages** (for the people being treated).

In any typical large group of adults, there are a few people with very low blood pressure, a huge number with middling values, and a few with very high values. The research shows that at every level of blood pressure, higher blood pressure means a higher eventual risk of stroke, heart attacks and other circulation problems. However, the risks of all these harmful outcomes relate more to recent pressures while under treatment than to the original pressures before treatment.

Assuming you have had enough careful measurements to classify your average blood pressure correctly (there is more information about measuring blood pressure in Chapter 3), the simple truth is that 'normal' blood pressure becomes 'high' at the point where you and your doctor consider that the **advantages of supervision** (and probably eventual medication) **outweigh** the disadvantages. There are other things besides your blood pressure to take into account in making this decision, for example the other predictable risks for similar harmful outcomes (notably whether you smoke, your blood cholesterol level and whether you have a family history of stroke or heart disease), the various drugs currently available, and your own ideas about medical treatment.

I'm 70. Does my age make any difference to whether I'm considered to have high blood pressure or not? And to whether I need treatment for it?

In all but a very few people in industrialised countries, average blood pressure rises throughout life up to about 80 years of age. Thereafter it tends to fall, but this seems to be part of the general effects of aging, and is not really relevant to this question. We can therefore say that average expected blood pressure rises with age.

However, risks of stroke, coronary heart disease and other common complications of high blood pressure also rise with age, not only because of this higher average blood pressure but also because the arteries become more fragile and liable to clotting inside. As the purpose of all drug treatment for high blood pressure is to prevent these harmful outcomes, the proportion of people who can be expected to gain more than they lose from treatment also rises with age. There is good research evidence that treatment is much more rapidly effective in people over 60 than it is in younger people.

Therefore, for practical purposes, the threshold for treatment (the borderline between 'normal' and 'high' blood pressure discussed in the answer to the previous question) should indeed be at least the same for older people as for the middle-aged, and possibly lower.

There is far less evidence about treatment for high blood pressure when it is diagnosed in people aged between about 20 and 40, although this situation is quite common. In theory, this group might benefit most, because without treatment they are likely to develop serious complications sooner and they might also be considered to have more life and health to lose. On the other hand, we also have no evidence yet about the possible harmful effects of taking any of the currently available drugs over the very long periods of time, perhaps 50 years or more, implied by starting treatment in youth. This remains very much a matter of clinical judgement for each individual case.

Types of high blood pressure

Is all high blood pressure the same, or are there different kinds?

Indeed there are, and probably more than as yet we know of.

High blood pressure was traditionally classified in two main groups: rare cases for which causes were known ('secondary hypertension' - in other words, where high blood pressure is secondary to some other condition), and common cases where no cause was known ('essential hypertension'). 'Essential' did not mean that the high blood pressure was necessary, but that it was 'of the essence': in other words, you had it because you had it, for reasons unknown. This ridiculous word (steadily becoming more ridiculous as we learn more about the many interacting causes of high blood pressure) is now beginning to give way to the more commonsense terms 'primary hypertension' or 'primary high blood pressure'.

Secondary hypertension is mostly caused by various sorts of kidney disease, but occasionally by coarctation of the aorta (a malformation of the large artery that carries blood from the heart); by overproduction of some hormones known to raise blood pressure; by tumours of the pituitary gland, adrenal glands or kidneys; or by disorders involving compression of the brain or brainstem. These 'classical' secondary causes altogether account for less than 1% of all treated cases of high blood pressure, if we exclude high blood pressure caused by the oral contraceptive pill (discussed in the section on *Contraception* in Chapter 7.

As 'essential hypertension' was by definition of unknown cause, the category has inevitably become more and more unreal, as more and more interacting causes for it are found. We now have the situation that many important causes of primary high blood pressure are known (which, if removed early, can lead to a fall in blood pressure), but these have not been reclassified as secondary hypertension. Examples are being overweight and a high alcohol intake in young men, mostly those with a family history of high blood pressure and therefore genetically susceptible to these causes. (You will find more information about all these in the section on *Causes* in Chapter 2.) As more causes are discovered, even primary high blood pressure will eventually have to be recognised as a diverse group.

If they know all this, then why do doctors still use terms like essential hypertension or primary high blood pressure?

The category remains useful because although the causes are diverse, the consequences of uncontrolled high blood pressure and the methods of controlling it are not. Whatever the cause of high blood pressure, the risks of stroke, heart failure, coronary heart disease and various other sorts of organ damage are increased. Perhaps even more importantly, no convincing or consistent evidence has yet been found that different causes benefit much from different sorts of drugs.

In practice, the aim of treatment for high blood pressure is usually not to find causes and treat them, but to find drugs that work and are well tolerated, and then keep on prescribing them. In some ways this is a realistic acceptance of the limits of current medical knowledge. However, it is not an acceptable attitude if it leads to a neglect of other measures (such as losing weight and drinking less alcohol) which can be equally effective, particularly in young people and people with borderline pressures.

Do children get high blood pressure? If so, what kinds of high blood pressure can they get, and is it serious?

Yes they do, but rarely. Most family doctors could spend a lifetime in general practice without seeing a single case. However, when high blood pressure does occur in childhood, it may cause very serious and irreversible damage to the brain, eyes or kidneys if it is not recognised and treated. Because high blood pressure is so rare in childhood, the possibility is often forgotten, so the diagnosis may be made too late.

Primary high blood pressure (or essential hypertension) can be said to occur in childhood: that is, there is a distribution of BP in children just as there is in adults, with a high end and a low end. As in adults, children at the high end of this distribution can be labelled as having high blood pressure: the question is what purpose such labelling serves? Adults with primary high blood pressure are at increased risk of coronary heart disease, stroke, and other types of organ damage, but children are not. There is no convincing evidence that children with unusually high blood pressure derive any benefit whatever from medication with BP-lowering drugs, and many good reasons for suspecting that they would not.

This certainly represents a consensus view of family doctors and paediatricians in the UK. I suspect this view is shared by many doctors in North America, but it has to be said that the United States Task Force on Childhood Hypertension recommended in 1977 that children in the top 5% of the distribution for BP be investigated fully and followed up, and some US experts in this field recommended that some of these children should be started on long-term medication, even in the absence of any evidence of organ damage. Few, if any, doctors in the UK agree with them.

For all practical purposes, when children have blood pressure high enough to need medication, then they have secondary high blood pressure – their high BP is a result of some other important disorder. In fact 95% of children with a sustained diastolic pressure of over 120 mmHg have an identifiable cause for their high blood pressures: this is nearly always a kidney disorder, occasionally coarctation of the aorta. They need accurate diagnosis and urgent treatment for these rare conditions.

I once heard someone say that they suffered from 'white coat hypertension'. What is this – is it a type of high blood pressure?

It's a nickname given to the effect that the medical profession has on some people – simply entering a hospital or a doctor's surgery can make them so nervous that their blood pressure shoots up. If they are allowed time to get over their initial nerves, then their blood pressure returns to its usual, lower level. The nickname comes from the fact that so many medical professionals (especially those in hospitals) wear white coats when they are working. While it is not a type of high blood pressure that needs any treatment, it does need to be allowed for when blood pressure measurements are taken, or somone could be diagnosed as having high blood pressure when all they actually have is a fear of doctors.

What is malignant hypertension? Does it have anything to do with cancer?

No, despite the name it has nothing to do with cancer, but it is the most serious form of high blood pressure and can cause immense damage (and even death) in a very short time. Its alternative name is 'accelerated hypertension'.

Malignant high blood pressure is a medical emergency. If it is not recognised and treated urgently, then irreversible damage to the kidneys, retina (the back of the eye) and brain is likely – any delays before starting treatment should be measured in hours rather than days. Before effective treatment of high blood pressure became available in the 1950s, people who developed malignant high blood pressure generally died within two years, mostly from heart failure, kidney failure, or massive stroke. Many people became blind or paralysed long before this.

As more and more people with high blood pressure are picked up early by routine blood pressure measurements, malignant high blood pressure is becoming rare. It only occurs when either very high blood pressure has persisted for a long time (usually several years), or when blood pressure has risen very fast indeed, with no time for the artery walls to thicken and resist this pressure. Today, anybody diagnosed with malignant high blood pressure is sent into hospital immediately, and their blood pressure is brought down gradually over the next two or three days. Treatment is usually the same as for all other cases of high blood pressure, but must always be maintained for life.

So what exactly happens in malignant high blood pressure?

If blood pressure remains very high for weeks, months or years, with a sustained diastolic pressure of at least 120 mmHg (usually much more) the walls of the arterioles (the smallest arteries) begin to crumble. Blood then leaks out of them, interrupting the arterial blood supply in whichever part of the body they happen to be. This usually begins in the kidney, where the damage leads to the release of hormones which push blood pressure up even higher, thus setting up a vicious circle of acceleration, in which already very high blood pressure pushes itself higher still.

The next site of damage is usually the retina (the back of the eye), causing leaks of blood (retinal haemorrhages) and leaks of plasma (retinal exudates). Finally there is damage to the brain, causing first swelling of the head of the optic nerve, then fits, and finally small strokes, unless the whole sequence is interrupted by heart failure.

Although some of those people who develop malignant high blood pressure get severe headaches, others may have severe kidney damage and very high blood pressures without any symptoms at all. Any severe headache deserves measurement of blood pressure, although high blood pressure is rarely the cause. Another common early symptom is blurred vision or patchy loss of vision starting in one eye. Malignant high blood pressure should be looked for in anyone with a diastolic pressure over 120 mmHg, by testing their urine for protein, and by examining both their retinas with an ophthalmoscope (either in a dark room, or after putting drops into the eyes to dilate the pupils).

The scale of the problem

How many people have high blood pressure?

High blood pressure is the commonest major disorder seen by doctors, and the biggest single health problem tackled by general practitioners. Blood pressure high enough to require some kind of medical treatment and continuing supervision affects between 10% and 30% of the adult population (this figure varies depending on age, ethnic mix, and social composition) – and 10% of the population of the UK means about five million people. This compares with between 2% and 8% of the adult population for diabetes, a disorder of comparable significance for health.

Is it a growing or diminishing problem?

There is no evidence that average blood pressure in the whole of the general population has risen over the 70 or so years over which measurements are available. There is some indirect evidence that it may have diminished, and may still be falling quite independently of medical treatment. Whatever definition of high blood pressure is used (and this has varied a good deal, since all definitions are arbitrary) the proportion of people with high blood pressure is directly related to average pressure throughout the population.

Standardised and accurate blood pressure measurements for large representative populations have only been available since the 1950s in the UK, Scandinavia and the USA, and more recently for other countries. There is some evidence from countries whose national diet has shifted from very high to much lower sodium (salt) intakes – notably Japan, Portugal and Belgium – that average blood pressure in the general population has fallen, probably for this reason. These reductions in sodium intake reflect shifts in methods of food preservation from the traditional methods of salting, smoking and pickling to the modern methods of refrigeration and rapid transport of fresh food. As these changes have occurred in all economically developed societies, average blood pressure has probably fallen everywhere, compared with average levels in the nineteenth century.

This view is supported by trends in death rates from stroke, which are known to depend more on average blood pressure than on any other factor. In every country that collects complete and reliable data on deaths by medically certified cause, stroke rates have been falling, probably since the 1920s and certainly since the 1950s.

Blood pressure and high blood pressure

Are you more likely to get high blood pressure if you're rich rather than if you're poor?

No, it's the other way around. Research in the USA has always shown higher average blood pressures in poorer people. Although research in this country in the 1950s and 1960s failed to show any systematic difference between social groups for average blood pressure, by the early 1980s this seemed to have changed, with higher average blood pressure in poorer populations throughout the UK.

These differences in average blood pressures are not large, but differences in other risk factors for heart disease show the same pattern. Alhough there is some evidence that coronary heart disease first became common after World War I and that it started among rich people, ever since the 1950s it has more and more become a disease of poorer people. This is partly because of differences in smoking habits, but some of the changes to the pattern may now be caused by these variations in average blood pressure, and perhaps by access to good diagnosis and treatment.

Does it vary around the world? For example, are there differences in blood pressure between races, or between different sorts of societies?

Yes, it does vary, but why it does is not an easy question to answer. A number of different factors have to be considered.

High blood pressure does not seem to exist in the few undisturbed Stone Age societies that still exist in the world, for example the Indians who live in the rainforests on the upper Amazon in South America, and the Highlanders of Papua-New Guinea. In the rest of the economically underdeveloped Third World, high blood pressure is a much more serious problem than in developed economies, with very high rates for stroke (particularly in rural areas) and corresponding burdens of care for these populations. In the economically less developed parts of southern Europe, death rates from stroke are still more than twice as great as death rates from coronary heart disease, whereas in developed European economies death rates from coronary heart disease are about three times as great as from stroke.

High blood pressure is a serious problem throughout black Africa, and black people in North America have much bigger blood pressure and stroke problems than whites. However, the differences between black and white North Americans disappear if differences in income are taken into account. In the 1960s and 70s, comparisons between British citizens of Afro-Carribean and European descent showed no such differences, but more recent studies have begun to show the same differences as in the USA.

These differences are social rather than racial, and social differences in average blood pressure seem to depend mainly on income differences. When North American incomes were much more polarised than British incomes, social differences in average blood pressure were much higher in the USA than in the UK, but there is evidence that as these societies converge, social differences in average blood pressure are becoming similar in the two countries.

It seems impossible these days to talk about anything to do with people's health without talking about money – so what are the economics of treating high blood pressure?

This depends first on how much treatment is rational, in conformity with good evidence of its effectiveness in preventing stroke and other outcomes of uncontrolled high blood pressure, and how much it is driven by other incentives and pressures. In private practice these include fees, in NHS practice they include satisfying the expectations of patients (real or assumed), and for almost everyone they include pressure from the pharmaceutical industry (which, like any other industry, wishes to increase its sales and profits). Secondly, it depends on whether we see benefits in terms of health gains for people or cash relief for taxpayers.

In the UK, as recently as 1986 (there is no more recent evidence) it remained true that roughly half the people with high blood pressure who would benefit from treatment were not known, half of those known were not having treatment, and half of those treated did not have their blood pressure controlled. This failure to deliver care is socially distributed: those in greatest need in the poorest sections of society often get the least care.

Evidence from the USA suggests that as a first step, the greatest gain from the least investment would be not to look for more undiscovered and untreated people with high blood pressure, but to reorganise the care of those already known and treated. This is probably true also in the NHS. General practice teams need to organise follow-up clinics so that they have lists of the people who need to attend, check whether they have actually done so, and if not, ask themselves why. For example, people are understandably unwilling to attend clinics where they may have to wait for long periods of time before being seen.

About 10% of the adult UK population needs treatment for high blood pressure, and roughly half of these are probably getting it. In most cases, management of high blood pressure is still isolated from management of other major risk factors for stroke and coronary heart disease, but this is changing.

Recent changes in the NHS contract for GPs should have led to most people with high blood pressure being identified, although it is much more doubtful whether most of these are being followed up with effective treatment. If all general practice teams developed cardiovascular follow-up clinics for high blood pressure on the same lines as the best have already done, and all their patients were treated to the level of quality attained in large clinical trials, an additional 15% of fatal strokes would be prevented, probably 5% of fatal coronary heart attacks, and similar percentages of nonfatal events.

These are realistic estimates, based on published evidence of what has already been achieved. If management of high blood pressure were fully integrated with management of other risk factors (such as persuading people not to smoke), these figures could be very much better, and coronary heart disease and stroke below 75 years of age could become exceptional rather than everyday tragedies.

2
Symptoms, causes and diagnosis

Symptoms

Do people with high blood pressure feel any different from people with normal blood pressure?

Usually, no. By itself, before it has caused organ damage, high blood pressure causes no symptoms at all. In fact there is some evidence that people with uncomplicated high blood pressure may feel slightly better, more alert and energetic, than people with lower blood pressure.

Symptoms may not be noticeable even after organ damage has started. Even very high pressures, very dangerous and already causing serious kidney damage, may sometimes continue for several months before they cause any symptoms. The only way to know if you have high blood pressure (and how high it is) is to have it measured with a sphygmomanometer, and there is more information about this in Chapter 3.

When my GP was checking my blood pressure, he asked me if I had a lot of headaches and if I got out of breath easily. Why did he ask that?

Headaches and breathlessness on slight exertion (eg on going upstairs) are symptoms which occur more frequently in people who have sustained blood pressures of around 180/120 mmHg or higher than in people with 'normal' blood pressure. Of course, both these symptoms are common anyway, but they happen more often in people with high blood pressure, and increasingly so as blood pressure rises.

Nearly everyone gets 'ordinary' headaches at some time or another – they can be caused by anxiety, tension or minor virus infections. Such innocent headaches are equally common in people with high blood pressure, but a careful doctor will always check your blood pressure first before dismissing associated headaches as insignificant, as they do occasionally signal sudden dangerous loss of control. Some of these headaches can be a warning of early damage to arteries in the brain or retina (the back of the eye), requiring urgent control of blood pressure to prevent serious complications.

Breathlessness in people with high blood pressure is usually simply a result of being overweight. However, if blood pressure has either risen out of control, or has unaccountably started to fall without any change in medication, then breathlessness may be the main symptom of early heart failure.

I would have thought that increased blood pressure would sometimes cause bleeding. Isn't this so?

The risk of bleeding from arteries into the brain (causing stroke) or into the retina (the back of the eye, where there can be patchy

Symptoms, causes and diagnosis

loss of vision if the bleeding is extensive) is increased by high blood pressure, particularly in people over 50, and is one of the main reasons why high blood pressure needs treatment. There is more information about this in the section on **What can go wrong** in Chapter 9.

Nosebleeds and subconjunctival haemorrhages happen more often in people with high blood pressure, although both are very common in people with normal blood pressure and need not be a cause for alarm. Subconjunctival haemorrhages sound very alarming, but 'haemorrhage' is simply the technical term for bleeding of any extent, great or small, and subconjunctival haemorrhages are simply a small amount of bleeding in the white of the eye. They can appear after coughing, sneezing or straining when emptying the bowels, and show up as a bright red area on the white of the eye which then disappears slowly over six weeks or so. They are completely harmless and have nothing to do with retinal haemorrhages.

Heavy periods and menopausal symptoms such as palpitations, night sweats and hot flushes (or the sensation of hot flushes without the appearance of flushing) all commonly occur in women with high blood pressure, but this is simply because high blood pressure is common at this age. None of these symptoms is caused by high blood pressure, nor are they cured by lowering it.

Since I was told I had high blood pressure, I've had awful palpitations. Is this one of the symptoms, and why didn't I notice it before?

Palpitations (feeling or hearing your own heart beating fast), tension headaches and overbreathing (breathing more rapidly than you need to) are symptoms of anxiety, and so are common in people who are anxious or frightened. If they already have these symptoms, and are then found to have high blood pressure, then the diagnosis may confirm their fears and reinforce the symptoms. Other people – like you – may get palpitations for the first time after they have been told that they have high blood pressure. They are not caused by the high blood pressure itself, but by fear of it and what it may mean. The symptoms usually disappear (although not always immediately) with sufficient explanation of what a diagnosis of high blood pressure actually means.

Although I'm only 35, my doctor says I have unusually high blood pressure. I've noticed that my heart often seems to miss a beat, and if I count my pulse, it's often irregular. Has this got something to do with high blood pressure?

Almost certainly not. There are two common causes of an irregular pulse in younger adults.

First if you take long, deep breaths, you may find your wrist pulse slows down as you breathe in, and speeds up as you breathe out. This is not a sign of disease, but of youth. It is caused by a link between the nerves controlling the breathing movements of your diaphragm and the point of origin of your heartbeats, which is called the atrial sinus. This type of irregular pulse is therefore called 'sinus arrhythmia'. Older people lose this link, although some still have it well into their sixties.

The other common cause, at all ages, is extra heartbeats (extrasystoles). These are smaller, relatively ineffective heartbeats, too small to reach your wrist pulse, but they cause an apparent delay before the next beat that is big enough to feel. They are completely normal and harmless, and always disappear if you start any vigorous activity.

Irregular heartbeats in older people may be much more complicated, and need sorting out by a doctor, usually with the help of an ECG (electrocardiograph) tracing.

If one of my children were to develop high blood pressure, how would I know? What symptoms should I look for?

Children very rarely develop high blood pressure. If they do, it is usually secondary rather than primary high blood pressure (see the section on *Types of high blood pressure* in Chapter 1 for an explanation of these terms).

Severe high blood pressure in childhood usually shows up first as headaches, but occasionally as fits or as impaired vision. A child with any of these symptoms, whether having them repeatedly or for the first time, should be taken to the doctor

Symptoms, causes and diagnosis 35

(something most parents would probably do in any case). The doctor should measure your child's blood pressure using an appropriately-sized small cuff and examine both retinas (the backs of the eyes) with an instrument called an opthalmoscope, or else arrange for these tests to be done by a specialist. Until this is done routinely in every case, we shall continue to see rare, but unnecessary, cases of severe organ damage in children with unrecognised and therefore untreated high blood pressure, usually arising from treatable disorders of the kidney.

However, it is important not to panic every time your child has a headache. Migraine headaches are common in children, and may cause temporary vision problems. Children with recurrent headaches should have their blood pressure measured.

Causes

Does anyone know what really causes high blood pressure?

There are many features which are commonly associated with high blood pressure - that is, they occur more often in people with high blood pressure than in people with lower pressures. It is not always easy to test whether these associations are also causes or simply coincidences.

For example, men who wear braces are more likely to have high blood pressure than men wearing belts. However, it is more likely that fat men find braces more comfortable than belts than that braces cause high blood pressure. In this case, we can test for causality by removing the braces and seeing whether blood pressure changes.

Things are less simple for less obviously absurd cases. We know from studies of many different kinds of secondary high blood pressure (there is more information about secondary high blood pressure in Chapter 1) that the original causes may be quite different from the continuing causes. For example, in a rare disorder called coarctation of the aorta the huge artery carrying blood out of the heart is tightly constricted a few inches beyond its origin, and then expands to its normal diameter. Obviously, blood pressure must rise above the constriction, and fall below it, just as it does when you pinch a hosepipe. Yet if this constriction is removed surgically and normal continuity is restored, blood pressure usually takes several years to fall to a normal value. The initiating cause is the constriction, but the continuing cause is probably complex changes in circulating hormones, designed to maintain blood flow through the kidneys despite the obstruction, which continue for a long time after the obstruction has gone.

Apart from inheritance (discussed later in this section), there is good evidence that there are four factors which are true and independent causes of high blood pressure. These factors are **being overweight, a high sodium intake, a low potassium intake and a high alcohol intake**. The effect they have depends in most (if not all) cases on inheritance: they have a much bigger effect on people from families with mostly high blood pressure than on people from families with mostly low blood pressure (there are questions about the inheritance of high blood pressure later in this section). They are also reversible causes: if they are controlled, blood pressure will eventually fall (although not necessarily to normal levels). This will happen sooner in young people and later in middle-aged and elderly people.

The evidence for these causes is consistent and convincing. That does not eliminate the possibility of other causes operating in some people, of which the most obvious and important are physical, psychological and social stresses of various kinds. These are discussed in other questions in this section.

Is it not likely that sustained stress, tension, and worry may cause a sustained rise in blood pressure, and therefore be the main cause of hypertension?

The 'tension' in hypertension refers to the tension in the artery walls, not to the sort of tension we mean when we talk about stress and worry. This confusion is one of the reasons I have used 'high blood pressure' throughout this book rather than 'hypertension'. 'High blood pressure' states a fact (your blood pressure is unusually high), without implying any known cause.

It does not suggest that we know more than we actually do.

To come back to your question – stress is one possible cause of otherwise unexplained high blood pressure, but it is not the only cause, and may not even be a common cause.

The theory that physical and psychological stress was the root cause of most high blood pressure was very popular in the 1960s and 1970s, but research since then has proved it not to be true. There may be a minority of people with high blood pressure in whom it is the main cause, but it does not explain most cases. Several large research studies have looked for (and expected to find) a link between the so-called Type A personality (people who are ambitious, aggressive and time-obsessed) and high blood pressure, but none could be found. Instead we find that lots of very nervous people have normal or even low blood pressures, and lots of easy-going phlegmatic people have dangerously high blood pressures. However, there is a tendency for some people with depression to have raised blood pressures: these fall when depression ends, either spontaneously or as a result of treatment with antidepressant drugs.

Clearly there are many other good reasons for avoiding or eliminating social and psychological stresses, regardless of any possible effects on blood pressure. Even if they are not causing

high blood pressure directly, they certainly affect your capacity to cope with treatment, and you should make sure that your doctor is aware of them. The sections on **Treatment without drugs** in Chapter 4 and on **Complementary therapies** in Chapter 5 include some information about stress reduction.

But surely physical or psychological stress and tension do raise blood pressure?

Yes, and this is where confusion can arise.

Stress can cause a large rise in blood pressure, lasting minutes or even hours. Such rises are normal and occur in everyone. They are brief additions to our usual average pressures, whether those be high or low. But they are temporary peaks in blood pressure – they go away when the stress that caused them is removed. As a possible cause of eventual organ damage, 'high blood pressure' refers not to the temporary peaks but to the average level (sustained over weeks, months or years) to which blood pressure returns when the stress is removed.

I'm very keen on sports, and I also do a lot of running. Will this give me high blood pressure?

No. Vigorous forms of exercise such as running certainly cause huge but brief rises in blood pressure, but there is almost no evidence to support the idea that physical stresses of this sort are a cause of high blood pressure which continues over days, weeks, months and years. On the contrary, there is good evidence that dynamic exercise (such as cycling, running, swimming or digging) can reduce blood pressure by as much as 10 mmHg, as well as reducing other risk factors for premature coronary disease (such as blood cholesterol and fibrinogen), and you will find more information about this in Chapter 5.

Static exercise (such as weight training, push-ups and other so-called body-building exercises) is a different matter. It can raise blood pressure substantially and can be dangerous in people who already have high blood pressure.

Are there any drugs that can cause high blood pressure?

Yes. They are in four groups: home remedies bought across the counter at the chemist; prescribed medication; herbal medicines; and drugs of addiction and abuse.

- **Home remedies bought over the counter**
  Many different preparations available for shrinking up your nasal air passages in colds, hay fever (allergic rhinitis) or 'chronic catarrh' (usually unrecognised hay fever) can raise blood pressure, because they contain chemicals (called sympathomimetic amines) which are closely related to naturally occurring chemicals in the body which act on blood pressure. If you are using any kind of nasal spray or decongestant drops, make sure you mention this to whoever is measuring your blood pressure. Despite their popularity, nasal decongestants containing these drugs only work for a short time, and the swelling returns worse than ever as soon as they are stopped. This leads many people to go on using them for days, months or even years on end, in which case they develop severe chronic nasal obstruction and catarrh, caused by the very drug they are using to treat it. This dependence is reinforced by the fact that these drugs tend to wake people up and give them a bit of a lift, in the same way as dexamphetamine (Dexedrine, 'speed'), so that (often unconsciously) they become addicted to them. The moral is, don't use them unless you have to, and never use them for more than a couple of hours. Traditional remedies such as menthol and eucalyptus are safer and just as effective, but check with your chemist that they don't contain amine supplements.

  NSAIDs are another group of drugs which can affect your blood pressure. They are prescribed for pains in bones, joints and muscles. Although some of them can be bought from chemists over the counter, most are only available on prescription, so they are discussed in the next group with other prescribed drugs.

- **Prescribed medication**
  Prescribed drugs include NSAIDs (which stands for non-steroidal anti-inflammatory drugs); corticosteroid hormones; and some drugs derived from liquorice which were at

one time used commonly to treat gastric ulcers but are now hardly prescribed.

NSAIDs are commonly used for joint pain. Although there are many different NSAIDs available, the most widely used is ibuprofen (which has many trade names, including Brufen, Cuprofen and Nurofen). NSAIDs cause a substantial rise in blood pressure in most people, pushing it up by about 5-10 mmHg diastolic pressure, about the same as most BP-lowering drugs bring it down. Because of this effect, it is important that you remind your doctor or pharmacist that you have high BP if you ever need painkillers, as they will be able to suggest more suitable alternatives for you.

Corticosteroid hormones include cortisone, hydrocortisone, prednisone, prednisolone, and adrenocorticotrophic hormone (ACTH). All of them, if given in high dosage, raise blood pressure by causing sodium and water retention and thus increasing the volume of blood in the body. This normally happens only if steroids are taken into the body as tablets or injections, but occasionally heavy use of steroid inhalers or some strong steroid ointments may penetrate sufficiently through the lungs or the skin to have the same effect. Large doses of steroid tablets or injections should never be used other than for serious, usually life-threatening disease, which will usually be under the care of hospital specialists. The only situations in which steroid treatment is at all likely to interfere with management of high blood pressure are severe asthma and rheumatoid arthritis, and you will find more information about these in Chapter 6.

- **Herbal medicines**
Herbal remedies are discussed in more detail in the section on *Complementary therapies* in Chapter 5, but among those that can cause high blood pressure or interact with BP-lowering medication are liquorice, ginseng, lily of the valley, foxglove and horse chestnut.

- **Drugs of addiction and abuse**
Dexamphetamine (trade name Dexedrine, nickname 'speed') and its more potent and even more dangerous relation

Symptoms, causes and diagnosis

Ecstasy cause a 'high' mood, wakefulness, indifference to food and transient very high blood pressure. Both drugs can cause hallucinations (which may be dangerous if people drive) and, combined with vigorous activity at high room temperature, Ecstasy may raise blood pressure high enough to cause death from acute heart failure.

Cocaine may also cause prolonged rises in blood pressure.

My uncle and my grandfather were both diagnosed as having high blood pressure, so am I going to get it? Is it inherited?

Yes, it is inherited (that is, it runs in families), but this does not automatically mean that you will develop it yourself.

We know that inheritance plays a very large part in who does and does not develop high blood pressure. Speaking mathematically, at least half of the variance in blood pressure within large groups of people can be predicted from knowledge of blood pressure in parents and brothers and sisters. However, we do not yet understand exactly how it is inherited. We know that some of our characteristics (like the colour of our eyes) and some rare diseases (like muscular dystrophy or haemophilia) can be caused by inheriting single genes. But we also know that (with certain rare exceptions) high blood pressure is hardly ever inherited in this simple way.

In all other cases, blood pressure depends on interaction between many different inherited factors, many of which operate only if certain environmental conditions exist. The most important of these conditions are probably birthweight (premature babies tend to have higher blood pressure in middle age); being considerably overweight in adolescence and as a young adult; sodium intake; and alcohol intake, particularly in younger people.

However, it is usually futile to argue about nature versus nurture, or inheritance versus environment. It is more important for you to realise that there may be a possibility of your developing high blood pressure, and that you should therefore be sensible about what you eat and drink, the amount of exercise you take, and not smoking. Your GP will advise you on how often you should have your blood pressure checked.

If I have high blood pressure myself, and high blood pressure is inherited, are my children likely to get high blood pressure? And if so, is there anything I can do to prevent it?

Yes they are, but not during their childhood. When they grow up, they are much more likely eventually to have high blood pressures than the children of parents with low blood pressures, even more so if both you and your partner have high blood pressures.

As to preventing it, there is as yet no evidence that this can be done (although studies which may eventually answer this question are now underway) but there are two likely possibilities. One is to reduce sodium intake, the other is to keep weight within normal levels for age and height (see Chapter 5 for information about how to go about both of these). We have some encouraging early data suggesting that control of obesity in childhood may lead to lower blood pressure levels in young adults, but no information yet on the effectiveness of salt restriction.

Does adult high blood pressure begin in childhood? If so,

Symptoms, causes and diagnosis 43

would it be worth screening children for high blood pressure, or do children with high BP not usually become adults with high BP?

Most of it probably does and, if you include inheritance (which precedes childhood) then nearly all of it does, if we leave aside the contribution of alcohol. However, as an extremely general statement, this is of little practical use. There is already fairly good evidence that controlling overweight in childhood, perhaps on a vegetarian diet, may prevent a lot of later high blood pressure in adults, but not much evidence to support any other specific preventive actions.

In general, screening children would not be useful. Screening of children for BP is essentially a research tool, not a useful activity in general practice and, if done at all, it must be done by specially trained and equipped teams. The fact that high BP begins with inheritance or in childhood does not mean that you actually have high BP in childhood – just that the tendency for you to develop it as you grow older is already there. All screening would show up would be the rare child who actually has primary high blood pressure – and primary high blood pressure in children does not need treatment. Screening is not useful for finding the equally rare cases of secondary high blood pressure, where BP rises rapidly over a short period, and is caused by some other illness (usually a treatable kidney problem).

Knowing that a child has an above-average BP is also not a very useful predictor of what will happen when that child grows up. Although there is a very general tendency for babies with higher BPs to become adults with higher BPs (just as babies with long noses tend to have long noses as adults), the links are very uncertain. In one study of 14-year-olds with untreated high blood pressure (average 170/100 mmHg) followed up for 20 years, only 17% had higher pressures 20 years later, and one third had diastolic pressures below 90 mmHg.

I'm 30, I don't smoke, and although I do enjoy an occasional glass of wine, I'm not a heavy drinker – but I've got high blood pressure, which I'd always thought only affected people who were much older than me. Are the causes of high blood

pressure in people of my age just the same as for people who are middle-aged or older?

Generally yes, bearing in mind that we still don't know most of the causes of most high blood pressure in middle age and later life. The main difference is that in younger adults like you there are more cases of secondary high blood pressure caused by other rare disorders (usually affecting the kidney or the adrenal glands). This is also true (but to a greater extent) of high blood pressure in children.

Doctors used to be taught that everyone aged under 40 found to have high blood pressure should be referred to a consultant for special investigations to see if it had been caused by such rare disorders. For the occasional person with extremely high pressure (sustained diastolic 120 mmHg or more) this rule probably still holds, but even then few such causes will be found. For the great majority of people in this age group who have raised pressures below this level, routine referral for these investigations is not necessary - providing your family doctor is prepared to take you seriously, organise a few simple tests, and make a careful evaluation of your response to treatment. The minority of people who then do need specialist referral (not for routine tests but for a serious and repeated search for these rare causes) can then usually be identified and get the attention they deserve, as many of these rare causes are very difficult to find.

Is getting older or just being old in itself a cause of high blood pressure? In other words, is high blood pressure normal in old age?

Blood pressure usually rises with age. All doctors used until recently to be taught, and many still believe, that higher BP is more or less normal as you get older, is less dangerous in the elderly than in middle age, and should only be treated if it rises to something like 180-200 mmHg systolic or 100-110 mmHg diastolic pressure, or causes definite organ damage. This is wrong. It is now generally accepted that although high BP in the elderly is certainly common, it should not be accepted as normal, for three reasons.

First, although average BP increases with age in all economically developed societies, this may not be 'normal'. In some societies that still have undisturbed Stone Age economies (eg Brazilian rainforest Indians, the Highlanders of Papua-New Guinea and some herdsman tribes in Kenya), blood pressure remains low throughout life with no rise in older people. In our Western developed economies, blood pressure that rises with age is therefore expected, but should not be assumed to be natural. This is not much help to people who don't want to live in a Stone Age economy, in which although the few who reach old age have low blood pressure, most die much earlier from a variety of accidents, infectious and parasitic diseases, and periodic famine. We still don't know exactly which aspects of Stone Age economy and culture cause lifelong low blood pressure. The current 'prime suspect' is a sodium intake around 15 mmol daily, less than a tenth of the average intake in our present European diet. The changes in diet required to reach such a low figure would not just modify our eating habits, it would wipe out all the traditional cuisines of Europe, India, and China. But, obviously, we can deduce from this that high blood pressure in old age is not inevitable.

Second, we now have consistent evidence from many long-term studies involving large groups of people that high blood pressure is more dangerous (ie it causes more heart attacks and strokes) in elderly people than in those who are middle-aged.

Third, we also have a lot of evidence that shows conclusively that bringing blood pressure levels down in elderly people is more effective in preventing stroke and coronary heart attacks than similar reductions of BP in middle age. In fact the only trials that have shown reductions in deaths from all causes (not just from stroke and heart disease) after treatment for mild or moderate high blood pressure have been in the elderly. Similar reduced all-causes death rates have not been shown for treatment of mild to moderate high blood pressure in middle-aged people, but only for fairly severe high blood pressure (diastolic 115 mmHg or over).

It is therefore wrong to regard high blood pressure in elderly people as normal or benign, or any less worthy of treatment than high blood pressure in middle age.

Diagnosis and initial investigations

How do doctors diagnose high blood pressure?

Simply measuring your blood pressure is by far the most important routine test. It is important for your doctor to make sure that enough reliable measurements have been made to provide evidence good enough to allow an average blood pressure value to be calculated accurately, and thus to assess how big a problem you really have. Except in extreme emergencies, at least three readings on separate days are necessary for this. For all but very severe cases, decisions on treatment can be made much better after two weeks or so of twice-daily home readings, which can teach you valuable lessons about how your own blood pressure behaves, and how it relates to how you feel from day to day.

Because blood pressure measurement is so important, it has a chapter of its own - Chapter 3.

I didn't know I had high blood pressure until I had to have a medical for my new insurance policy. Why wasn't it diagnosed before?

Probably because you had not had your blood pressure measured for some years. If you read the section on *Symptoms* at the beginning of this chapter, you will see that - like you - many people with high blood pressure have no symptoms at all. The only way to know if you have high blood pressure is to have it measured (there is more information about this in Chapter 3). If the only medical check-ups you have are for insurance or perhaps before you start a new job, then those are the only times when anyone has a chance to measure your blood pressure and find out that it is high.

Chapter 7 on *Living with high BP* includes sections on both work and insurance.

Do doctors and nurses try to find out what causes high blood pressure in particular people? If so, what sort of questions do they ask?

Yes, they do. There are some questions which I think health

Symptoms, causes and diagnosis

professionals should ask about everyone found to have blood pressure at or over about 150/90mmHg.

- Questions about your blood pressure measurement.
  Was the blood pressure measurement likely to represent your normal blood pressure? Did this measurement worry you, did you hurry to this appointment, was it very cold outside, did you have a full bladder, or was there any other reason why any kind of discomfort or anxiety might have pushed up your blood pressure? Doctors or nurses measuring blood pressure are all taught to look for reasons of this sort for unexpectedly high values. A rapid pulse often gives a clue to anxiety or vigorous exercise within the previous 10-15 minutes.
- Questions about your family.
  Were either of your parents or any of your brothers or sisters known to have high blood pressure? People without any family history of high blood pressure are more likely to have a rare, surgically treatable cause of high blood pressure, such as a kidney disorder or coarctation of the aorta. (You may be examined for absent or suspiciously reduced pulses over the femoral arteries, felt in your groin creases. This is the classical sign of coarctation of the aorta, rare but easily detected, with very effective surgical treatment.)
- Questions about your drinking habits.
  How much alcohol do you drink in a usual week? Drinking more than 4 units of alcohol a day if you are a man or 3 units a day if you are a woman is a common and readily removable cause of high blood pressure, particularly in people aged under 40 (a unit of alcohol is one glass of wine OR one single measure of spirits OR half a pint of average strength beer or lager).
- Questions about your weight.
  Do you look overweight for your height? All your doctor or nurse needs to do is look at you and think. Again, this is a readily treatable cause.

Your doctor may also suggest that you have some other tests, which are discussed in the answer to the next question.

When my doctor told me that she thought I probably had high blood pressure, she said that she wanted me to have some blood and urine tests (and probably some other tests as well) on top of having my blood pressure measured a lot. Why?

For two main reasons. The first is to assess how much (if any) organ damage has already been done, and to establish baseline values so that any possible damage can be assessed in the future. Unless your normal pattern is recorded from the beginning (ie from the baseline), apparent changes later on may be misinterpreted. The main 'target organs' for damage by high blood pressure are the large and small arteries everywhere in your body, but especially in the brain, eyes, heart, and kidneys. Measurable damage of this sort is rare under 40 years of age, except in people with diastolic pressures sustained above 120 mmHg for many years.

The other reason is to find out if your high blood pressure is of the less common secondary type rather than the more common primary type (the difference between them is explained in Chapter 1). 'Classical' causes of secondary high blood pressure are all rare, accounting for less than 1% of all cases of treated high blood pressure. In practice they are usually searched for in two stages: before treatment begins (as in your case), and then later on if treatment unaccountably fails. For example, if after several months of treatment your blood pressure was still not under control, or if after several years of good control your blood pressure became uncontrollable despite continued treatment, then a secondary cause might be sought, starting with investigations to see whether one of your kidney arteries had been blocked by a clot. Some very rare causes, such as the adrenal tumor phaeochromocytoma, are extremely difficult to find and require great persistence.

Depending on your individual case and on what your doctor thinks is necessary, you may have any (or even all) of the following tests.

- **Urine and blood tests**

Before starting treatment, you should have your kidneys

Symptoms, causes and diagnosis 49

checked, which involves having simple urine tests for protein, bacteria and glucose, and by having your blood urea and creatinine levels measured. All these tests require as far as you are concerned is providing a urine sample and having a small amount of blood taken from your arm. The results of these tests will provide a baseline measure for assessment of possible future organ damage and act as a check for possible causes (they may indicate a cause in the kidneys, which account for more than half of all cases of classical secondary high blood pressure).

At the same time your GP may ask for a number of other routine blood tests to be carried out, including three that often give clues to high alcohol intake (raised mean corpuscular volume, gamma-glutamyl transferase, and triglyceride), and one that indicates rare adrenal tumours that raise blood pressure (reduced blood potassium).

- **Checking pulses**

Not, in this case, the pulse in your wrist, but those in your groin and your feet and ankles.

A quick check on groin pulses is enough to exclude a very rare condition called coarctation of the aorta.

The pulses in your feet and ankles provide information about the state of your leg and coronary arteries. If you are over 40, then the health of your leg and coronary arteries should be assessed by taking these pulses and by asking you a few questions about how you feel. (For example, if you regularly get pain in your calves or in the front of your chest after exercise such as prolonged walking or climbing stairs or hills, and these pains are worse in cold weather, then this would suggest that you may have some artery problems.) Artery pulses below the inner side of the ankle and in the forefoot should be checked, as even in people with no artery damage, one or other of these pulses may be absent (usually on both sides). Unless your normal pattern is recorded from the start, apparent changes later on may be misinterpreted.

- **Eye tests**

Damage to the eyes usually only occurs in people with very

high pressures, and so most people will not need to have their eyes examined. However, people with very high pressures (diastolic 120 mmHg or more) do need careful examination of the retina (the back of the eye) with an ophthalmoscope, in a darkened room or with eye drops to dilate their pupils. This is to look for swelling and bleeding around small retinal arteries, which reveal imminent high risk of serious damage to the eyes, brain, and kidneys. When found, this is a medical emergency requiring urgent admission to hospital.

- **X-rays and ECGs**

At one time chest X-rays and special X-rays of the kidney (pyelography) were thought to be essential before starting treatment. We now know that these are not efficient ways of looking for secondary high blood pressure at this stage (unless there are other definite indications of heart failure or lung or kidney disease), and so they are not necessary or useful for routine initial assessment.

The same applies to ECGs (electrocardiograms). These give much less information about heart function than you might think, they require careful evaluation, and interpretation is full of pitfalls. Interpretation is far easier if a baseline ECG is available, before there are any reasons to suspect heart damage. One single ECG trace is therefore a useful investigation for everyone before they start treatment for their high blood pressure. Should you ever develop suspicious chest pains then an ECG would be essential, and will be easier to interpret if an earlier trace is available to compare with it.

- **Other tests**

Some other rare causes of secondary high blood pressure are obvious just by looking at you, for example acromegaly and Cushing's disease.

Examination of your chest and heart with a stethoscope is only important for elderly people or those with pressure high enough to cause heart failure.

In people with very high pressures or who already complain of symptoms suggesting little strokes (transient giddiness; speech impairment; double vision; weakness of one side

Symptoms, causes and diagnosis

of the face or of one hand or of one leg; and sudden loss of memory for recent events) brain damage can be assessed mainly by assessment of brain function. The most sensitive way to do this is is for the doctor simply to ask the person and their family the right questions (about memory for recent events; difficulties in finding the words they want to say or grasping the words spoken to them; double vision or other vision disturbances; weakness of one side of the face; difficulties in chewing or swallowing; difficulties with fine finger or hand movements; difficulties in walking or balancing) and really listening to the answers. Formal neurological tests of eye movement, face or limb weakness, co-ordination and balance, and various nerve reflexes are also useful, but usually less sensitive than the perception by the person or their experienced carers that something is wrong. If these tests are done at all, they must be done well, which takes a long time. They are not necessary or useful for the large majority of people found to have high blood pressure.

3
Measuring blood pressure

Sphygmomanometers

What is a sphygmomanometer? Are there different kinds?

'Sphygmomanometer' is simply the technical term for an instrument used to measure blood pressure (a manometer is an instrument for measuring the pressure of fluids; 'sphygmos' is the Greek word for pulse). These instruments could equally well just be called 'blood pressure monitors' or something similar, but sphygmomanometer was the name chosen when they first

Measuring blood pressure

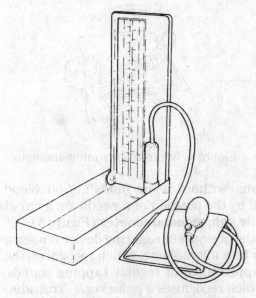

Figure 3: Mercury sphygmomanometer

came into use in the late nineteenth century and so is still used today.

The sphygmomanometers in everyday use in doctors' surgeries consist of a device for measuring pressure connected to an inflatable cuff which is wrapped around your upper arm. The differences between the three basic types - mercury (Figure 3), aneroid (Figure 4) and electronic (Figure 5) - lie in the pressure-measuring devices they use.

- **Mercury sphygmomanometer** (Figure 3)
  This is the type of sphygmomanometer still used by most doctors. Its pressure-measuring device is a long hollow glass tube with a mercury reservoir at its base. Your blood pressure pushes the mercury up the tube, and the level it reaches can then be read off on the scale.
- **Aneroid sphygmomanometer** (Figure 4)
  These balance your blood pressure against pressure in a thin metal capsule containing air ('aneroid' comes from the Greek,

54 High blood pressure at your fingertips

Figure 4: Aneroid sphygmomanometer

and means 'without using fluids'). Your blood pressure is indicated by the position of a needle on a circular dial.
- **Electronic sphygmomanometer** (Figure 5)
In these the pressure-measuring device is a sensor in the cuff. This may be a microphone, which recognises the appearance and disappearance of regular tapping sounds, or a transducer, which recognises a pulse wave. Transducers are more efficient (but more expensive), less prone to pick up irrelevant signals, and are now almost universally used. Microprocessors (the ubiquitous 'chips' found in everything from pocket calculators to computers) then convert the information received by the sensor into blood pressure readings which are either printed out or shown on the machine's display screen. With some electronic sphygmomanometers, the cuff may be inflated by an electric pump and deflated automatically.

Figure 5: Electronic sphygmomanometer

Measuring blood pressure

What's the point of the doctor listening to my arm through a stethoscope when he's taking my blood pressure?

To hear the sounds of your heart pumping blood through the main artery in your arm (the brachial artery), which are heard best through a stethoscope placed in the crook of your elbow. The pressure required first to start and then to stop these pumping sounds is used as the measure of your blood pressure.

When your blood pressure is taken, the cuff wrapped around your upper arm is inflated until the pulse in your wrist can no longer be felt: this indicates that the flow of blood through your brachial artery has been stopped. The cuff is then inflated a little more, until the sphygmomanometer reading is about 20 mmHg higher than the point at which your pulse could no longer be felt.

This is the point at which your doctor or nurse (or you yourself if you are taking your own measurements) starts listening through the stethoscope. The air is then slowly released from the cuff until clear, regular tapping sounds are heard through the stethoscope. The level of pressure at which these sounds are heard is your systolic pressure, and the figure shown on the sphygmomanometer scale is recorded.

The pressure in the cuff is then released further. First the tapping sounds disappear and then, at a pressure about 50-100 mmHg lower, soft, regular whooshing noises are heard through the stethoscope. When these sounds disappear, it indicates that the blood is once again flowing smoothly through your brachial artery. The level of pressure at which the sounds disappear is your diastolic pressure, and the figure shown on the sphygmomanometer scale is again recorded.

In an electronic sphygmomanometer, a sensor in the cuff replaces the stethoscope. The sensor perceives the appearance and disappearance of pulse sounds or movements, rather than someone's ears, and the machine notes the systolic and diastolic pressures for you automatically.

Are all the different sorts of sphygmomanometer equally accurate?

Mercury sphygmomanometers are accurate to the nearest 2 mmHg if they are well maintained and used carefully. They have a great advantage over the other types in that when they go wrong, it is usually obvious and can be easily corrected.

Aneroid sphygmomanometers are small, and are more convenient to carry than the larger mercury sphygmomanometers. Modern machines developed in the past five years or so are accurate and reliable; older machines are not.

Because of the way they work, electronic sphygmomanometers have the potential to eliminate several important sources of error. They are also easy to use, particularly by people measuring their own blood pressure at home. Unfortunately their futuristic appearance is no guarantee of accuracy and this is especially true of the machines on sale to the public at an affordable price. Also, unlike the traditional mercury machines, it may not be obvious if anything goes wrong with an electronic sphygmomanometer, so you may go on recording systematically incorrect and misleading readings. However, electronic machines are constantly improving and, once their accuracy is beyond doubt, they will certainly replace mercury machines.

In my opinion, sphygmomanometers of all kinds should (like other measuring instruments) be compelled by law to conform to some common minimum standard of accuracy. Two published standards are now available, one from the British Hypertension Society and the other from the American Association for Advancement of Medical Instrumentation (AAAMI), but nothing has been done to enforce them in this country. A European Union directive on standards of performance and safety is due to come into force shortly and has already been applied in Germany: machines that meet this standard will be marked 'CE', but this does not guarantee that they will have been tested by an independent organisation.

I've read about portable measuring instruments which give 24-hour readings. Are these a better way to measure blood pressure?

These machines first became widely available in the late 1980s. Unlike electronic sphygmomanometers used for isolated readings, they do measure blood pressure almost as accurately as a traditional mercury machine. However, they cost much more

Measuring blood pressure

than ordinary sphygmomanometers (whether electronic or mercury). They are now widely used by many GPs and some hospital departments, and may be lent out for home use for initial assessments.

Most of the models now available are rather cumbersome, usually because of heavy batteries (which should soon be a thing of the past, as technology improves). As with most other sphygmomanometers, they depend on an inflatable cuff wrapped around the upper arm. This can seriously disturb sleep for many people, and may also be distracting while driving a car. They do not interfere much with ordinary activities of a more sedentary kind, but heavy work is impossible.

These machines are usually set to measure blood pressure at 30 minute intervals (the best for statistical analysis), but most people prefer them to operate hourly. Although they are designed to be used over 48 hours, few people can put up with them for more than 24 hours at a time.

They are a great help in sorting out 'white coat hypertension' from 'real' high blood pressure, and thus preventing people being started on a lifetime of treatment merely because they are afraid of doctors. ('White coat hypertension' refers to the effect that the medical profession has on some people - simply entering a doctor's surgery can make them so nervous that their blood pressure shoots up.) As these people probably account for

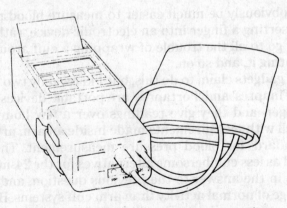

Figure 6: 24-hour blood pressure monitor

at least one-third of those with borderline high blood pressures, the general use of these machines would probably be cost-effective if they were made easily available on loan to GPs through NHS Health Authorities.

The information these machines provide is not always easy to interpret. At present, all the important evidence we have on the value and limitations of long-term treatment for high blood pressure at various levels is based on ordinary readings, with people sitting down and having their blood pressure measured in the traditional way by a doctor or nurse. These values cannot easily be translated into the average values measured by these new portable instruments. A major long-term study of the predictive value of 24-hour measurements compared with traditional isolated measurements began in Europe in 1989 in an attempt to settle this question. Until we have the results of this study or some similar evidence, making your own series of readings at home (as discussed later in this chapter) will probably continue to be a simpler and more useful way of getting more representative blood pressure measurements before treatment begins.

All this wrapping a cuff around your arm, inflating it and so on is a bit cumbersome. Why can't blood pressure be accurately measured more simply, perhaps by machines applied to a finger?

It would obviously be much easier to measure blood pressure just by inserting a finger into an electronic device, rather than having to go to all the trouble of wrapping a cuff around your arm, inflating it, and so on.

Several gadgets claim to do this, but I know only two that are reliable. 'Finapres' and 'Portapres' are portable devices applied to the finger, and they give readings over a few hours which match well with measurements made inside an arm artery, the 'gold standard' for blood pressure measurement. They were developed as less cumbersome alternatives for the 24-machines discussed in the answer to the previous question, and allow a wider range of normal activity than arm cuff systems. However, they are very expensive, and unlikely to be available outside a few major hospitals actively involved in research.

I would not recommend that you buy any of the finger sphygmomanometers sold for home use.

Accuracy and reliability

How reliable can one measurement be?

The short answer is not very reliable – you need to take several to get a reasonable picture.

Figures 1 and 2 (in Chapter 1) show just how much blood pressure varies throughout the day. As you can see from those examples, even if a single measurement is made absolutely accurately, you can't safely assume that it represents an average reading. Doctors now generally agree that you need at least three readings (preferably made on separate days) before you take any really big decisions, such as starting or stopping treatment. Many GPs would now go further than that, and will ask you to measure your own blood pressure at home for a few weeks (there is more about this in the section on *Measuring blood pressure at home* later in this chapter).

Even at those immediately dangerous levels of pressure where drug treatment is almost always needed (roughly, above 200 mmHg systolic or 125 mmHg diastolic), it is still wise to take several readings at least a few minutes apart before taking action to reduce pressure. Pressures often fall by as much as 20 mmHg even in this short time, as patients, doctors, and nurses all become less alarmed.

Is there scope for human error in making blood pressure measurements?

Yes, of course, as with everything else that humans do. Blood pressure measurements need to be made carefully and by people who have been trained in how to make them.

For example, I know of some hospitals where all the blood pressure measurements recorded end in zeros for both systolic and diastolic pressure. If you read to the nearest 2 mmHg (the marks on the scale) then on average only 20% of accurate measurements should end in a zero. This means that the doctors and nurses in those hospitals were measuring only to the nearest 10 mmHg. Hospitals are now tending to use electronic machines, which are incapable of preferring zeros, but this apparently greater accuracy can conceal readings which may be just as inaccurate if the machines are carelessly used, for example by lowering the cuff pressure too fast.

Apart from carelessness, the main sources of human error come from using a cuff that is too small (discussed in the answer to the next question) or deflating the cuff too fast. In order to get an accurate reading, the pressure in the cuff must be deflated at roughly 2 mmHg per second. If it is deflated faster than this, then blood pressure will be systematically underestimated, by an amount proportional to the speed of deflation. In other words, the faster the deflation, the less accurate the reading.

Why would someone deflate the cuff too fast? One simple reason is that they might be in a hurry. Another is that having an inflated cuff around your arm squeezing it tight is uncomfortable, sometimes even painful, and it can be tempting to deflate it quickly to remove the discomfort. Some of the better electronic sphygmomanometers can solve this problem, as they do have mechanisms for deflating the cuff automatically – but then someone has to set this mechanism at the correct slow rate.

Obviously these problems are not insurmountable – they can all be easily avoided by being careful and paying attention to detail.

Is the accuracy of blood pressure measurements affected by whether I'm fat or thin?

Yes. The cuff used to block the flow of blood through the brachial artery when measurements are made contains an inflatable rubber bladder. This should reach right round the full girth of the arm. If it is too short, blood pressure measurements may be overestimated by about 20 mmHg, a serious margin of error.

This is a common cause of incorrect diagnosis and unnecessary treatment. It can be avoided only by using a larger cuff.

Well-equipped GPs and hospitals have such cuffs, but don't always remember to use them (and, unfortunately, some GPs and hospitals don't even possess outsize cuffs). If you have large upper arms (more than about 30 cm or 12 inches in circumference) I'm afraid you must learn to insist (gently and courteously but firmly) on the use of an outsize cuff. If you don't do this, you may easily be overtreated.

Electronic sphygmomanometers present a similar problem. Because they depend on a sensor sewn into the cuff, serious measurement errors can result if the cuff used is too short. If you have large upper arms, you will again need to insist on an outsize cuff being used. However, some models do have long cuffs as standard: cuffs containing a 35 cm (14 inch) rubber bladder inside will do for arms up to 42 cm (16 inch-17 inch) circumference, and few arms are bigger than this.

Measurements on people with exceptionally thin arms underestimate blood pressure by 5-10 mmHg however carefully they are performed. There is no way round this, and it is probably the reason why research studies generally show that high blood pressure in very thin people appears to carry greater risks than the same levels of blood pressure in fatter people.

Does the fact that blood pressure varies during the day mean that it matters whether it is measured in the morning or the evening?

Most people have higher blood pressure for a couple of hours before and after waking. In theory, this means that blood pressure measured in a GP's surgery early in the morning should therefore be a bit higher than if measured in the evening. However, comparison of millions of blood pressure measurements in a large survey in USA showed no significant difference between measurements made in the morning and in the afternoon - so in practice it makes little or no difference.

Does my state of mind affect my blood pressure measurements?

Indeed it does. Simply entering a doctor's surgery can make some people so nervous that their blood pressure shoots up, a condition sufficiently well known to doctors to have its own name – 'white coat hypertension'. If you know you are anxious or frightened when you see your doctor or nurse, it is important to tell them this. You can then either arrange to have more measurements at the clinic, so that you get used to the procedure and become less anxious, or you can arrange to measure your own blood pressure at home (there is a section on **Measuring blood pressure at home** later in this chapter).

Are my blood pressure readings affected by hurrying to keep my appointment?

They may be, if you have only five or 10 minutes to wait before your blood pressure is measured. If you ran for the bus, you need to sit quietly for about half an hour before any measurement.

Are my blood pressure readings affected by my menstrual periods?

No, unless your periods are painful, in which case pain is the cause, not menstruation itself.

Some of the drugs commonly used to relieve period pains – for example, mefenamic acid (Ponstan) and other NSAIDs such as ibuprofen – may raise blood pressure by up to 10 mmHg, so you need to remind your doctor or nurse if you are taking these. Aspirin and paracetamol have no effect on blood pressure.

Are there any other important causes of misleading blood pressure readings?

Apart from recent exertion, pain, fear, anger, embarrassment and so on, the other important causes are alcohol, some kinds of medication, and a full bladder.

Large quantities of alcohol, whether taken slowly and steadily over months or quickly in a binge, can raise blood pressure substantially in many people. This is a common cause of sustained high blood pressure in young men.

Several commonly used drugs, both prescribed and bought over the counter at the chemists, tend to raise blood pressure: there is more information about these drugs in the section on **Causes** in Chapter 2. Never forget to remind your doctor or

Measuring blood pressure

nurse what drugs you are taking, whether they were bought over the counter or prescribed for you.

A stretched bladder causes a huge rise in blood pressure: people whose blood pressure is normally around 130/70 mmHg may easily raise it to about 200/120 mmHg in this way. This can happen easily in a doctor's waiting room, if someone wants to go to the toilet, but is afraid of losing their place in the queue. It can also happen to men with benign enlargement of the prostate admitted to hospital with acute retention of urine. Inexperienced junior house surgeons, alarmed by finding an apparently severe high blood pressure, may call in a house physician colleague who prescribes BP-lowering drugs, and the man then leaves hospital with his prostatic obstruction relieved but wrongly labelled as suffering from high blood pressure, to spend a remaining lifetime on unnecessary medication.

Once a stretched bladder is emptied, blood pressure falls quickly to its usual value. The lesson is – if you need a pee, say so.

If blood pressure measurements are so variable, why does it matter whether they are accurate?

I explained in the answer to the first question in this section why it is necessary to take several measurements before making any important decisions about treatment. Inaccurate readings will distort this overall picture. If they were all inaccurate, the picture would be very distorted indeed, and you could find yourself either not receiving the treatment you need, or being overtreated. So accuracy is important, but the way to make single blood pressure measurements more representative of your average blood pressure is to take plenty of readings, and not just to rely on one measurement, however accurately it has been made.

If my blood pressure measurements vary so much, how can figures for my 'average blood pressure' have any meaning?

Several very large research studies of the behaviour of untreated blood pressure (all levels, whether 'high', 'normal' or 'low'), made in large groups of people over many years, have all shown that even single measurements of blood pressure can predict future group risks (that is, according to group average blood pressure) for stroke, coronary heart disease, and other consequences of high blood pressure. Individual risks, on the other hand, can only be predicted with similar accuracy if they are based on at least three readings (and preferably more) made on separate days, to give a reasonable estimate of your average pressure.

Can blood pressure be measured in children in the same way as in adults?

Generally no, for two reasons. Firstly, children in general, right up to and probably during adolescence, tend to have even more variable blood pressures than adults, with huge differences between readings even when these seem to have been made in exactly the same circumstances. Even more than in adults, many separate readings are necessary to define even a rough average pressure in a child, and even these need to be viewed sceptically in the absence of any symptoms or evidence of organ damage.

Secondly, until children reach a more or less adult size, there are big problems about matching the measuring device to the size of a child's arm. For at least the first year of life, systolic BP can be measured only with either an infrasound or an ultrasound device, using a very small cuff, with a specially trained and experienced observer taking the measurements. Diastolic pressure cannot be measured at all. For older infants and children, ultrasound machines are still necessary up to about 8 years of age, with a range of cuff sizes, and again require specially trained and experienced staff to use them. From about 10 years on, ordinary adult sphygmomanometers can be used, but only with special small-sized cuffs.

Measurements by doctors and nurses

I've heard that experienced doctors can estimate blood pressure just by feeling the pulse. Is this really true?

Measuring blood pressure

No, and I would not trust anyone who claims to be able to assess blood pressure accurately by feeling the pulse.

Sphygmomanometers came into routine use in hospitals shortly before World War I. Before then, the only way to estimate blood pressure was to place two fingers on the radial artery at the wrist, using the one nearest the elbow to press on the artery, and the one nearest the hand to feel when the wrist pulse disappeared. The amount of pressure required to stop the pulse gave an extremely rough estimate of systolic blood pressure (they didn't bother with diastolic pressure). So, with a lot of experience, it probably is just possible to get some idea of how high blood pressure is, without using a sphygmomanometer, but this would be like trying to thread a needle by candlelight rather than electric light.

If you had to put money on it, who would you back as the best people to measure your blood pressure – specialists, GPs or nurses?

I wouldn't take the bet, as it depends on the individual person, not on their job title. How well either doctors or nurses measure blood pressure in practice depends on how well they have been trained, the quality of their equipment, and how carefully they use it. Having said that, nurses do generally seem to have a less alarming effect on people than doctors, particularly in hospitals, so to that extent they can measure BP more accurately. Hospital specialists running high blood pressure clinics generally insist on good measurements, but other specialists measure blood pressure no better or worse than most GPs.

In my opinion, very few doctors and nurses get sufficient training in taking blood pressure measurements while they are students. There are many reasons for this, one of which is certainly lack of time. As approximately one person in every six has some degree of high blood pressure, I feel that this is an area where training should be improved, and where continuing education and emphasis on accuracy is required during their professional lives. Doctors and nurses who have been on courses for better management of high blood pressure have generally unlearned common bad habits, and measure blood pressure accurately. We have a long way to go before everyone reaches this standard.

Measuring blood pressure at home

Might it be useful for me to measure my own blood pressure at home?

Indeed it might. Home measurements have the great advantage that they can be made when you are relaxed and unflustered and that you can make them as often as you like, without worrying about taking up your doctor's or your nurse's time. They are usually lower than measurements made in hospitals, but little different from measurements made in a GP's surgery by a doctor or practice nurse.

Many general practice teams now like to have 28 home measurements (usually made twice daily every day for two weeks) before starting treatment, especially in borderline cases. They are extremely useful early on, before any treatment starts, mainly in order to decide whether to start treatment now, or whether to wait for a while to see if your apparently high pressure is sustained.

Most people have no problems with taking their own blood pressure measurements accurately once they have had some basic training and practice. However, a few people may have difficulty. People with an irregular pulse caused by atrial fibrillation or frequent extra (ectopic) heartbeats may produce lots of odd sounds at levels above systolic and below diastolic pressure, so it may be impossible for them to take an accurate blood pressure measurement. The best anyone can do in these cases is to make a rough estimate of the level at which sounds appear and disappear. There are also a few people in whom sounds are still audible down to 0 mmHg, which again makes accurate readings extremely difficult. Many of these can get a diastolic pressure by removing all clothing from their arm, or sometimes by using the other arm.

Measuring blood pressure

Do all doctors agree that people should do their own measurements at home?

No - many specialists and some GPs disagree with home readings. These doctors either suggest that it is not possible for people to learn to measure their own blood pressure accurately or, alternatively, that the procedure will frighten people and make some of them obsessed with excessively accurate control of their blood pressure.

There is now plenty of published research evidence on this topic, and all of it supports the view that any literate person who can drive a car, use a typewriter or word processor, or understand how to use a programmed electric cooker or washing machine is certainly able to measure blood pressure as accurately as any doctor or nurse, and possibly better than many. It also shows that for nearly everyone who wants to do these measurements themselves, anxiety is thereby reduced, not increased. Anxiety does increase in about 5% of people, but only if they are pushed into doing measurements against their own inclination.

Should I go on doing my own readings once my treatment's been established?

Home measurements are probably less useful for follow-up once treatment has started. Nobody with blood pressure high enough to need medication, not even doctors or nurses, should attempt to manage their problem entirely alone. Judgements about starting, changing, interrupting or stopping treatment need to be made objectively, against a background of experience with many other cases, and knowledge about other complicating risks. Such judgement is not possible for a person with high blood pressure acting alone, however much they may know. Home measurements of blood pressure can be useful in follow-up, if they add to the evidence normally available at a blood pressure clinic, but they cannot replace regular skilled and independent advice.

I personally do not recommend home measurements for follow-up after treatment has started, except in two circumstances. The first is if you have to be away from your usual medical centre for more than three months, and would otherwise have to transfer supervision to a different medical unit. Continuity of good care is important, and you may be better off continuing your own supervision on the same lines you are already used to. The second is if you fall into the minority of 10-20% of people whose blood pressures do not respond as expected to standard treatment. A series of home measurements then often helps to establish what is really going on between visits to your doctor.

I'm not at all mechanically minded or good with my hands – will I find it difficult to learn to measure my own blood pressure?

Probably not. Given help from an experienced practice nurse, it takes most people about five minutes to learn how to use an electronic sphygmomanometer as accurately as most doctors or nurses. Learning to use a mercury sphygmomanometer takes a little longer – about 20 minutes on average. The answers to the next few questions tell you what you need to know about taking your own measurements, but you do really need a few minutes of personal teaching first, using whatever instrument you will actually have.

I'm not at all sure how and where to find my pulse – does this matter?

Yes. All types of sphygmomanometer require accurate location of your brachial artery pulse, and you will also need to know how to find the pulse in your wrist.

Figure 7 shows you how to find your brachial artery pulse, looking down at your own left elbow crease from above, as you would during the measurement (left-handed people will need to imagine a mirror image of these instructions). First find the tendon in the middle of your elbow crease – it feels tough and stringy. Just inside (to the right of) the tendon you can easily feel the pulse from the brachial artery. That's where you must put your stethoscope, or place the marked part of the cuff on your machine.

Figure 8 shows you where your wrist pulse is, just above the

Measuring blood pressure

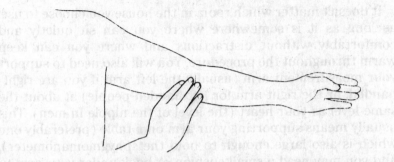

Figure 7: Locating the brachial artery pulse

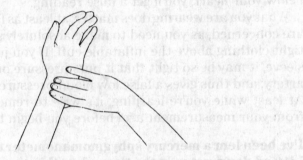

Figure 8: Locating the wrist pulse

top wrist crease, right over on the thumb side. You use the fingers of your right hand to find the wrist pulse on your left hand.

When I'm taking my measurements, do I have to do them at particular times of day? Where in the house should I be when I take them, or doesn't it matter?

If you've been asked to measure your blood pressure twice a day, the most convenient times to do this - and not to forget to do it - will probably be on getting up in the morning and on going to bed at night. Your morning blood pressure will usually be a bit higher than your evening blood pressure, and there may easily be differences of 20-30 mmHg between different measurements, even when carefully performed under apparently identical conditions.

It doesn't matter which room in the house you choose to use, as long as it is somewhere where you can sit quietly and comfortably without distractions and where you can keep warm throughout the procedure. You will also need to support your measurement arm (usually the left arm if you are right-handed, or the right arm for left-handed people) at about the same level as your heart (the level of the nipple in men). This usually means supporting your arm on a table (preferably one which is also large enough to hold the sphygmomanometer), and you may need a small cushion or book under your arm to ensure that it is at the right height. If your arm is far above or below your heart, you'll get a false reading.

What you are wearing does matter, at least as far as your arms are concerned, as you need to make absolutely sure there is no tight clothing above the inflatable cuff. If you just roll up your sleeve, it may be so tight that it puts pressure on your brachial artery, and thus gives a false low blood pressure measurement. At least while you're learning, it's wise to remove all clothing from your measurement arm before you begin the reading.

I've been lent a mercury sphygmomanometer to use at home. I jotted down notes at the time when the nurse was teaching me how to use it, but I'd like to be reminded of exactly what to do in case I've missed anything out.

First get yourself comfortable with your measurement arm supported, as described in the answer to the previous question. Make sure that the sphygmomanometer is placed so that you can see the scale easily, and put your stethoscope around your neck. The most convenient kind of stethoscope to use has a diaphragm at the end, not a 'bell'.

Wrap the inflatable cuff neatly round your upper arm. If it has a Velcro fastening, make sure that this isn't full of fluff or it won't anchor properly (you can clean it with an old toothbrush). If it's the older cloth type of cuff without Velcro, tuck in the end.

Fit the earpieces of the stethoscope into both your ears, and jiggle them around a bit till you have a good fit. Find your brachial artery pulse, and put the diaphragm of the stethoscope over it. If you tuck half the diaphragm under the cuff, it will leave

Measuring blood pressure

your right hand free to operate the bulb that inflates the cuff. (Your left hand will be need to be free if you are left-handed – as usual, left-handers are being asked to imagine mirror images of instructions.)

Turn your left hand palm upwards. With the fingers of your right hand, find the wrist pulse on your left hand. This is just so you know how to find it later.

Now take the inflating bulb in your right hand. With your left hand, tighten up the knurled screw clockwise until the valve is closed (after a bit of practice you'll find you can do this easily with your right hand while you hold the bulb in your palm). By repeatedly squeezing the bulb with the valve closed, pump up the pressure to about 90 mmHg on the glass column, and then feel again for the pulse in your left wrist. It will still be there. Now resume pumping up the pressure, now and then checking your pulse in your left wrist. You may be slow and clumsy at first, and

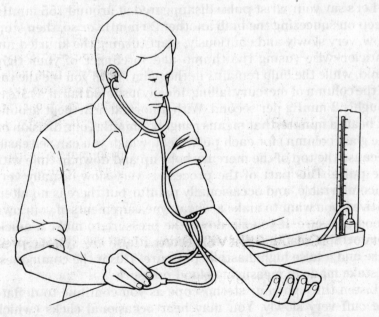

Figure 9: Measuring your own blood pressure with a mercury sphygmomanometer

if your left arm is beginning to feel as though it might burst or drop off, release the valve by turning the knurled nut anticlockwise, stop for a while, and start again when your arm feels comfortable.

The reason you have to keep checking the pulse in your left wrist is that when it disappears, it's a signal that you've pushed the pressure in the cuff above your systolic pressure. As blood pressure varies so much, different people need to start measuring it from different levels. Of course, we could suggest that everyone started from 350 mmHg or more, higher than any expected systolic pressure even in people with severe high blood pressure, but this would inflict a lot of uneccessary pain on the enormous majority of people whose systolic pressures lie 150 mmHg or more lower than this – so you tailor the procedure to 20 mmHg or so above your own systolic pressure. After a while, you'll be able to do this without checking your wrist pulse, because you'll have a rough idea of what to expect.

Let's say your wrist pulse disappeared at around 155 mmHg. Keep on squeezing the bulb another 20 mmHg or so, then stop. Now, very slowly and cautiously, start turning the knurled nut anticlockwise (using the thumb and forefinger of your right hand, while the bulb remains in the palm) until you see the top of the column of mercury falling. Ideally it should fall at a rate of roughly 2 mmHg per second. With a normal heartbeat around 72 beats a minute, that means roughly 2 mmHg (one division on the glass column) for each pulse beat, which you can see easily because the top of the mercury bobs up and down in time with the pulse. This part of the process is very slow, usually very uncomfortable, and occasionally painful, but there is no alternative if you want to make accurate measurements of your own blood pressure. If you zip down the pressure to make a quick, comfortable reading, you will record a false low systolic pressure and a false high diastolic pressure. This is the commonest mistake made in measuring blood pressure.

Listen through your stethoscope as you continue to deflate the cuff very slowly. You may hear occasional clicks (which mean nothing at all) but after 10 mmHg – 25 mmHg or so you'll start to hear a regular tapping sound. This is systolic pressure.

Measuring blood pressure

Look at the level of the mercury column, measure it against the scale on the glass tube, and read off the measurement to the nearest 2 mmHg. Say the number out loud, and write it down before you've forgotten it.

Keep on dropping the pressure. While you're learning, keep dropping the pressure at the same very slow rate. Eventually, as you get used to the procedure, you'll be able to drop the pressure faster until you're about 20 mmHg above your expected diastolic pressure, and you'll find this much less uncomfortable.

Probably somewhere around 50 mmHg – 60 mmHg below your systolic pressure, the regular tapping sound will first become much softer (often quite suddenly), and then disappear. When it disappears, this is diastolic pressure. Look again at the column of mercury, and again measure its height against the scale on the glass tube. Again, say the figure out loud and then write it down, under the first figure.

After you've recorded both systolic and diastolic pressures, turn the knurled knob fully anticlockwise to open the valve completely and release all pressure on your left arm. It may ache for as long as half an hour after, but the discomfort will get less as you get used to the procedure and do it more quickly.

I've now had one try at measuring my own BP, but I'm not convinced that I'm going to be able to distinguish the different sounds. The practice nurse is going to give me another lesson, but am I right to be worried?

No, not really – once you've had some more training from your nurse and some more practice at taking your measurements, you should be able to distinguish the sounds quite easily. As with anything new, our worries beforehand soon disappear as we become accustomed to what we are doing.

What you will actually be hearing is the sound of the blood flowing through your brachial artery. When the cuff is inflated enough to stop the blood flowing, there is no sound. As soon as the pressure from the cuff falls below this peak pressure, blood starts to flow. At first, at or below systolic pressure but above diastolic pressure, it flows in spurts. At or below diastolic pressure, it flows continuously. As you slowly reduce pressure in the cuff and listen with your stethoscope over the artery, you can hear these spurts of blood, first as a tapping sound, later as a longer, softer whooshing sound, and finally the sound disappears. When you first hear the regular tapping sound, that's your systolic pressure. As you keep on slowly reducing the pressure in the cuff, the sounds soften, and eventually (usually about 60 mmHg lower) they disappear – that's your diastolic pressure.

If you do find that you have problems hearing the sounds, ask if you can switch to using an electronic sphygmomanometer, which will detect the sounds automatically for you through its sensor, and doesn't require you to listen through a stethoscope.

Is the procedure different when you use an electronic sphygmomanometer at home?

Electronic sphygmomanometers all come with an instruction book, which nowadays is usually adequate. As they vary in how fully they are automated, and in the various symbols and icons they use on their displays (designed to ensure equal comprehension – or bewilderment – in all languages), you will need to read the book of words that comes with your machine for full information on how to use a particular machine.

You need to get yourself comfortable with your measurement arm supported (just as described earlier in this section) and the cuff wrapped around your arm before you start to take your readings. Electronic sphygmomanometers recognise systolic and diastolic pressures through a sensor in the cuff, and the part of the cuff containing the sensor must be placed over your brachial pulse. Failure to do this is the commonest cause of inaccurate readings.

Exactly what happens next depends on your particular machine. Most of them have some sort of automatic inflation of the cuff, followed by automatic deflation which is triggered by recognition of systolic pressure. The rate of deflation may or may not be variable. If it is, set it to the slowest rate possible and don't speed this up later, even if it makes the procedure more comfortable. If it is not variable, check the time it takes to go from say 140 mmHg to 80 mmHg against the second hand on your watch. This should take 1 minute 20 seconds. If it takes less than a minute, don't buy or use the machine – the deflation rate is too fast and it will not give you accurate readings.

The machine will take the readings for you automatically and will either show them on a digital display screen (in which case you will need to write them down as they appear) or print them out for you.

Virtually all electronic sphygmomanometers measure how fast your heart is beating (your heart rate or pulse rate) as well as your blood pressure. These are useful indicators of your state of mind while measuring your BP. Rates over about 80 beats a minute suggest some anxiety.

What can go wrong when I'm taking my own measurements at home?

It is, of course, possible for any machine to go wrong but this is not very common (although you should check that the battery of an electronic sphygmomanometer is not running low, as this can cause inaccurate readings). You also need to make sure (as I have mentioned several times in previous answers in this chapter) that you are not deflating the cuff too quickly.

The most common causes of false measurements at home are anxiety, fear, anger, pain, embarrassment and cold. If you feel relaxed and are not distracted by other things going on, you can be reasonably confident that the pressures you record are correct. If you really cannot relax, and always feel anxious when measuring your own blood pressure, then say so, because this factor needs to be taken into account by your carers. Cold is a powerful raiser of blood pressure, and if you have come in from a frosty winter's day, take half an hour or so to warm up before taking your measurements.

Another occasional but very powerful cause is a full bladder, or one that will not empty completely because of obstruction from the prostate gland, a common condition in men over 50.

Is it a good idea to buy my own sphygmomanometer if I'm going to be doing readings at home?

Usually no, unless your doctor advises it for some particular reason.

Why not? After all, these days people with diabetes measure their own blood sugar levels, people with asthma measure their airways obstruction with instruments called peak flow meters, and people with weight problems have always been encouraged to weigh themselves.

For people with diabetes, blood glucose varies from hour to hour and day to day, requiring variations in treatment. People with insulin-dependent diabetes have to take dosage decisions at least once a day, sometimes more often, and cannot go to a doctor each time. The aim of diabetes treatment is as far as possible to simulate the natural output of insulin from the pancreas, which varies greatly according to food intake and energy expenditure, and has a very rapid effect on blood glucose, acting within seconds. This is not yet true for blood pressure, although one day it may become so. The aim of treatment for high blood pressure is to shift average blood pressure downwards throughout all day and every day, regardless of different activities, using drugs with slow and long-sustained effects measured in hours rather than seconds.

Even more importantly, unlike measurements of blood pressure, measurements of blood glucose are unaffected by one's state of mind when making them. The aim of treatment for high blood pressure is usually to shift your average resting blood pressure to below about 160/90 mmHg, but worrying about the result is quite likely to raise your blood pressure above this target level, even though most of the time it is much less than this – and this could lead to overtreatment. The dose of BP-lowering medication required to maintain this target level is not likely to change much from day to day, and so once your blood pressure is controlled, decisions seldom have to be taken more often than once every three months. If you measure your blood pressure yourself each day in order to tailor your treatment to that day's special requirements, your blood pressure is likely to go out of control (either too low or too high), and both you and anyone else who lives with you will become a nervous wreck.

Another reason is that the easiest sphygmomanometers to learn how to use are electronic. As I mentioned in the first section of this chapter, the cheaper electronic machines sold for

Measuring blood pressure

use at home are seldom accurate enough for good treatment decisions. Unless you have a good deal of medical or nursing experience, you will find it very difficult to recognise the difference between unusually high, low, or in other ways bizarre readings which truly represent what is going on in your body, and equally strange readings caused by a fault in the machine. If an electronic machine goes wrong in any way, even just a low battery, you may not recognise this, and if your decisions are based on these measurements, they will be wrong. Traditional mercury sphygmomanometers go wrong in simpler and more recognisable ways, but they are more difficult for untrained people to use.

If you are asked to make a series of home measurements, it will usually be possible for your GP's practice to lend you a suitable sphygmomanometer and train you in how to use it.

If I do decide that I want to buy my own sphygmomanometer, how do I decide which one is best to buy?

Sphygmomanometers commonly used for home readings are of two basic kinds, the traditional mercury machines, and the newer electronic machines.

Mercury sphygmomanometers are relatively cheap and very reliable if they are reasonably well looked after. As they are not used so often as the machines at GPs surgeries and hospitals, mercury sphygmomanometers used at home normally perform well for at least five years without any maintenance. For people who want to measure their own blood pressure during treatment (which I do not advise in usual circumstances), they are usually the best choice. They take a bit longer to learn how to use than an electronic machine, but after an average 20 minutes teaching by an experienced nurse, you should be able to measure your own blood pressure accurately.

For doctors, portability is important, but for your own home measurements a machine standing on a fixed metal base is just as good as a folding machine, and much cheaper. If you have a large upper arm with a circumference of 30 cm (12 inches) or more, ask for an outsize cuff and make sure you get it (there is a discussion about cuff sizes in the section on *Accuracy and reliability* earlier in this chapter). Whoever supplies you with the machine can get you an outsize cuff, but it may have to be specially ordered.

Electronic machines are much easier to use, and most people can learn how to use them after about five minutes of instruction by a nurse. A few can print out readings, and all the others display figures which can simply be read off, whereas with a mercury sphygmomanometer you have to measure the top of the mercury column against a glass scale marked at 2 mm intervals.

There are two problems with the electronic machines. First, none of the many different electronic machines on sale to the public at an affordable price is as reliable or accurate as a mercury sphygmomanometer. The only really satisfactory electronic machines are expensive – the price makes them a reasonable purchase for a medical centre which lends them out for home readings, but they cost too much for most people to buy for themselves. Secondly, because they depend on a sensor sewn into the cuff, people with large upper arms will need an outsize cuff – often difficult to obtain with the cheaper machines.

Other points to bear in mind if you are buying an electronic machine are that it should have some sort of signal indicating a low battery (which may otherwise give misleading readings without warning), and whether the machine claims to conform to the approved quality standards of either the British Hypertension Society, the American Association for the Advancement of Medical Instrumentation (AAAMI), or the European Union (apparently German machines already adhere to this standard).

4
Managing high blood pressure

Aims of treatment

My doctor tells me that I have high blood pressure, and that I will need treatment for it. But I feel perfectly well - there aren't any symptoms as far as I can see. If high blood pressure doesn't cause symptoms, why does it need to be treated?

The only reason anyone needs treatment for high blood pressure is to prevent its likely consequences. Many serious sorts of organ damage are eventually caused by high blood pressure, including stroke, heart attacks and heart failure, damage to the retina (the back of the eye) and the kidneys, and many more (they are all are discussed in more detail in Chapter 9). All of these happen more often in people with uncontrolled high blood pressure – and the higher the pressure is, the more likely they are to occur. Your doctor is recommending treatment for your high blood pressure to reduce your risks of any of these unpleasant things happening to you in the future, not to make you feel better today (high blood pressure does not usually cause symptoms – there is more information about this in the section on *Symptoms* in Chapter 1).

The good news is that careful treatment works. After treatment, your chances of developing any of these forms of organ damage should be much reduced. The risks become roughly proportional to the lower blood pressure level you have reached with your treatment, not to the blood pressure level you had before your treatment started.

A cautionary note: high blood pressure is not the only cause of any of these kinds of organ damage, so reducing your blood pressure cannot wholly prevent them. Smoking is another very important cause of all of them, and so are high blood cholesterol levels and poorly-controlled diabetes, which are often associated with overweight and insufficient regular exercise. Effective prevention depends on attention to all of these causes.

What pressure should my treatment be aiming for?

Very generally speaking, treatment usually aims at a target below about 150–160/90 mmHg. If it can be maintained below 140/85 mmHg, so much the better.

Does everyone with high blood pressure get the same treatment?

The treatment your doctor recommends will depend on how high your blood pressure is and what sort of lifestyle you have. The recommendations might be different, for example, for a younger person who is overweight, smokes, takes no exercise and has a blood pressure level that only needs to be brought down slightly than for someone much older who already leads a very healthy lifestyle and whose blood pressure needs to be brought down quite a lot. The various options for treatment are all discussed in this chapter.

How do doctors know what treatment to give? Do they have any guidelines to follow?

Doctors obviously have their training and experience to help them in deciding what treatment to recommend for high blood pressure, just as they do for any other problem or illness that they see. In addition, the British Hypertension Society has published a set of guidelines for the management of high blood pressure (details of this publication are given in Appendix 3). These guidelines are too long to reprint in full here, but they set out details of how most people with high blood pressure should be assessed and evaluated, when treatment should start, and the most suitable treatment options available in different circumstances. The advice given in this book is in line with their recommendations.

A doctor told me that although my systolic pressure was high (over 200 mmHg), this was all right, because my diastolic pressure was OK (under 90 mmHg) and so I wouldn't need any treatment. Is this true?

No. Without knowing how old you are, or how long ago you got this information, it is difficult to understand why you were told this, but I can suggest one possible reason. Doctors used to be taught that high systolic pressure was caused by hardening of the arteries, that this was a normal ageing process, and that high blood pressure in the elderly only mattered if diastolic pressure was also high (over 90 or 100 mmHg). All the studies on blood pressure in large groups of people have shown all these beliefs to be false. Hardening of the arteries (from gradual build-up of cholesterol and blood clots as plaque) is common in the elderly, but not normal. As one of its main causes is high blood pressure, to regard it as as evidence against the significance of high blood pressure is absurd.

At all ages over 40, systolic pressure is a better predictor of future risks of stroke, coronary heart attacks and so on than diastolic pressure. Under 40, diastolic pressure seems to be a better predictor. Having a low diastolic pressure does not reduce the significance of a high systolic pressure.

It sounds as if it would be sensible for you to go to your current doctor and have your blood pressure checked again, so that you can start appropriate treatment if it is still high.

Treatment without drugs

Can I really bring my blood pressure down to normal without taking drugs?

The answer depends on how high your average blood pressure is. You discover your average blood pressure by having your doctor or practice nurse take a series of readings spaced over three months or so, or by taking 28 twice-daily measurements yourself at home (there is more information about this in Chapter 3 on *Measuring blood pressure*).

Generally speaking, if your blood pressure averages 160/105 mmHg or more, you will probably need some medication, whatever else you may do to bring your blood pressure down. Even so, you may need fewer drugs at a lower dosage if you modify your life in some ways.

However, most people found to have high blood pressure have an average pressure less than this. If you are one of these people, you should be able to bring your blood pressure down by about 10 mmHg without needing drug treatment just by modifying your lifestyle (your age will also affect this - these measures tend to be more effective in younger people). You will still need to be followed up once a year to make sure your blood pressure is not rising again.

So exactly what do I need to do? Will I have to make a lot of changes to the way I live now?

Possibly. There are five main areas where you may need to make changes.

Managing high blood pressure

- Smoking (if you smoke, then stop)
- Exercise (regular exercise reduces blood pressure)
- Weight control (if you are overweight)
- Diet (what you usually eat)
- Alcohol intake (how much you usually drink)

You will find information about all these subjects and the hows and whys of any changes you need to make in Chapter 5.

I notice that this list doesn't include any mention of stress. Doesn't reducing stress by winding down and learning to relax help?

This is a very debatable point. A doctor called Chandra Patel has devised a treatment plan for helping wound-up people with high blood pressure to wind down. Controlled studies of her work suggest that it has an effect on people with moderately raised blood pressure that lasts for at least a year, and that it reduces blood pressure almost as much as BP-lowering drugs.

However, published accounts of attempts by other doctors to follow her treatment plan have so far failed to obtain the same good results. Her treatment is based on the assumption that the main cause of high blood pressure is nervous response to stress, but the results of numerous scientific studies on this question have yielded inconsistent and contradictory evidence, with the most rigorous studies giving least support to this idea. It is possible that the people in her studies, who were self-selected volunteers, were not representative of the general population. All we can really say is that people with moderately raised blood pressure in the diastolic range 90-105 mmHg may get some benefit from relaxation exercises of this sort. However, there is no convincing evidence that blood pressures in the range normally needing drug treatment can be effectively controlled in this way.

Sedative drugs and tranquillisers are not alternatives to BP-lowering drugs (there is a question about these in the section on *Treatment with BP-lowering drugs* later in this chapter).

BP-lowering drugs

What BP-lowering drugs are available, and is there much difference between them?

There are currently some 60 different BP-lowering drugs listed under their generic names (ie their true or scientific names) in the official reference books (such as the *British National Formulary*) and they are available under well over 100 different brand names (ie the names they have been given by the pharmaceutical companies that make and sell them). The number of different drugs available and, especially, the bewildering confusion of different names, is more a reflection of the needs of the pharmaceutical industry than the needs of the people who take them or the doctors who prescribe them. The position is constantly changing, as new drugs are introduced and those which are less effective or which do not sell well are withdrawn.

The BP-lowering drugs that are most usually prescribed can be divided into the groups listed here, according to the ways in which they work (their mechanism of action).

- Diuretics (this group includes thiazide and thiazide-like diuretics, potassium sparing diuretics, diuretics with potassium supplements and loop diuretics)
- Beta-blockers
- Angiotensin Converting Enzyme (ACE) inhibitors
- Angiotensin inhibitors
- Vasodilators
- Alpha-blockers
- Calcium-channel blockers
- Drugs acting mainly on the brainstem

You will find lists of drugs currently available in each group and information about their mechanisms of action and possible side-effects in Appendix 1. (That appendix also contains information on two other groups of drugs – the ganglion-blocker drugs and the adrenergic neurone blockers – which are used only rarely, normally only in specialist hospital departments.)

Within each group, differences between different drugs are

small, and rarely as significant as manufacturers claim. Studies comparing drugs from all five of the main groups in common use (diuretics, beta-blockers, ACE-inhibitors, alpha-blockers and calcium-channel blockers) show few important differences either in their effectiveness or their side-effects. As usual, the biggest differences are in price: the older diuretic drugs at a few pence a month, or the newer ACE-inhibitors costing over 100 times more. Even less significant are the differences between branded and generic drugs. Providing you stick either to one or the other, the main difference between branded and generic drugs is who makes the profit, and how much. Doctors who prescribe drugs by their generic names (as they are now encouraged to do) are not just saving money for the National Health Service, but are also helping themselves to think clearly.

How do BP-lowering drugs work?

They manipulate - in various ways - the body mechanisms normally used to control distribution of blood flow between different organs. Blood pressure can be lowered by reducing the total volume of blood in the body; by relaxing the spiral muscles around small arteries and thus widening their bore (diameter); or by reducing heart output (the amount of blood that your heart pumps out each minute). All drugs now in use operate through one or more of these final pathways, but they vary greatly in the way they reach them: some act first on the brain, some on different functions of the kidney, some directly on the heart or small arteries. The nature of possible side-effects depends on which of these routes they take.

We now have many different drugs which usually lower blood pressure, but our exact knowledge of how many of them work is still incomplete. For example, there is still no full agreement between experts on how diuretics reduce blood pressure, although they are the second oldest group of BP-lowering drugs in common use (and among the most effective). We know they increase output of sodium, but they also affect blood volume and relax small arteries. Just as we are still discovering new effects of aspirin (first derived from willows in 1825 and first synthesised in 1899), we shall probably still be discovering new effects of diuretics well into the next century, to say nothing of more recent drugs.

By how much do these drugs lower blood pressure?

Used on their own, the BP-lowering drugs in current use usually reduce blood pressure by about 5-10 mmHg of diastolic pressure. If drugs from different groups are combined, their effects are usually additive so the reduction will be greater. Very high pressures (systolic pressure over 200 mmHg or diastolic pressure over 120 mmHg) tend to fall more than borderline pressures: so someone with extremely high pressure (the highest I personally have seen was 370/180 mmHg) may need and obtain a fall of 100 mmHg or more. Such huge reductions are unusual, and have to be made carefully and slowly.

Although they were originally thought to have less effect than other BP-lowering drugs, diuretics are actually among the most effective, with an average reduction of 10-11 mmHg diastolic pressure in people whose average diastolic pressure before treatment was around 120 mmHg.

Can they lower blood pressure too much?

Providing you have normal kidney function, and no ECG evidence of impaired blood supply to your heart, the lower your blood pressure is the better (down to a systolic pressure of about 110 mmHg). If your systolic pressure is consistently below this figure, you are probably being overtreated, and your medication can be reduced or simplified. (If you are measuring your own blood pressure, don't try changing your medication without medical advice.)

Some BP-lowering drugs are much more likely than others to cause excessive falls in pressure. Diuretics, beta-blockers, calcium-channel blockers, and drugs acting mainly on the brainstem such as methyldopa are all extremely unlikely to reduce systolic pressure below 100 mmHg, which is roughly the threshold for fainting. Alpha-blockers do so commonly after the first dose, which should therefore always be given at bedtime, as you can't faint when lying down flat in bed. They are unlikely to have this effect after the first dose, but are generally not used for

Managing high blood pressure

elderly people, in whom profound falls in blood pressure happen more easily and are more likely to have serious results. ACE-inhibitors may also cause profound falls in pressure when first used, particularly if they are given together with diuretics, or to people whose kidney function is impaired.

Do BP-lowering drugs have side-effects? If so, what are they?

There are very few drugs which have no side-effects at all, and BP-lowering drugs are no exception. The different groups of drugs all have different possible side-effects, and these are outlined in Appendix 1. Reading lists of side-effects can be alarming, so it is worth remembering two things. First, that the fact that side-effects are possible does not mean that they are either inevitable or severe; and second that it is possible to have beneficial side-effects as well as unpleasant ones.

There are two side-effects which are common to several groups of BP-lowering drugs. The first is impotence: all BP-lowering drugs can occasionally cause partial or complete failure of erection in men. The effect is reversible (ie normal function returns when the drug is stopped) and is discussed in more detail in the section on *Sex* in Chapter 7.

The second is fainting: a few BP-lowering drugs can cause either feelings of faintness, or an actual faint with momentary unconsciousness. The same thing can happen if your blood pressure is brought down too low by overtreatment.

Faints occur because of sudden drops in blood pressure, so that blood supply to the brain falls below the level necessary to maintain consciousness. Before all such faints there are usually brief warning symptoms of sweating, nausea, and a feeling of impending 'blackout'. If you sit down with your head between your legs for a couple of minutes, the faint can be avoided. If you do actually faint, then once you are lying down, the blood gets back into your head simply by gravity and you quickly recover. Fainting should never be treated by propping someone up before they are fully conscious, as this only prolongs unconsciousness and can cause brain damage by impeding the natural process of recovery.

I understand that diuretics may be the most commonly prescribed drugs for high blood pressure and also that they are very effective – but I've also read somewhere that they can cause other problems. Is this true?

I suspect that you have been reading about the thiazide diuretics, which have an undeserved reputation for causing dangerous falls in blood potassium (hypokalaemia).

Low blood potassium is important because it may cause dangerous disturbance of heart rhythm. At one time this was thought to be a common side-effect of thiazide diuretics, but we now know that it is rarely a problem. It can be prevented in most people simply by eating a well-balanced diet which includes foods that are high in potassium, such as green vegetables, fruit and fruit juices.

People who are ill and who eat badly because of their illness (especially people with heart failure) will need potassium supplements, usually potassium chloride. This is not easy, because even when this is very carefully formulated in slow-release preparations such as Slow-K, many people develop ulcers in the gut, occasionally leading to serious bleeding or scarring. These gut ulcers are often painful.

Concerns about low blood potassium led to the development and promotion of two types of branded preparations: thiazide diuretics combined with potassium supplements, and a separate group of potassium-sparing diuretics. We now know that thiazide diuretics rarely lead to low blood potassium in otherwise healthy people leading a normal life. For the vast majority of people treated for high blood pressure with thiazide diuretics, low blood potassium is not a significant risk, and neither of these preparations should be routinely used for treatment of high blood pressure. Combined preparations contain enough potassium to cause gut ulcers, but not enough to prevent low blood potassium for the few people who really are at serious risk. Although they are still very widely prescribed, this is a hangover from the past which should be corrected.

High blood potassium (hyperkalaemia) is also an important cause of disordered heart rhythm, and commonly occurs in kidney failure. Early kidney failure (an important complication of high blood pressure which is more common in people who also have diabetes) often causes few or no symptoms, and may be detectable only by blood tests. If thiazide diuretics are routinely prescribed with potassium supplements (either in combined preparations or together with potassium tablets such as Slow-K) or if potassium-sparing diuretics are routinely prescribed, there is a serious danger that people with early, undetected kidney failure may develop dangerously high levels of blood potassium. For the large majority of people with high blood pressure who are apparently well and lead a normal life, this danger of high blood potassium now seems much greater than its opposite, low blood potassium. Experts therefore agree that potassium supplements are normally unnecessary, and potassium-saving diuretics are inappropriate (after all, there are plenty of other BP-lowering drugs available which cannot cause this problem). Unfortunately they are still promoted for routine treatment of high blood pressure.

How do we know that all these drugs do more good than harm?

Nearly all the BP-lowering drugs in common use seem to be remarkably safe and well tolerated, considering how widely they are prescribed. We have evidence about this from the many drug trials and research projects which have been carried out on them (explanations of what is involved in the different types of trials can be found in the section on **Drug testing and clinical trials** in Chapter 10).

For the older drugs (ie those introduced before 1980), we have good evidence from randomised controlled trials that drug treatment does substantially more good than harm for certain groups of people who are at high risk.

For the newer drugs (mainly the ACE-inhibitors) we obviously have less evidence so far. The trials show they are generally effective and may be better tolerated than their older competitors, but unexpected long-term effects not only cannot be ruled out, but on past experience are likely to be found eventually. Such unexpected effects might be either beneficial or harmful, and they might not occur very often, but it is well to remember that the newer a drug is, the less we know about it. This will apply most of all to the newest group, angiotensin inhibitors, which are just beginning to reach the market.

Since the 1950s, treatment with BP-lowering drugs has transformed the management of severe high blood pressure (about 200/120 mmHg and over), greatly reducing risks of stroke, heart failure, eye and kidney damage, with smaller reductions in coronary heart attacks. There is also hard evidence justifying treatment well below this figure for people who already have symptoms of transient ischaemic attacks (TIAs), small strokes, diabetes, or damage to the arteries, eyes, kidneys or heart, or who have strong family histories of these problems.

For the large majority of people who have lower pressures but who are still at increased risk of the consequences of high blood pressure, dogmatic rules are not justified. Decisions about whether to start BP-lowering drugs or whether to wait and see, perhaps with annual blood pressure checks, depend on judgement of probable gains and possible losses: the experts in this must be you together with your own doctor. As all good doctors willingly admit, nothing in medical care is ever certain, and each individual case treated must in some ways be a human experiment. Probabilities may approach certainty, but because each individual is genetically different from every other, and has a body modified by different experiences, no predictions can ever be completely accurate.

Some BP-lowering drugs seem to be labelled SR, which I'm told means slow release. What does this actually mean, and what is the point of them? Do they have advantages over 'ordinary' tablets?

Slow-release (also called SR or sustained-release) tablets or capsules are designed to delay drug absorption in the gut. They usually do this efficiently, but transit time through the gut (ie the time it takes the tablet or capsule to travel through your digestive system) varies between different people, and from time to time in everybody. If you have diarrhoea, you may see your SR medication go apparently unchanged down the toilet.

SR preparations are much more expensive, more profitable, and are rarely available as generic preparations, so manufacturers sometimes promote them more energetically than is justified by their real advantage. However, in a few cases (eg calcium-channel blockers and clonidine) SR preparations are not just an advantage but an essential for safe care.

Manufacturers claim that SR preparations help to supply drugs more evenly through the day, with consequent better control of blood pressure. This is rarely important, because most of the drugs have a long half-life (the time taken for the level of a drug in your blood to fall to half its peak value), and so do their active metabolites (the simpler but still usefully active chemicals resulting from the chemical breakdown by your body of the original drug). Manufacturers also claim that SR drugs give better control at night. As blood pressure falls by as much 100 mmHg during sleep (even in people with untreated severe high blood pressure), this argument is rather unconvincing.

The real justification for SR preparations is in drugs which may otherwise cause unpleasant side-effects when they are at their peak blood levels, or which cause rebound high blood pressure when their blood levels fall. For these reasons, all calcium-channel blockers and clonidine (one of the drugs acting mainly on the brainstem) should only be taken as SR preparations.

Do BP-lowering drugs ever have to be given by injection?

Generally, no. Most of the drugs given by mouth act quickly, so nothing is gained by giving them by an injection into a muscle or a vein, even for malignant hypertension (discussed in the section on *Types of high blood pressure* in Chapter 1). Indeed, much may be lost by lowering blood pressure too much and too fast, resulting in brain damage. For people who are unconscious in hospital with very high pressures, blood pressure can be reduced slowly and carefully using a slow intravenous infusion (a 'drip' into a vein) of sodium nitroprusside.

Treatment with BP-lowering drugs

How can I be sure that I really need drugs to control my blood pressure?

Whether or not you need drugs depends on how high your blood pressure actually is.

If you have mildly raised blood pressure (average reading below 160/100 mmHg), then there is no convincing evidence that you will get worthwhile benefits from treatment with BP-lowering drugs, unless you already have evidence of organ damage or have diabetes. You are, however, likely to benefit from doing the things discussed earlier in this chapter and in Chapter 5 on *How to help yourself*: stopping smoking, losing weight, reducing alcohol and salt intake and taking regular exercise.

If your diastolic pressure is in the intermediate range (100–110 mmHg) then you need more measurements, taken over three months or so, to see what your average pressure really is before any decisions are made about treatment. The best way to do this is probably with home readings using a sphygmanometer on loan from your doctor (you will find more information about how to do this in Chapter 3 on *Measuring blood pressure*), but some doctors prefer to use repeated measurements made by a practice nurse. After these you can discuss the options with your doctor.

If your average blood pressure over a whole three month period is 150/90 mmHg or higher, then you probably need BP-lowering drugs. If:

- you also have diabetes;

Managing high blood pressure

- or you already have evidence of organ damage, for example angina, arterial leg pain, or stroke (however small);
- or you have suffered transient ischaemic attacks (TIAs), a coronary heart attack, or heart failure;
- or you have a strong family history of any of these occurring in close relatives who are under 50 years of age;
- or your average BP is around 160/110 mmHg or more;

then you will probably gain more than you will lose by starting BP-lowering drugs.

Other things you do may reduce the dose of these drugs that you need, but they are unlikely to make BP-lowering drugs unnecessary. However, if as well as taking medication, you also stop smoking, lose weight, drink less alcohol, take more exercise and stop eating very salty foods, your treatment will be more effective at lower doses.

I've had high blood pressure for many years. One of my neighbours, who's just been diagnosed with high blood pressure, has also been given tablets to take, but they are not the same as mine (although we go to the same GP). Why is she on different tablets? How do doctors decide which tablets you should have?

The various groups of BP-lowering drugs came into use at different times, as you can see from the following list (the years are those in which the first available drugs in that group were introduced). You will find more detailed information about all of them in Appendix 1.

1949 Drugs acting mainly on the brainstem
1951 Vasodilators
1957 Thiazide and related diuretics
1966 Beta-blockers
1976 Alpha-blockers
1979 Calcium-channel blockers
1981 Angiotensin Converting Enzyme (ACE) inhibitors
1994 Angiotensin inhibitors

As you started treatment many years ago, you are probably still taking the drugs that were considered the best available at that time – and rightly so, if you have good control and minimal side-effects (there is no point in changing treatment that works just for the sake of change). As your neighbour was diagnosed more recently, she may well be on a newer drug, or your doctor may have decided that she would respond better to being on a different drug (people react differently to BP-lowering drugs – see the answer to the next question), or she may have other problems which suggest that one type of drug would suit her better than another. There are no particular advantages in being on a newer rather than an older drug – what is important is that everyone has a treatment that works for them.

Doctors use their training and experience in deciding which drugs to prescribe, and also have a set of guidelines from the British Hypertension Society (you will find details of the report in which these guidelines were published in Appendix 3). No doctor, not even the greatest specialists, can possibly have personal experience of all the different drugs available. Good doctors make themselves familiar with one or two from each group, and stick to them.

Different people with high blood pressure seem to respond differently to BP-lowering medication. Why?

There are sometimes large and usually unpredictable differences between people in their response to different kinds of BP-lowering drugs, for two main reasons.

First, each of us (unless an identical twin) inherits a unique set of genes which, together with our even more individual personal life histories of exposure to different foods, chemicals in the environment and so on, determine the exact way in which our bodies work. No two people are exactly alike, and nor is their response to medication.

Secondly, we are now certain that people with primary (essential) high blood pressure have many different causes of high blood pressure: all they have in common is that these causes are not yet known (there is more information about this in the section on *Types of high blood pressure* in Chapter 1). As the causes are different, it is not surprising that they respond differently to the various drugs available.

Do black people differ from white people in the way they respond to BP-lowering drugs?

No, with one exception which has more to do with where they come from than skin colour. There is fairly consistent evidence that people of sub-Saharan African descent respond less well to both beta-blockers and ACE-inhibitors than do other ethnic groups, whether black or white. On much less convincing evidence, it has been suggested that they respond better than other ethnic groups to thiazide diuretics and calcium-channel blockers.

Will the side-effects of the drugs affect me?

Because individuals vary so much in their response to treatment, this is a question I can only answer in general terms. Most people aged over 30 notice little or no change whatever, and minor changes usually disappear after a week or two. People who are under 30 and older people who do hard physical work often find they are less energetic and tire more easily. It is quite likely that some of these effects are inseparable from a reduction in blood pressure: they are not really a side-effect, but an inevitable part of the intended effect of the drug. Fortunately such effects seem either to wear off after two or three months of treatment, or people forget how they used to feel, so it's usually worth carrying on for a while before changing medication.

If you feel that you are having problems with side-effects, then it would be worth discussing this with your doctor, and deciding between you whether to wait and see if they wear off, or if it would be worth you changing to a different type of drug.

There is a question about side-effects in the section on **BP-lowering drugs** earlier in this chapter, and Appendix 1 includes information about the side-effects associated with the different BP-lowering drugs.

I've got to take two different drugs for my high blood pressure. Why do I need more than one kind?

Combinations of two (or even three) BP-lowering drugs from different groups (they are listed in the previous section on **BP-lowering drugs**) are often the only way to reduce blood pressure effectively at low enough doses to avoid unpleasant side-effects. Many drugs have a much bigger effect at low doses if they are combined with a diuretic. Many of these combinations are marketed as single tablets or capsules, which makes medication easier to take and reduces prescription charges, but may lead to problems if there are side-effects (because it may not be obvious which drug is causing the trouble). This can be avoided if drugs are started separately, and only combined after a trial period.

It is rarely necessary or useful to take more than three different BP-lowering drugs. If this seems to be happening, take all your tablets in their containers to your doctor, and make sure that you are really meant to be taking all of them. Even the best practices can lose track of repeat prescriptions, which may still be issued to people long after their treatment is supposed to have changed.

Can I start two different BP-lowering drugs at the same time?

This is often done without apparently doing much harm, but it seems more sensible always to start all drugs one at a time, unless treatment is truly urgent.

First of all, you may not need more than one drug. Individual responses to BP-lowering drugs are often surprising, some people with very high blood pressure getting a large fall with only a small dose of one drug, while others still have poor control despite full dosage of two or even three BP-lowering drugs from different groups.

Secondly, if there is some unpleasant side-effect, you won't know which drug is causing it. Except in real emergencies, the best rule seems to be always to start, change doses, or stop BP-lowering drugs one at a time, with at least one blood pressure measurement between each decision. To avoid too many visits to your doctor, this can often be arranged with a practice nurse.

Are my BP-lowering drugs likely to become less effective as time goes on?

No. If your blood pressure begins rising substantially after years

Managing high blood pressure

of good control on medication, this is very unlikely to be because your drugs have become ineffective. There will almost certainly be another cause - the first thing your doctor will look for is obstruction of one of your kidney arteries.

Are there any alternatives to the BP-lowering drugs - for example, could I take sedatives or tranquillisers instead and get similar results?

No. So-called minor tranquillisers or sedatives, such as diazepam (brand name Valium) or chlordiazepoxide (Librium), have no consistent effect on high blood pressure and are not an alternative to specific medication.

The major tranquillisers, such as chlorpromazine (Largactil), used for psychotic mental illnesses and schizophrenia do cause big falls in blood pressure, but this is a direct effect of these drugs on parts of the brainstem controlling blood pressure, not an effect on anxiety or tension. This has to be borne in mind if people being treated for such illnesses also seem to need specific medication for high blood pressure, because they may get huge falls in blood pressure with unusually small doses. It does not make them suitable drugs for treating high blood pressure and they are not designed (or used) for that purpose.

I really don't like taking tablets, even when I know that they're doing me good. Will I ever be able to stop taking my BP-lowering tablets?

Probably not. Providing you really needed them in the first place, it is very unlikely that you will ever be able to stop your drugs completely, although you may well manage with simpler medication and/or a lower dose. Most people who stop taking their BP-lowering drugs have a gradual rise in their blood pressure, and this may not start until several months after stopping medication.

People often need less medication as they get older, either because they become more sensitive to BP-lowering drugs as their livers and kidneys become less efficient at removing them from their bodies, or because their hearts can't pump so well so their blood pressure falls. After many years of good control, a few elderly people can stop their medication without any consequent rise in their blood pressure, but this is surprisingly rare, at least before about 80 years of age.

A few people, rightly treated for definitely raised blood pressure when in their 30s, seem to be able to stop taking medication after many years of good control without returning to their original high pressures, but this seems to be unusual. Even these people need careful supervision, and should have their blood pressure checked at least once a year for the rest of their lives.

All this is not surprising, because in most cases we don't know the causes of high blood pressure and are only suppressing effects; and because the initiating causes of high blood pressure are usually different from the maintaining causes (all this is discussed in the section on *Causes* in Chapter 2).

My blood pressure has been well controlled for many years now and I really would like to try doing without drugs. What should I do?

If your blood pressure really has always been well below target pressure for several years, you should discuss with your doctor whether it is worth you considering doing without your drugs for a trial period.

The first thing to do is to look through your medical record to see what your last three or four blood pressure measurements were before the decision was made to start your medication in the first place. If these averaged less than about 160/100 mmHg, and you had no other special reasons for starting treatment (these reasons include diabetes, evidence of heart damage or a small stroke or similar problems, or a strong family history of any of these), then perhaps you never really needed medication anyway, in which case you should obviously try stopping. Even if your initial blood pressure readings were a bit higher than this, there are probably a few people who do - after many years of good control - maintain normal pressures without medication. Such people are rare, and have usually started treatment young, certainly under the age of 40.

Any attempts to do without your drugs should be undertaken

cautiously, with close supervision. If you and your doctor decide to go ahead, taper off the tablets (ie don't suddenly stop taking them), and make sure you have weekly blood pressure checks for the first month, then monthly checks for at least three months, and then annual checks. If your blood pressure stays down, the chances are that you never really needed drug treatment for it in the first place. In most cases blood pressure slowly climbs up to its original pre-treatment level (sometimes months after stopping medication), and medication must then be resumed – but there are exceptions and there's no harm in looking for them, providing this is done carefully.

Clonidine, methyldopa and beta-blockers should all be tapered off, not stopped abruptly, because of the risk of rebound high blood pressure if they are stopped suddenly.

Treatment for young adults

I'm in my late 20s and I've just discovered that my blood pressure is on the high side. My doctor says that providing I get my weight down and take some more exercise then I don't need any other treatment for it at the moment. Do lots of people my age get high BP, and is he right about my not needing tablets?

Most people found to have high blood pressure when they are middle-aged or older probably already had high BP when they were in their 20s and 30s – it was simply never measured when they were younger or, if it was measured, it fell below the conventional threshold for starting treatment, even if it was on the high side. In fact until recently high blood pressure was generally considered only to be a problem for people in these older age groups, and it was uncommon for younger people to have their BP checked in any systematic way. This practice is now changing, so more and more young adults are now having their BP measured routinely every three years or so.

In my own practice, because of my interest in high blood pressure, we regularly checked the blood pressures of about

2000 people of all ages. Using a high threshold for high blood pressure (around 160/100 mmHg), we found 25 men and 16 women under 40 years old with BP sustained at or over this figure, over a period of 18 years from 1968. So it is a fairly common problem, and you are not unusual.

When it came to deciding about treatment, we found no proper studies had ever been done in this age group, and this is still the case at the time of writing this book. Your doctor's decision not to prescribe tablets may well be right, especially as you seem to have been given sensible advice about ways of bringing your BP down without taking any medication (for more details about ways of doing this, see the section on **Treatment without drugs** earlier in this chapter, and the whole of Chapter 5 on **How to help yourself**).

This does not mean that you should ignore your high blood pressure or take it lightly. When we followed up those young men and women in my practice, we found that several of them had developed some of the unpleasant consequences of high blood pressure by the time they reached 40 (the women did rather better than the men, but there were still cases of non-fatal heart attacks or strokes among them). We came to the conclusion that many of these unpleasant consequences could have been avoided if we had started them on BP-lowering drugs at a younger age, as we increasingly did.

However, the results of our small study do not mean that your doctor is wrong in not putting you on BP-lowering drugs immediately, as there are strong arguments both for and against doing that (see the answers to the next two questions). What is important is for you to follow his advice, to attend regularly for follow-up, and to report any symptoms you may have that may indicate that some other problem is developing (you are unlikely suddenly to develop a problem without there being some early symptoms that something is going wrong).

What are the arguments for and against early medication for high blood pressure in young adults?

The single most important effect of high blood pressure is the damage it does to arteries, particularly to the coronary arteries. This effect builds up over a very long period, probably starting in in childhood or adolescence, causing a steady build-up of cholesterol plaque which obstructs blood flow, resulting both in organ damage and in yet higher blood pressure (because of increased resistance to the flow of blood through the arteries). In theory, the sooner this vicious circle can be broken, the better the results of treatment should be.

Earlier treatment might improve on the currently disappointing figures for the prevention of coronary heart attacks when treatment for high blood pressure is begun in middle age. Coronary disease seems to develop slowly over many years, and is therefore difficult to reverse by reducing blood pressure in middle age.

There are two strong arguments against this. First, whatever the risks – known and unknown – of BP-lowering medication, they probably increase with the duration of the treatment. A man starting medication for high blood pressure at age 30 may have to take BP-lowering drugs continuously for another 50 years or more. Even if we had good evidence from controlled trials of treatment started in this age group, it could not tell us about very long-term side-effects.

Second, all controlled trials of treatment for high blood pressure in middle-aged and elderly people have confirmed that the greatest benefits are gained by those groups of people who already have organ damage when they start treatment. Obviously no event can be prevented once it has already occurred, but given close medical supervision, very few people get either coronary heart attacks or strokes without any preceding symptoms. Once there is objective evidence of organ damage from high blood pressure, rigorous control can usually prevent it getting any worse. Before there is any objective evidence of organ damage, it is much more difficult to be confident that treatment really will do more good than harm.

So if there is so little good evidence on what to do with young adults with high blood pressure, and you feel the theoretical

arguments are so finely balanced, how can any doctor reach a sensible decision on whether to treat someone in their 20s or 30s?

In my opinion, all the ways of treating high blood pressure without medication must be considered and usually tried seriously in cases of this kind (in other words, I would always treat a young adult with high blood pressure, but not necessarily with drugs). For smokers, although stopping smoking will not reduce high blood pressure, it will enormously reduce its risks, and that is the point of all treatment. For heavy drinkers (men who drink 3-4 pints or more of average strength beer or the equivalent in wines or spirits a day, about half that in women), stopping alcohol will usually bring blood pressure down substantially within three months. For overweight young adults, there is now good evidence that effective weight reduction combined with a regular exercise programme reduces blood pressure as much as usual BP-lowering medication, but both weight control and exercise have to be kept up indefinitely.

A serious approach to these non-drug treatments (discussed in more detail in the section on **Treatment without drugs** earlier in this chapter, and the whole of Chapter 5) is time-consuming. It requires careful initial evaluation of blood pressure and other coronary risk factors, an assiduous and repeated search for evidence of organ damage, and regular follow-up at least once a year for the foreseeable future.

If blood pressure does not fall after about six months of serious effort on these lines, then BP-lowering drugs need to be considered as an immediate possibility and a long-term probability, but even so there's no hurry in the absence of any evidence of organ damage. However, if there is evidence of organ damage or if the person with high BP also has diabetes, then they are likely to gain far more than they lose by starting medication.

Which BP-lowering drugs are most suitable for treating high blood pressure in people in their 20s and 30s?

The first choice should still probably be the simplest, the drugs of which we have longest experience – thiazide diuretics in low doses. Many people get a good sustained fall in blood pressure without any other drugs and without any perceptible side-effects.

By far the most popular second-line drugs are ACE-inhibitors, which probably cause fewer short-term side-effects in young adults than any other BP-lowering medication. They are not yet backed by any large scale controlled trials in any age group, so this is still a shot in the dark compared with thiazide diuretics. In most cases ACE-inhibitors are ineffective unless combined either with thiazide diuretics, or with fairly severe salt restriction. Anyone who has already been on thiazide diuretics will need to stop them for at least a week before starting on ACE-inhibitors, otherwise their blood pressure may fall much too far and too fast. If thiazide diuretics are needed as well as ACE-inhibitors, they can be added later.

There is more information about both these types of drugs in Appendix 1.

Treatment for elderly people

I'm now 73, and have just started on tablets for my high blood pressure. Does my age make my having this treatment any more difficult, and am I more likely to have side-effects from the drugs than younger people?

Yes and no. Generally speaking, people of your age and older tolerate all drugs less well than younger people because their kidneys and livers eliminate drugs less efficiently and their bodies are generally less able to tolerate big changes, including changes in blood pressure. Other concerns are that some elderly people may be more likely to make mistakes in remembering to take their tablets as prescribed, and many also have to take other drugs for other health problems, which may cause complicated interactions between different drugs (both these concerns are dealt with in the next section on the ***Practical aspects of drug treatment***).

On the other hand, elderly people generally respond to BP-lowering drugs just as well as younger people, perhaps rather more so. They often show a good fall in blood pressure with smaller doses of BP-lowering drugs than are required by middle-aged people.

Are there any particular BP-lowering drugs which are more suitable for elderly people to take – or any that we should avoid?

Apart from those decribed below, most commonly used BP-lowering drugs seem to be relatively trouble-free and effective for the elderly, particularly the thiazide diuretics at low doses, which are almost always the best first choice in this age group (as well as for younger people). Their theoretical drawback is that they tend to make the underlying body chemistry of diabetes worse, but even for elderly people who already have diabetes the benefits greatly outweigh harmful effects. ACE-inhibitors also seem to be effective, and (so far – in drug terms they're still fairly new) trouble free, except for provoking a dry cough in about a quarter of all people who take them. Beta-blockers can be used safely in people who do not have either asthma or heart failure.

The drugs which are best avoided are the alpha-blockers, which can cause fainting in the elderly, and the drugs acting mainly on the brainstem – methyldopa and clonidine. Elderly people starting on BP-lowering drugs for the first time are unlikely to be prescribed these drugs acting mainly on the brainstem, but those who have been on medication for some years may still be taking them, because they were the best drugs available for them when they started their treatment.

Methyldopa (brand names Aldomet and Hydromet) commonly causes liver damage in elderly people, often bad enough to cause severe jaundice. As well as making them ill, it can be very difficult to sort out the diagnosis, because blood test results in this condition closely resemble those for other common causes of jaundice such as gallstones, virus infections of the liver, and side-effects of other drugs. It should be avoided in elderly people, and unlike other BP-lowering drugs, even people who have taken it for many years without trouble should probably switch to a less risky alternative by their late 60s.

Clonidine (brand name Catapres) often causes depression. As elderly people develop severe depression more commonly than younger people, and more frequently go undetected, this drug should be avoided when medication is started for the first time in elderly people. People who have taken clonidine for years, starting in middle age, can reasonably continue as they get older, providing they don't have any trouble.

You will find more information about all these drugs in Appendix 1.

My father has been treated for high blood pressure for more than 30 years, and has now reached his 80th birthday, in apparently good health. He is fed up with doctors and tablets. Could he safely stop taking his blood pressure tablets now?

If he started on his medication when he was 50, he probably had fairly severe high blood pressure at that time, and really needed his treatment. If his doctor has a record of the actual pressures recorded when this first decision to start treatment was made, you can check whether that decision was really justified. Unless that decision was based on, say, a single reading of under 160/100 mmHg, even at 80 he would probably be unwise to stop his medication now. Blood pressure nearly always rises steeply after stopping medication, often after a delay of three months or even more, with serious danger of precipitating a stroke.

If his BP is now well controlled below 160/90 mmHg, he could try slowly reducing his medication, with weekly blood pressure checks at his GP's surgery for the first month, and monthly checks thereafter for at least another three months. Most practices can now arrange for this to be done by a nurse. If his blood pressure remains below 160/90 mmHg for over three months after stopping all his BP-lowering medication, it would be probably be safe for him to carry on without it, providing that he has annual BP checks.

BP-lowering medication should never be stopped abruptly, because this can cause a steep 'rebound' rise in blood pressure, to even higher levels than before treatment started, with a serious risk of bringing on a stroke or heart attack. Of course, having reached 80, your father may just want to take a chance with this. This is his right, but he needs to think seriously before making such a choice. Sudden death from a heart attack or a massive stroke may seem a better way to go than some of the alternatives, but there is no way of ensuring that strokes or heart attacks will follow this swift, neat, clean pattern.

Another thing that you may wish to think about is whether or not he is suffering from depression (not that being fed up with doctors and tablets is a sign of depression, but it is something to consider). As he has been on BP-lowering drugs for 30 years, he may well be taking one of the older drugs which are known to cause depression (as outlined in the answer to the previous question), and his doctor may feel that a change of treatment should be considered.

Practical aspects of drug treatment

I'm on drugs for my blood pressure, but I also have drugs to take for other things which are wrong with me. I'm not quite sure which is which – how do I find out?

You are certainly not alone in having this problem. Drug names can be very confusing, and tablets or capsules of different drugs can be surprisingly similar in appearance. The problem becomes even more complicated if you are having treatment for more than one problem or illness at a time.

Most drugs have at least two names, the generic (scientific) name and the brand (or trade) name given by the company which makes the drug. The generic name is usually written with a small first letter; capital first letters are usually used for the brand name. In this book I have normally used the generic names, in an attempt to reduce this confusion, but there is no way to avoid it altogether.

To find out about your own medication, first look at the names printed by your chemist on the containers. If you make a note of these, you can then ask your chemist, your doctor or your practice nurse which are your blood pressure drugs and which are the drugs you need for other conditions (doctor's receptionists are not usually trained to decide questions of this sort, so don't ask them).

When you have found out which tablets are for your blood pressure, you may want to look them up in the table in Appendix 1, where you will find lists of the generic and brand names of most BP-lowering drugs, as well as information about the way they work and their possible side-effects.

How often do I have to take my BP-lowering drugs?

None of the BP-lowering drugs in current use need to be taken more than twice a day, which means with roughly 12-hourly intervals between doses. As well as being more difficult to remember, traditional three-times-a-day doses are not evenly spaced through the 24 hours, leading to uneven blood pressure control.

Many BP-lowering drugs can be taken in a single daily dose. This is obviously even more convenient, but there may be problems if you forget to take a dose. With twice-daily doses, one forgotten dose will be less important.

You will normally find that the chemist's label on your tablets or capsules tells you how many you need to take and how many times a day. However, if the label just says 'take as directed' or something similar, you may want to check back with your chemist, your GP or your practice nurse to make quite sure what you should be doing.

Should I take them before, during or after meals?

All slow-release (SR) drugs are designed to be taken either with a meal or soon after. Otherwise, timing in relation to meals is unimportant, except that a fixed routine is easier to remember.

Can I swallow them at the same times as other drugs for other problems?

Yes.

Does that mean that any of the BP-lowering drugs can be

combined with any drugs for any other problems, or are there some rules about this?

You are right to be cautious and yes, there are some rules. However, providing these rules are followed, swallowing the different sorts of tablets at the same time is all right.

The first area where there could possibly be problems is in combining ACE-inhibitors with diuretics (if you are not sure if your drugs fall into either of these two groups, the advice given in the answer to the first question in this section will help you find out). Diuretics are used to treat heart failure and oedema (dropsy) from kidney and heart problems, as well as for their BP-lowering effect. To make it more complicated, ACE-inhibitors are used to treat both high blood pressure and heart failure, but are often more effective when combined with a thiazide diuretic. If you start taking ACE-inhibitors and diuretics at the same time, you may have a sudden very severe fall in your blood pressure which could put you into kidney failure. ACE-inhibitors must always be started on their own, although once they are established, diuretics may be cautiously added to increase their effect. Anyone who has already been on diuretics will need to stop them for at least a week before starting on ACE-inhibitors.

Otherwise the main problems are with non-steroidal anti-inflammatory drugs (usually abbreviated to NSAIDs) used for treating arthritis and other bone, joint and muscular pains; with steroid drugs used to treat severe rheumatoid arthritis and asthma; and with some antidepressant drugs. These are all discussed in Chapter 6 on **High blood pressure plus . . .**

I don't drink heavily, but I really do enjoy a drink occasionally. Can I still drink alcohol now I've got to take BP-lowering drugs?

Yes, within reason. None of the BP-lowering drugs has any specific harmful effects when combined with alcohol, but you must bear two things in mind.

First, alcohol in excess of the amount your body can easily tolerate (which means MORE THAN 4 units of alcohol A DAY for a man or 3 units A DAY for a woman - a unit of alcohol is one

Managing high blood pressure

glass of wine OR one single measure of spirits OR half a pint of average strength beer or lager) is itself an important cause of high blood pressure. People who cannot get good control of their high blood pressure despite normally adequate BP-lowering medication often find that if they cut alcohol intake by half or more, they obtain good control with smaller doses of their drugs.

Secondly, all BP-lowering drugs which cause drowsiness (mainly methyldopa and clonidine) will do so much more if combined with even small doses of alcohol. All other BP-lowering drugs cause some drowsiness in some people.

Even without BP-lowering medication, you take unnecessary chances when you drink and drive. With medication added and in charge of a lethal weapon like a car, there is no such thing as a safe level of blood alcohol.

What about food – are there any foods I should avoid while taking BP-lowering medication?

The only specific interactions between foods and any BP-lowering drugs are between ordinary salt (chemical name sodium chloride) and both diuretics and ACE-inhibitors. Both of these are more effective if you substantially reduce the amount of sodium in your diet (by about 50%). The same dose will then have a greater effect on your blood pressure, or you will be able to get the same effect from a lower dose. A reduced-sodium diet is worthwhile if you can manage it without too much trouble, and without increasing the amount of fat in your diet, but it is not worth making yourself miserable over it. There are some suggestions about how to reduce the amount of sodium in your diet in the section on *Sodium and salt* in Chapter 5.

I'm worried that I'm going to forget to take my tablets – how can I remember to take them?

The commonest problems are either forgetting completely, or wondering whether you really did take a tablet a few minutes after you actually took it.

Getting into a routine can help, so try to always take your tablets at the same time of day each day. Ask your doctor to prescribe them to be taken once or twice a day, not three times (it is more difficult to space out tablets to be taken three times a day, and that makes it more difficult to remember to take them). Shiftworkers can usually stick to the same times each day if they are taking tablets only once or twice a day.

Some branded tablets come in foil packs marked with the days of the week (just as the contraceptive pill does) and these are a great help. If your tablets don't come in this type of pack, your chemist should be able to help you with a range of special containers designed to help you remember your medication. These containers range from the very simple to the very sophisticated, and which you choose will depend on whether you just have your BP-lowering drugs to take, or whether you have to take other drugs for other problems.

All these suggestions can help, but only you can decide what will really help you remember. Devise your own method, stick to it, and make sure your partner or a friend or family member knows it too, so that they can help you remember.

But what if I still forget to take my tablets at the right time?

Take your usual dose as soon as you remember it. Don't take a double dose, and don't worry about a couple of hours either way on dosage times.

What if that means I accidentally swallow a double dose?

This usually happens when people have just swallowed their tablets, but forget a few moments later that they have done so. None of the drugs used to lower blood pressure is harmful in any important way if a single normal dose is doubled, although some of them could make you a bit drowsy.

If I run short of tablets, can I borrow some from my friend, who is also being treated for high blood pressure?

This is not really a sensible thing to do. Although there is little difference in effectiveness or tolerability between the absurdly large number of different tablets available, they work in different ways, and it is very unwise to start mixing up treatments yourself.

Managing high blood pressure

If you really must take your friend's tablets, do so only if you are completely certain that they are identical to your own. Check both the name and the strength on the chemist's label, and look carefully at the tablets themselves. If there's the slightest doubt about this, don't take chances.

A much better course is to keep an eye on your tablets, and make sure you get a repeat prescription well before they run out (you may need to devise a system to remind you to do this). Trying to get prescriptions at weekends can be difficult, and won't make you popular.

Can I vary the dose of my BP-lowering drugs according to how I feel from day to day?

No. Symptoms are not related to blood pressure except at very high and dangerous levels, which are rare. The only way to know your blood pressure level is to measure it properly with a sphygmomanometer. One of the values of making your own blood pressure readings at home (as described in Chapter 3) is that you will learn this from experience – it will show you that there is no connection between how you feel and how high or low your readings are.

If you feel ill you should consult your doctor or practice nurse. If you are convinced your medication is making you ill, see your doctor as soon as possible and ask if you can stop taking it or change to a different drug.

What should I do if I can't swallow my tablets because my throat's too sore, or if I can't keep them down because I'm vomiting?

If you are ill enough not to be able to swallow or keep down tablets, you need to see your doctor, both for treatment and to have your blood pressure checked. However, your illness is not likely to continue long enough for your blood pressure to rise out of control.

Neither aspirin, paracetamol, antibiotics, nor any other medication likely to be bought or prescribed for a sore throat has any harmful interaction with BP-lowering drugs.

Some drugs used to treat nausea and vomiting, for example

phenothiazine drugs such as prochlorperazine (Stemetil), can interact with methyldopa (Aldomet) to cause involuntary movements of the face and limbs. This effect is reversible, won't last, and is not serious, but it can be very frightening. Metoclopramide (Maxolon) is an effective prescribed alternative. It may also cause involuntary movements of the same kind, particularly in children and young women, but does so more rarely. Otherwise you can buy hyoscine (sold under various brand names, eg Joyrides, Kwells, Scopoderm). This is less effective but does not have the same side-effect.

What should I do with my drugs if I have to go into hospital?

The most sensible plan is usually to take with you just enough of your tablets to last for a day or two, putting them in envelopes with their names and strengths written on the outside.

Much will obviously depend on the hospital's policy on letting people continue on their usual drug treatment and, of course, on why you are going into hospital. A few hospitals still confiscate and destroy all tablets brought in by patients, and wait for hospital doctors to prescribe a new lot of whatever they prefer. This is not only wasteful and confusing, but often leads to stopping treatment altogether, or at least to interrupting it. Most admissions to hospital are for planned surgery, when the doctor most likely to show interest in your high blood pressure is the anaesthetist. Encouraged by sensible anaesthetists who understand how important it is to control blood pressure during and after surgery, most hospitals will now allow you to continue with your usual medication, but may still insist on supplying their own drugs rather than using yours.

What will happen if I just stop taking my tablets altogether?

Your blood pressure will probably rise to its pre-treatment level, usually within a day or two, but occasionally up to three months after stopping.

If clonidine is stopped abruptly, this commonly causes a sudden rise in blood pressure, often to extremely high and dangerous levels, much higher than pre-treatment levels. It should therefore always be tapered off slowly, by gradually reducing the dose over several days. It should also always be taken as slow-release (SR) tablets, so that this rebound rise will not occur if a dose is forgotten or delayed. The same thing occurs occcasionally after stopping methyldopa and beta-blockers.

Some BP-lowering drugs, mainly beta-blockers and calcium-channel blockers, also control angina, which may also get much worse for a time if they are stopped suddenly.

If you really want to stop taking your tablets, then it is worth doing it slowly and sensibly and under your doctor's supervision. There is some advice about how to do this in the previous section on *Treatment with BP-lowering drugs*.

Are BP-lowering drugs dangerous if taken accidentally or misused? What if a child gets hold of them?

If taken accidentally by an adult, no harm will be done. It is also difficult to misuse them. None of the drugs commonly used for high blood pressure is much good for killing either yourself or others. All have a wide tolerance between the lowest and highest effective doses, and a large margin between the highest effective dose and a fatal dose. Nor will they expand the minds of experimenting teenagers.

Some are dangerous to children, and all should be locked out of the way (this is true of all drugs, including those we take for granted such as aspirin and paracetamol). Many childproof containers seem designed to deny access not only to children but also to any normal adult, so locked medicine cabinets seem to be the only solution.

Monitoring treatment and follow-up

How often will I need to have my blood pressure checked now that I'm on treatment for my high blood pressure? And why? After all, they measured it a lot before I started treatment.

Before anyone starts on treatment for high blood pressure, several measurements need to be made on different days – at least three and often many more. This is to get some idea of your average blood pressure, and to decide whether you need treatment at all. These measurements will usually be made by a practice nurse, or you may be taught how to measure your own blood pressure at home (there is more about this in Chapter 3), and then asked to return to your doctor with your own twice-daily record of your blood pressure over a week or two.

Presumably something similar has happened to you, and the results showed that you were likely to benefit from medication. Now that you have started your treatment, you will probably need weekly measurements at first to assess your response to different doses of your drugs or to different drug combinations. This has to continue until your blood pressure is controlled. It may take only a week or two, but in roughly one third of people this process of trial and error takes several months, occasionally more than a year. It's worth persevering, because eventually almost everybody either reaches their target pressure, or at least has a very substantial fall in their blood pressure (which greatly reduces associated risks). Once your treatment has been shown to be effective, you will probably only need your blood pressure measured every three months or so.

Are there any special symptoms I should look out for while on treatment for high blood pressure?
As long as your blood pressure is well controlled, you are much less likely to develop any of the serious consequences of uncontrolled high blood pressure. Your vigilance can be more effectively applied to making sure you attend regularly for follow-up, with routine blood pressure checks about every three months.

Drugs used for treatment of high blood pressure often cause minor symptoms or side-effects (discussed in general terms earlier in this chapter, and covered in more detail in Appendix 1). It is important to report these to your doctor, because they can nearly always be avoided by changing the drug or changing the dose.

Angina (pain over the front of the chest on exertion) and claudication (leg pain from obstructed leg arteries) are increasingly common in men from middle age onwards, and are much more likely in people with high blood pressure, even if this has been controlled by treatment. They are much less common in women, unless they have been heavy smokers. Often they are not recognised, angina being dismissed as 'indigestion' and claudication as arthritis. Both should be reported to your doctor. (There is more information about angina and claudication in Chapters 6 and 9.)

When I go for follow-up, what other things ought to be checked besides my blood pressure?

The reason your high blood pressure needs treatment is to reduce your risks of eventually suffering from stroke, coronary heart disease, or any of the other complications that it can cause (discussed in more detail in Chapter 9). The other major causes of these outcomes therefore also need attention. This is not possible unless the relevant symptoms and signs are initially measured and assessed, and then regularly followed up. How much you smoke, your blood cholesterol level, your weight for your height and your regular exercise habits should all have been recorded before your treatment started. Whoever is doing your follow-up will want to check these (for example, to see how you well you are doing with any diet or exercise plan that has been suggested or if you have succeeded in giving up smoking). They will also want to know how you are getting on with your medication (if you are having any problems or side-effects) and if you have any other problems you wish to discuss.

About once every five years, you should also have a urine test (to check your kidney function by testing your urine for protein) and a blood test to check your urea and creatinine levels. The urine test for protein will automatically include a test for glucose, which is important because diabetes is a not uncommon complication of high blood pressure. These tests should also have been done before you started treatment, and they are discussed in more detail in the section on ***Diagnosis and initial investigations*** in Chapter 2.

Any other tests you have will depend on your own particular circumstances. For example, if you also have diabetes, then you will have a routine examination of your retina (the back of the eye) once a year; but if you have good control of your blood pressure and no signs of diabetes, then this will not be necessary.

Should I be told exactly what my blood pressure is when I attend follow-up?

Yes If you are not told, ask, and then write the figure down in your diary. Doctors used to be taught never to tell people what their blood pressures were, on the grounds that this made them worry. As far as I know, nobody teaches this now.

It doesn't seem to matter what I do, whenever I attend for follow-up, my blood pressure still seems to be high. What can be done about this?

Between 20% and 30% of people treated for high blood pressure are unable to reach target pressures during their first year or two on medication, even on combinations of two or three different drugs. The commonest causes of failure to respond to BP- lowering drugs are:

- people forgetting or not wanting to take their tablets, but being too afraid to admit this;
- a high alcohol intake (more than about 21-25 pints of average strength beer or the equivalent in wine or spirits a week for a man, or about half that for a woman);
- taking ACE-inhibitor drugs without either reducing the amount of salt in the diet or without also taking a thiazide diuretic; or
- fairly severe depression.

These four common causes of apparent drug-resistance should be excluded by doctors or nurses asking you the right questions and really listening to your answers (some nurses are better at this than some doctors). If all these causes are excluded, the next possibility is a rare cause of classical secondary high blood pressure, which will need special investigations (if you need such investigations, you will find they are quite simple – they have been explained in the section on *Diagnosis and initial investigations* in Chapter 2).

In about half of this 20-30%, none of these causes of apparent drug-resistance can be found. For them (and for you, if you are one of them) it is reasonable to set an interim target well below their pre-treatment pressure, but well above the ideal target pressure (which is about 150-160/90 mmHg). Half a loaf is better than no bread. Most of them eventually get good control, but perhaps only after several years of continuous medication.

Much to my surprise, whenever I attend for follow-up my blood pressure seems to be very low. Should anything be done about this?

Generally speaking, low blood pressure means low risk for stroke, heart attacks, and the other consequences of high blood pressure, and there is no evidence that it increases risks of other diseases.

Some people feel tired more quickly and more often if their systolic pressure averages less than about 110 mmHg, even if this occurs naturally rather than as a consequence of taking BP-lowering drugs. Between 5% and 10% of people on any BP-lowering drug feel tired because of the medication itself. Below a systolic pressure of about 100 mmHg occasional feelings of faintness or actual faints are possible, and at systolic pressures below about 90 mmHg they are common.

Reducing blood pressure below a systolic pressure of about 120 mmHg seems pointless. If yours is consistently below this threshold you are probably being overtreated, and you should talk to your doctor about reducing your medication.

Where should I go for follow-up – would I be better off in a hospital outpatient clinic or should I just see my GP?

Providing your GP has a well organised follow-up system, you are likely to be better off with this than with any hospital clinic. There is likely to be more continuity, and it is much easier to integrate care of any other problems you may have with control of your blood pressure.

Some GPs still have no organised follow-up system, but rely instead on people asking them to do things when they come to the surgery for an appointment. With well-informed people this can work, but you must make sure that your blood pressure is checked every three months or so, and that you have a more general check (including a urine test for kidney function) about once every five years.

If your GP is really not interested, you will probably be better off with an endless succession of young doctors in training in a hospital clinic. They won't know you, but they will check the most important things that need checking.

Is it just as good to be followed up by a practice nurse as by a doctor?

As a rule, yes. Very generally speaking, practices which have developed enough of a team approach to delegate follow-up to nurses are likely to be more thoughtful and up to date than practices which have not, but there are many exceptions, particularly in practices too small to allow division of labour.

More and more practice nurses are getting special training to run blood pressure follow-up clinics, and often clinics for other related problems such as diabetes or coronary prevention. Those with recent training may even be more up to date than the doctors who employ them. Nurses usually have more time, and are often more in touch with the practical problems of living on an average income.

I usually see a practice nurse for my follow-up, and I'm perfectly happy about this, but I wonder if I should sometimes see my doctor and, if so, when?

However well you seem to be doing, you should certainly see your doctor for a review at least once every five years, and many doctors do this annually. Unless the practice has some computer-based reminder system, it can be very easy to let this slide, because GP practices are so busy.

Your nurse should be operating within guidelines which indicate when a doctor's opinion is needed. This should include a target pressure, usually less than 160/90 mmHg or thereabouts. If your measurements are consistently higher than this, either the nurse will change your medication (within guidelines) or you should see a doctor.

Managing high blood pressure

If you are concerned about other problems which may or may not be related to either your high blood pressure or to its treatment, there's no harm in asking your nurse about this first. If she's not sure of the answer, she'll probably either ask a doctor, or arrange for you to see one.

Problems may arise where nurses are under pressure to protect doctors from an excessive workload, often real enough. If you suspect this is the case, and you really do want to see your doctor, you must insist on your right to do so. In the last resort, you can change to another doctor.

I'm worried, because when I go for my follow-up checks, I usually seem to see a trainee doctor. Is a trainee fully competent for this responsibility?

Trainee doctors are fully trained in hospital medicine, but are by definition not yet fully trained in general practice, which follows on from their hospital training.

Trainees are more recently trained than their senior colleagues, and therefore sometimes better informed and more up to date. Management of follow-up for high blood pressure is usually fairly straightforward compared with many of the tasks facing GPs, and you may well be better off with an interested and unhurried trainee than with an uninterested and time-starved senior doctor.

5
How to help yourself

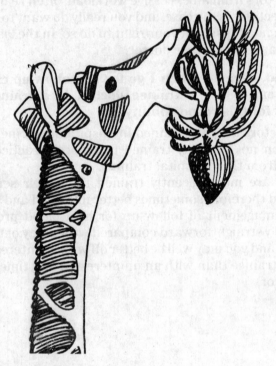

Weight control

How does my being overweight affect the management of my high blood pressure?

Being overweight is an important and reversible cause of high blood pressure, particularly in young people under 40. If you can get your weight down - and keep it down - so that you have a BMI of 25 or below (BMI stands for Body Mass Index and is explained later on in this section) then you have a good chance of normalising your blood pressure.

Although middle-aged and older people may get some fall in blood pressure with a fall in weight, it is likely to be much less than in younger people. Still, many overweight people whose blood pressures fail to come down with apparently adequate medication find their drugs are more effective once they lose a stone or so (about 6 kg) in weight.

You must also bear in mind the possibility that a standard sphygmomanometer cuff applied to a large arm is probably giving very misleading blood pressure readings. Simply using an outsize cuff that fits correctly will often bring readings down by about 20 mmHg.

I know that I'm a bit overweight and I've now been told that I have high blood pressure. If I get my weight down, will it help my blood pressure?

It almost certainly will if you are under 40, and probably will if you are older than that. It will probably also reduce your risk of developing other health problems associated with being too fat, such as diabetes. (Although the connections between the causes of high blood pressure and the causes of diabetes are not yet fully understood, they are certainly important: people with high blood pressure are more likely to get diabetes later on in life. For this reason diabetes keeps cropping up throughout this book, although it's a book about high blood pressure. Human biology has little respect for labels.)

Having said that, what you really need to consider is not just what you weigh, but how much body fat you have. Simply weighing yourself will tell you if you are overweight, but it will tell you nothing about the proportions of fat and muscle in your body. It is excess fat, not muscle, that causes high blood pressure and increases the risks that have to do with being overweight. To improve your general health, to reduce blood pressure and the risk of coronary heart disease or stroke, to prevent diabetes (or to improve control of diabetes if you have it already), you require not only energy balance (calories in = calories out, don't eat more calories than you use), but a higher energy throughput (ie more energy both in and out) – which means taking more exercise as well as watching what you eat.

The combination of a sensible diet and regular exercise will build muscle and reduce fat stores. Do not be discouraged if you do not immediately seem to lose weight when following such a programme – while you are replacing your fat with muscle, the change will not readily show up on the scales. In the longer term you will see your weight fall. What is important for you to remember is that losing weight on a calorie-reduced diet but without an exercise programme will have less effect on your blood pressure (and the accompanying risks of coronary heart disease and stroke) than the same weight loss achieved with an exercise programme.

There is a section on *Exercise* later in this chapter.

Why do people put on weight?

We all need energy from food and drink to fuel our many body processes which must continue even when we are asleep. All forms of physical activity (such as walking, shopping, typing and so on) require additional energy. Energy is measured in calories (or in joules, which is the metric equivalent – one calorie equals 4.2 joules).

Ideally your calorie intake from the food you eat each day should balance the amount of energy used up by your body, and when this happens you will neither gain nor lose weight. If the amount of food and drink you consume provides more energy (calories) than you use in your daily activities, then the extra food will be converted into body fat and you will put on weight. If you reduce your daily intake of calories so that you are taking in less energy than your body needs, then your body will make up the difference by using up its fat stores, and you will lose weight.

Incidentally, if we are to be strictly correct, we should really be talking about kilocalories (often abbreviated to kcal or written as Calories with a capital first letter) or kilojoules (abbreviated to kjoules or kj), and these are the units you will probably see on the nutritional information labels on food packaging. But most people simply use the shorthand term 'calorie' when they mean kilocalories, and that is what has been used in this book.

How to help yourself

Does it matter where you're fat? All my weight seems to be in my hips and thighs.

Yes, it does seem to matter as there is some strong evidence that your body shape is important. Overweight people whose body fat is concentrated round the middle (as shown in Figure 10) are more likely to have higher blood pressure and are at much higher risk of coronary disease than those overweight people whose body fat is mainly in their arms, legs, breasts and buttocks (as shown in Figure 11). The best way to measure this is to divide your waist measurement by your hip measurement, both at their widest point: a healthy result is less than 1.00. Coronary risk rises steeply in people whose belly girth is greater than their hip girth - the classic beer-drinker's pot belly.

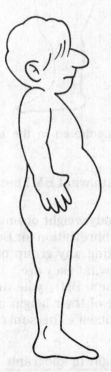

Figure 10: Body fat concentrated around the middle of the body

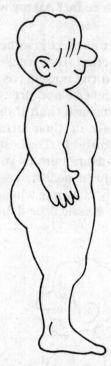

Figure 11: Body fat concentrated in the arms, legs, breasts and buttocks

Could you please explain what BMI means and how I work it out?

Your normal or 'ideal' body weight obviously depends partly on your height. BMI is the abbreviation for Body Mass Index, which is a useful way of ranking any group of people with various heights according to how fat they are.

To calculate someone's BMI, you divide their weight in kilograms by the square of their height in metres (to square a figure you multiply it by itself). This sum can be written down as a formula:

$$\text{BMI} = \frac{\text{weight in kilograms}}{(\text{height in metres})^2} \quad \text{or} \quad \frac{\text{kg}}{\text{m}^2}$$

How to help yourself

Your BMI is in the normal range if it is between 20 and 25. People below BMI 20 are underweight, and above BMI 25 are overweight. The formula works well for most adults, but not for children or very short people under about 5'3" (1.60 m), or for very tall people over about 6'2" (1.87 m) or so. Within these limits, BMI is a good predictor for life expectancy (which is why insurance companies have always been so interested in heights and weights). Very skinny people and very fat people both have lower than average life expectancy. The rise in death rates for obesity rises rapidly from a BMI of about 30, so this is generally used by doctors as a borderline between simply being overweight and serious obesity, and BMI 40 as a borderline between serious obesity and giant obesity, which is very difficult to control.

An example may help to show how BMI can be used. Imagine a fit young man who plays rugby, weighs about 10 stone and is 5'7" tall (metric equivalents 63.5 kg and 1.7 m). Using the formula, we can calculate his BMI by squaring his height in metres (ie $1.7 \times 1.7 = 2.89$) and dividing that figure into his weight in kilograms (ie $63.5 \div 2.89 = 21.9$). He has an excellent BMI of 21.9. Ten years later he has stopped playing rugby but still drinks with the team, his height is unchanged, but his weight has risen to 14 stone (88.9 kg), and so his BMI has risen to 30.8. He is unlikely ever to be able to get his BMI back to 22, but he might reasonably settle for 26, still slightly on the heavy side but not seriously so. He could use his BMI to calculate what his weight should be. The formula for this is

$$(\text{height in metres})^2 \times \text{BMI required} = \text{target weight in kg}$$

In his case, this will be $2.89 \times 26 = 75$ kg (165 lb, or 11 st 11 lb). So he needs to lose just over two stones (14 kg) to reach his target weight.

Admittedly all this fiddling about with converting stones into pounds into kilos is irritating, but the answer is either to become a good European and start measuring and thinking in metric terms, or invest in a pocket calculator that will do the conversions for you.

What weight should I aim for?

As you will have seen in the previous question, you can use what you now know about BMI to work out a suitable target weight for yourself. Alternatively, there are plenty of published charts and tables which will show you the range of weights that are considered average for your height (have a look at the books in the section on health and diet in your local library – one of the books is bound to include such a chart). Or you could ask your GP or practice nurse to suggest a suitable target weight for you.

The most important thing is simply to commit yourself to a definite target with your partner, some other friend, or with somebody in your family doctor's team; to weigh yourself once a week on reliable scales; and to be honest about your results.

Can I weigh myself on bathroom scales? I'm prepared to buy some new ones.

If you are willing to pay a lot for really accurate home scales, that's fine, but few bathroom scales meet this specification, however smart they may look. This is because you should lose weight slowly, at a rate of less than a pound a week, and these amounts need to be measured accurately. Ordinary bathroom scales vary from hour to hour and day to day, depending not only on real changes in your weight, but also on temperature and humidity. These variations are generally larger than the expected changes in your body weight in one week – so that when you have stuck to your rules and actually lost weight, the scales may show a small gain, or when you know you have broken your rules, your actual weight gain may be misrepresented as a small loss.

The most difficult part of any diet and exercise programme is to keep up your morale and motivation. Nothing reinforces these so much as real progress, however small, but nothing destroys them faster than misleading feedback. Balance arm scales (at your chemist or at your doctor's surgery) will give you accurate measures of progress; cheap bathroom scales will not. Remember to stick to more or less the same clothes and shoes each time you weigh yourself, and don't bother to weigh yourself more than once a week.

If you do decide that you want to buy yourself a good set of scales, then it would be worth looking at copies of *Which?* magazine in your local library to see if they have carried out any recent tests and, if so, which models they recommend.

Why do I have to lose weight so slowly? I'd much rather go on a crash diet and get it all over with in a couple of weeks.

Because if you do that you will probably put all the weight back on again fairly quickly as soon as you stop following your diet. Small regular losses may be less dramatic than the gimmicky crash diets which are designed to sell more magazines or so-called slimming foods, but they are far more effective. A slow weight loss really is the most efficient weight loss: there is plenty of evidence to show that people who lose weight too quickly tend to put it all back on (and more) within just a few years.

More importantly, losing weight slowly and steadily is the healthiest way to go about it – if you lose weight too fast you will not only lose your fat, but also the types of body tissue (such as muscle) that you need to keep.

So what's the best way to go about reaching and maintaining my target weight?

By following a sensible diet such as the one suggested in the answer to the next question and by increasing the amount of exercise you take (see the section on *Exercise* later in this chapter). If you do this, you can expect to lose a bit less than a kilogram (just over 2 lb) in your first week (probably less), and perhaps 250 gm (9 oz) a week thereafter. A small fall in weight such as this, sustained over several months, is the right way both to lose weight and to maintain the loss (which is where most people fall down). If you combine diet with exercise, you will be replacing some fat with muscle, so the beneficial changes in your body cannot be measured only by weight loss.

Every time I open a magazine there seems to be yet another diet article and they are all different. I find it all very confusing. Can you suggest a suitable diet to help me lose weight?

There are six golden rules.

- **Eat less fat**
  Fats are the most concentrated kind of energy available, so they contain more calories per gram or ounce than any other foods. A diet high in fats or oils is therefore a diet high in calories, and the main reason that people become overweight in the first place is because they are eating too much fat and not using it up through exercise. You will find more information about fats and how to reduce your intake of them in the section on *Fats and oils* later in this chapter.

- **Eat less sugar**
  Sugar has no nutritional value as it contains nothing but calories, whether you eat it on its own or in sweets, soft drinks, jams and honey, or in foods such as biscuits and cakes, or hidden in processed or convenience foods (check the labels, and on savoury products as well as sweet ones, as sugar can be an ingredient of those as well). Reduce the amount of sugar you eat and you reduce your calorie intake.

- **Stop nibbling between meals, but do not miss meals**
  Nibbling between meals can add a lot of surplus calories to your diet without you noticing (especially as many snack foods are high in fats and/or sugar), so one of the best things to do when you want to lose weight is to stop nibbling. (If you really do need a snack, then a piece of fruit is probably the best choice.) Your body prefers to have a regular supply of food, so do not be tempted to go over the top and miss meals altogether. If you do, you will either eat too much at your next meal to make up for it, or you may even develop an obsessive relationship with food which will almost certainly be bad for your health and could even lead to eating disorders such as anorexia or bulimia.

- **Eat more vegetables, fruit and bread**
  Reducing the amount of fats and sweet foods you eat is easier if you replace them by those foods which, weight for weight, contain less energy (ie fewer calories). They are generally more bulky and need more chewing (so that overeating is more difficult), and as they are also digested more slowly, you

How to help yourself 129

tend to feel full for longer. And, of course, they provide the vitamins and minerals that are essential in a healthy diet.

- **Take regular exercise**
  This has been discussed earlier in this section, and there is also a section on *Exercise* later in this chapter.

- **Measure your weight honestly and regularly on accurate scales**
  See the earlier questions and answers in this section for the reasons why.

If you follow these rules, you will be eating a healthy diet, and you will lose weight without consuming expensive (and probably tasteless) 'diet' foods or having to count each individual calorie.

Your golden rules are quite general – where can I get some more detailed information?

There are a number of books and leaflets available about diet and nutrition, and we have listed some of them in Appendix 3. You may find some of the leaflets available in your doctor's surgery, especially if they run a weight-reduction group. If you need more detailed advice, you could ask your doctor to refer you to a dietitian, who will look at your individual needs and advise you of any changes that you need to make to your diet.

Is it a good idea to cut down on sugar by using artificial sweeteners instead, or choosing 'diet' foods which contain them? Would this help me lose some weight?

This might seem to be a good idea, because you are replacing something high in calories (sugar) with a low-calorie or no-calorie equivalent, and so you are reducing your total calorie intake. However, there are a few drawbacks.

One of the most commonly-used artificial sweeteners is saccharin, which is often in the form saccharin sodium. If you want to cut down on the amount of sodium in your diet (the reasons for this are discussed in the section on *Sodium and salt* later in this chapter), then you will want to avoid saccharin.

Other artificial sweeteners do not present this problem.

Used in moderation, all the artificial sweeteners available in this country are safe. However, a government body called the Committee on Toxicity does make recommendations about the maximum amount (called the acceptable daily intake) of artificial sweeteners that you should eat. This is because there is still some debate among scientists about the safety of these chemicals when they are eaten in large quantities. For most people, exceeding this acceptable daily intake would be quite difficult, but it is something you may want to consider. (If you want to know more about this, then *Which?* magazine produced an excellent article on the subject in their September 1994 edition.)

Opinion is also divided on whether using artificial sweeteners will actually help you lose weight. They certainly won't help you lose your sweet tooth (if you have one). The foods that contain them can be quite low in fibre (so they don't fill you up and you feel hungry again sooner) and quite high in fat (which you also need to cut down on if you want to lose weight). There are ways of cutting down on sugar without using artificial sweeteners: for example, instead of eating a 'diet' yoghurt, you could stir some fresh fruit into a low-fat plain unsweetened yoghurt – the combination would be just as sweet, low in fat, more filling (because of the dietary fibre in the fruit), and probably both cheaper and tastier.

What about weight-reduction groups – are they any real help?

Yes, they can be – group methods are generally more effective than trying to do it on your own. Commercial weight-reduction groups are well known, widely advertised in the media (especially in 'slimming' magazines) and are available in almost all towns. If you join one of these, you are more likely to lose weight and maintain your new lower weight than if you try to do it by yourself – and the average standard of dietary advice is better than you will get from some family doctors. The groups require you to attend regularly, and as they make a charge this makes them expensive enough to be out of reach for many people.

Equally good results have been achieved by non-commercial

voluntary groups, often based on NHS health centres or group practices. Most have been started by local enthusiasts, who may be members of the public, or health centre staff such as practice nurses, health visitors or community dietitians. If the sort of group you think you need does not exist locally, and you fancy the task of starting one, you should get in touch with others with real experience of doing this. Dietitians at your local hospital or your community dietitians (if there are any in your area) will probably be able to help you.

Healthy eating

Now that I'm being treated for high blood pressure, what are the most important changes I should make in what I eat and drink?

Available evidence suggests that to reduce both your high blood pressure and its consequent risks for stroke, coronary heart disease and so on, the most effective changes you can make are to reduce your intake of alcohol, fats, and salt (sodium). You should also increase the amount of bread, vegetables and fruit you eat. If you are overweight, you will also need to make a general reduction in your total energy (calorie) intake, as was discussed in the previous section on *Weight control*.

The reasons for cutting down on alcohol are given in the answer to the next question, and there are sections on *Fats and oils* and *Sodium and salt* later in this chapter.

Why do I need to watch the amount of alcohol I drink?

Drinking more than 4 units of alcohol A DAY for a man or 3 units A DAY for a woman is a common and easily avoided cause of high blood pressure, particularly in people aged under 40 (a unit of alcohol is one glass of wine OR one single measure of spirits OR half a pint of average strength beer or lager).

Regular heavy drinking raises blood pressure, particularly in young men. This response varies, but it is substantial in some people – so much so that many young men whose diastolic pressures are over 100 mmHg can reduce their BP to normal without medication, once they reduce their drinking to not more than a pint or two of beer a day. High alcohol intake is a common cause of treatment failing to work, and if your BP refuses to fall despite apparently adequate treatment, you should think about what you are drinking.

Acute heavy drinking (bingeing) can cause a rapid though brief rise in BP, and this may bring on a stroke in older people.

There is consistent evidence that moderate drinking (ie drinking no more than the previously-mentioned recommended daily limits) reduces the risk of coronary heart disease, probably through its effects on blood cholesterol and blood clotting factors. Heavier drinking (15 pints of beer a week or more for a man) increases the risk.

Do red meat or spicy foods cause high blood pressure?

No. On average, vegetarians have lower blood pressures than meat eaters, but there's nothing special about red meat as opposed to any other sorts of meat.

Spicy foods may make your face flush, but they have no effect at all on your blood pressure.

My daughter has become a vegetarian and is keen for me to become one too. Would a vegetarian diet be good for my high blood pressure?

Yes, it would be. Blood pressure is on average lower in vegetarians than meat-eaters. Switching to a vegetarian diet lowers blood pressure in people whose BP is high enough to need treatment, although rarely enough to avoid any need for BP-lowering drugs. We have good evidence that potassium (which comes mainly from fruit and vegetables) reduces BP, and this may be the main way in which a vegetarian diet works, although we are not entirely sure.

Vegetarian diets have a high fibre content, and high-fibre foods are digested and absorbed slowly (which means that you tend to feel full for longer – very helpful if you are trying to lose weight). They usually include plenty of pulses (peas, beans and lentils) which contain a particular type of fibre (called soluble fibre) which appears to lower blood cholesterol levels. As well as all these benefits, some kinds of cancer seem to occur much less in vegetarians. Of course, people who become vegetarians tend to avoid various other sorts of dangerous habits, notably smoking, but the consistency of the evidence is impressive. Omnivores wait impatiently for evidence on just how much meat they may eat, without losing all the apparent benefits of vegetarianism.

If you decide that you want to be a vegetarian, you could contact the Vegetarian Society (address in Appendix 2) for information.

What about eggs and dairy foods in a vegetarian diet?

Strict vegetarian diets can easily become deficient in protein, which is essential for building new cells. Eggs, milk, cheese and other dairy products are important sources of protein as well as variety for most vegetarians. They are not available for vegans (a group of vegetarians who eat no animal products at all) who must rely on pulses (beans and peas), soya products and nuts as their most protein-rich foods.

Egg yolks are high in cholesterol, but as a source of high blood cholesterol they are no more important than other foods containing animal fats which, when digested, are changed into body cholesterol. Prudent diets generally recommend not more than two eggs a week, but if you cut down on other fats, you can eat more.

All cheeses except cottage cheese contain large amounts of sodium, so cheeses have to be virtually eliminated from any serious low-sodium diet (you will find more information about this type of diet in the section on *Sodium and salt* later in this chapter). They also contain a lot of saturated fat, which raises blood cholesterol. The same applies to butter, except that you can easily get low-salt butter. For reasons which so far remain unexplained, people who drink a lot of milk tend to have lower blood cholesterol levels than people who drink little or none. Evidence for this is consistent and apparently reliable. However, milk does contain a lot of salt, and has to be restricted in low-sodium diets.

I don't want to become a vegetarian. Are there any alternatives? What if I gave up red meat altogether and stuck to chicken and fish – would that be enough?

There are differences between vegetarian and meat-eating diets other than the exclusion or inclusion of meat. For example, vegetarians tend to eat less fats and more fibre than meat-eaters, so exactly what accounts for the difference in blood pressure between them is still unclear.

Giving up red meat is not necessary even if you have been told that you need to reduce your cholesterol levels (there is a section on *High blood cholesterol* in Chapter 6). However, chicken (with the skin removed) and fish contain less fat than red meat, and a low-fat diet is helpful for people with high blood pressure (there is more information about this in the next section on *Fats and oils*). Perhaps you would find a compromise acceptable – reducing the amount of red meat you eat by replacing it at some meals with chicken or fish, while at the same time cutting down on fats generally and eating more high-fibre foods. A dietitian would be able to give you more detailed advice.

Fish is something that we keep being told is a 'healthy food'. Is this true for people with high blood pressure? I hope you are going to say 'no', because I don't enjoy eating it.

I'm going to disappoint you. Fish, particularly oily fish such as mackerel, herrings, salmon and trout, have an important protective effect against coronary heart disease, and are therefore an important part of any prudent diet for people with high blood pressure. The effect is probably through omega-3 fish oils, which reduce blood levels of triglyceride, the form in which fat is transported from the gut to the liver. They can be taken as capsules if you really can't stand the taste of fish.

What is dietary fibre? If I need to increase the amount of fibre in my diet, which foods should I eat?

'Dietary fibre' usually means everything in your food which you cannot digest, and which therefore passes through your body until it is expelled in your stools (faeces). Although we use the term 'fibre', dietary fibre includes lots of important materials

How to help yourself

which are not fibrous at all, such as gums and mucilages, which affect both the way in which your food is absorbed, and the quantity you want to eat before you begin to feel full and tired of chewing.

As well as breakfast cereals whose fibre content you can hardly miss if you ever watch television, wholemeal bread and all fruit and vegetables have a high fibre content, although how much you actually get from your fruit and vegetables depends on whether you cook them, and how much. Regularly adding sodium bicarbonate to your cooking to keep vegetables green rapidly destroys their fibre content, and so does boiling them for a long time. Fresh fruit and raw salads are ideal.

Pulses (peas, beans, lentils etc) have the highest fibre content of any cooked vegetables. They also generate a lot of methane, which is noisy but odourless (unless combined with onions or garlic).

Increasing the fibre content of your diet by eating more wholemeal bread, fruit and vegetables is one of the most effective steps you can take in any reduced-fat, weight-reducing and cholesterol-lowering diet.

Isn't bread fattening, and therefore bad for high blood pressure?

All foods are fattening if you eat too much, that is if you take in more energy (calories) than you use up. Because bread used to be the biggest single item in any ordinary person's diet, it was a good target for general calorie reduction, but now that almost everyone eats a much more varied diet, this is no longer true.

All breads contain fairly high proportions of fibre, but wholemeal or granary loaves contain much more than ordinary bread (white or brown) and are therefore healthier. This is partly because you have to chew them more – which means that you will probably eat a bit less – and partly because they improve digestion of fat in your gut.

A major problem about bread is what we choose to put on it. If you always add butter or margarine to every slice of bread, you enormously increase both your energy intake and the proportion of fat in your diet. Much of this is just habit, and it is often easy to miss it out without noticing the difference when you eat bread with cheese, peanut butter, or many other spreads.

Is sugar as bad for you as people say?

Sugar is important because it contains many calories (and nothing but calories), so if you include a lot of sugar in what you eat, you will find it more difficult to achieve energy balance (calories in = calories out, don't eat more calories than you use) and so you are more likely to put on weight. This is a good reason for adding as little as possible to your food, for avoiding foods high in sugar, and for resisting the demands of your children for unlimited sweet-eating. However, there is no evidence that sugar of any kind has any specific harmful effect either on blood pressure or on the heart, or that eating sugar causes diabetes in any specific way other than contributing to energy imbalance (if energy in exceeds energy out, then surplus energy is stored as fat).

There is also no evidence that brown sugar is better than white, or that naturally occuring sugars such as fructose, lactose and honey provide any special health benefits.

There is also no evidence that glucose drinks are of any benefit whatever to health except in people with vomiting or diarrhoea, or who for some other reason are unable to eat ordinary food. Of course they 'provide energy', but no more so than spotted dick or treacle pudding. Glucose is simply another variety of sugar.

I can't tolerate eating salads more than once a week. What can I do?

Breathe a sigh of relief – salads aren't compulsory. The important thing is to include plenty of fresh fruit and vegetables in your diet, whether raw or cooked (providing that you don't overcook them).

The other thing you could try is experimenting with the type of salads you eat and the dressings you put on them. The cookery books listed in Appendix 3 will give you ideas for salads which contain interesting and tasty ingredients, and for dressings that are low in fat but which still help to make even a simple

How to help yourself

lettuce leaf taste better. For example, you could use an olive oil dressing on your salads: this will contribute monounsaturated fats to your diet, and this will be beneficial for your heart. There is more about fats and oils in the next section in this chapter.

Would eating more garlic have any effect on my high blood pressure?

Garlic has no significant effect on high blood pressure, but there is good evidence that it reduces blood cholesterol, and therefore in turn reduces the risks associated with having high BP (such as heart attacks and strokes). Large quantities of fresh (not powdered) garlic used in cooking reduce LDL cholesterol ('bad' cholesterol) by an average 12% (about 0.7 mmol) but have no effect on HDL cholesterol ('good' cholesterol). (There is more information about cholesterol in the section on **High blood cholesterol** in Chapter 6.) You will have to put up with the smell, as garlic pills are much less effective, but if the whole family eats it, you can all share both better health and a Mediterranean indifference to puritan values. Alternatively you could chew some parsley after your meal to sweeten your breath.

You're suggesting an awful lot of changes, and I don't think I could alter what I eat so much all in one go. Do I have to do everything at once?

No, you can make changes gradually. This would in fact be better than doing it all at once, as it will give you a chance to get accustomed to your new eating habits, and then you will be more likely to keep to them. One approach would be to make just one change a week: for example, in the first week you could have a piece of fruit instead of biscuits or crisps for your elevenses, in the next week you could also switch from white to wholemeal bread for your sandwiches, and so on. It's also worth remembering that a healthy diet doesn't have to include foods that you dislike or be tasteless or uninteresting.

Fats and oils

Why do I need to cut down the amount of fat that I eat?

Firstly because they are the most concentrated kind of energy available, so they contain more calories per gram or ounce than any other foods. A diet high in fats or oils is therefore a diet high in energy. Most people eat more energy than they need, and therefore gain weight, which is in turn another cause of raised BP, particularly in young people.

Secondly because fats and oils are the main source of blood cholesterol, which is a risk factor for coronary heart disease and (to a smaller extent) for stroke. You will find more information about cholesterol in the section on *High blood cholesterol* in Chapter 6.

By how much do I need to cut down, and how do I go about it?

Over 40% of the calories in an average diet comes from fats of various kinds (including cooking oils and less obvious fats such as those found in cheese and pastry). There is medical agreement that to improve our health we should reduce this level to about 35% or less, but there is no evidence yet that this is happening. People have greatly reduced their intake of milk, cream and butter, but evidently many food manufacturers (particularly of snacks, fast-foods and convenience foods) put the fat back in again during processing. As with salt (discussed in the next section in this chapter), the fat and oil content of food seems to be an important factor in its immediate appeal to most people.

Percentages, although interesting, are not really very helpful when it comes to practical advice about cutting down on fats. The books and leaflets listed in Appendix 3 will give you some more detailed information, but you could start with the following suggestions.

- Grill or bake foods rather than frying them or roasting them in fat.
- Choose lean cuts of meat and cut off any visible fat.
- Skim any visible fat off the top of cooked dishes.

- Remove skin from chicken and other poultry (most of their fat is in or just under the skin).
- Replace high-fat foods (whole milk, cream, butter, high-fat cheeses) with their low-fat or reduced-fat equivalents (skimmed or semi-skimmed milk, yoghurt, low-fat spreads, reduced-fat cheeses).
- Cut down on the amount of butter or margarine that you put on your bread, or switch to a low-fat spread.
- Cut down on snack foods (which are often high in sugar or salt as well as high in fats).
- Cut down on biscuits, cakes and pastries (which all contain hidden fat – and lots of sugar).
- Read the nutrition labels on food and choose those that have the lowest fat content.
- Whenever possible, replace saturated fats or oils with monounsaturated or polyunsaturated fats or oils (there is more information about these in the answer to the next question).

Please can you explain the difference between saturated, monounsaturated and polyunsaturated fats? And what's the difference between a fat and an oil?

The terms saturated, monounsaturated and polyunsaturated all refer to the chemical make-up of fats and oils. Chemically speaking, fats and oils are made from long-chain molecules containing carbon, hydrogen and oxygen atoms. If there is no more space on the chain for any more oxygen atoms, then we have a saturated fat; if there is space for more oxygen, then the fat is unsaturated (monounsaturated if there is room for only one more oxygen atom; polyunsatured if there is room for more than one).

Saturated and unsaturated fats are handled differently by your body: saturated fats raise blood cholesterol (and thus the risk of heart disease) much more than unsaturated fats. At the same total fat intake, diets containing a higher proportion of unsaturated fats and oils are probably healthier.

Fats and oils differ only in their consistency – fats are usually solid at room temperature, whereas oils are usually liquid. They all contain a mixture of saturated and unsaturated fats: the difference is in the proportions. This is why we often hear talk about an oil or spread being 'high in polyunsaturates' or 'low in saturates'.

What does all this chemistry mean in practical terms? How do I know which fats or oils to use?

In practical terms it means that you should not only reduce your total fat intake but also, where possible, switch from fats high in saturates to those high in unsaturates (and preferably high in monounsaturates rather than polyunsaturates). This applies both to the fats and oils you use in cooking and those you spread on your bread.

Saturated fats come mostly from animals: examples of fats high in saturates include butter, lard, suet and dripping. Coconut oil and palm oil are also high in saturates, and cheap cooking oils tend to include more saturated fats.

Unsaturated fats come mostly from vegetable oils or from animals fed on grass rather than grain or cattle cake (which thus excludes fats from most farmed animals). Vegetable oils high in polyunsaturates include corn, sunflower and soya oils. Olive oil is high in monounsaturates, as are rapeseed and groundnut (peanut) oils.

I can't stand the taste of margarine. Do I have to give up using butter?

The short answer, if you do **not** have a raised blood cholesterol, is no. Butter and ordinary margarine have the same fat content, so they both contribute the same amount of energy (calories) to your diet. So, whichever fat spread you use, spread it thinly and avoid adding it unnecessarily to food on your plate (eg to vegetables and potatoes).

If you are trying to lose weight, you may find a 'low fat' spread (from either a butter or margarine source) useful, but do remember that this it will still contain a lot of calories and so should be used sparingly.

If you do have a high blood cholesterol, then you could change to a spread high in unsaturated fat. Once again you will need to remember these still have the same total fat and calorie content as butter – it is just that the proportions of saturated and unsaturated fats have been altered by the manufacturers. Some soft margarines and spreads have been heavily promoted as polyunsaturates, with a protective effect against coronary disease. However, recent research has shown that eating too much polyunsaturated fat can also be linked to the development of coronary heart disease. In practical terms, this means that you will probably be better off switching to a spread high in monounsaturates. The evidence in favour of olive oil as an alternative covering for bread is convincing, and it tastes delicious.

What about cooking oils just labelled 'vegetable oil' – is it OK to use them?

If the label is not specific about the source, that is if it does not say that it is sunflower oil or rapeseed oil or whatever, then it is not really to be recommended. The chances are that it will be a blend of oils and contain a higher proportion of saturated fats than an unblended oil.

Some of these oils are expensive. Can I reuse them?

You should not reuse oils as each time they are heated more of the fats become saturated – which defeats the object of using an oil that is high in unsaturates in the first place. We would nearly all benefit from eating less fat, so perhaps we should look at it like this: using a 'better' source of fat may be more expensive initially but by using less of it, the cost works out the same.

Would it be a good idea to switch to 'low fat' varieties of sausages, crisps, etc?

Although these are lower in fat than the 'normal' varieties, they still contain a considerable amount of fat, and you will also need to remember that they still have salt in them. They are probably best kept for occasional treats or to help you make the transition from a diet high in fat to one with a lower fat content.

You also need to keep an eye open for the sugar content of sweet foods and puddings described as low fat – some low-fat yoghurts have been known to contain the equivalent of five teaspoons of sugar.

Sodium and salt

What's the connection between sodium and salt?

Sodium is one of the minerals which your body needs to keep it functioning properly. While we all need some sodium, most of us eat far more than we need and could easily cut down without in any way damaging our health. Sodium intake is measured in units called millimoles (abbreviated to mmol). The average intake in this country is about 150 mmol a day – about 10 times the amount that is essential for health.

The main source of sodium in most foods is sodium chloride, which is the chemical name for ordinary cooking or table salt (that's the connection between sodium and salt). Because salt is such a major source of sodium in our diet, doctors often refer interchangeably to low-salt or low-sodium diets – reduce the amount of salt in your diet and you automatically reduce the amount of sodium.

Sodium is also found in other substances used in cooking and food processing, such as bicarbonate of soda (chemical name sodium bicarbonate), sodium nitrite (a preservative), saccharin sodium (an artificial sweetener) and monosodium glutamate (used in Chinese food and many sauces).

How do we know that the amount of salt we eat affects our blood pressure?

High blood pressure does not exist at all, nor does average blood pressure rise with age, in some tribes in Brazil and Papua-New Guinea whose sodium intake is at the bare minimum essential for life (less than 15 mmol a day), about one tenth of the present average intake in the UK (about 150 mmol a day). On the other hand, in countries with very high sodium intakes, such as rural Portugal with about twice the UK sodium intake (300 mmol a day), or rural northern Japan with more than two and a half times the UK intake (400 mmol a day) both high blood pressure and stroke are extremely common.

So, in general, evidence points towards salt intake being an important cause of the general rise in blood pressure with age in nearly all societies. This evidence is not absolutely conclusive, because the people who consume natural rather than medically prescribed low-sodium diets are extremely poor, often hungry, and generally can expect to live less than 40 years even if they survive infancy.

There are good biological reasons why sodium intake might affect blood pressure, mainly through its effects on the kidneys. The idea that salt overload is the cause of primary high blood pressure, with susceptibility to sodium overload genetically determined, seems quite likely and is currently fashionable. However, the evidence is not consistent and there are still many experts who doubt the truth of this theory.

Evidence that substantial salt restriction is an effective or practical treatment for high blood pressure is much less convincing.

Which foods are high in salt?

The main source of sodium in most foods is sodium chloride, which is ordinary salt. This is present not only in added cooking salt or table salt, but also in usually unsuspected foods such as milk, cheese and bread, and in virtually all tinned or ready prepared foods such as most breakfast cereals, sausages, burgers, pizzas and soups. A diet sufficiently low in sodium to reduce blood pressure by up to 5 mmHg, with sodium intake reduced to about half normal at 60-70 mmol a day, must virtually eliminate all these foods, as well as more obvious ones like kippers, bacon, olives, hummus, Marmite and snacks such as crisps and salted nuts.

Is it really worth me going on a low-salt diet?

This is debatable, and reducing salt alone is not enough – you must reduce the amount of fat in your diet as well as reducing the amount of sodium. This is a very important although generally neglected feature of any effective diet for blood pressure control because, as everyone knows who has actually followed a low-sodium diet (rather than merely written about it or researched it on other people), for the first few weeks all food tastes like a mixture of cardboard and wallpaper paste, and you then tend to eat more fat in an attempt to make it taste of something. As fat certainly raises LDL blood cholesterol (there is more about cholesterol in the section on **High blood cholesterol** in Chapter 6) and therefore the risk of coronary disease and stroke, you stand to gain nothing at all by reducing your salt intake if at the same time you also raise your fat intake.

If you follow a moderately low-sodium diet and if you have very mildly raised BP in the diastolic range 90–100 mmHg, you may not need any medication. If it is much higher than this, you may need lower doses, or fewer different drugs, than you would on your usual diet. You will never eat out again, because if you really are sticking to a low-sodium diet, all restaurant food will taste unbearably salty. Speaking for myself as a food addict, I doubt if the game's worth the candle; so much deprivation for such a trivial result is simply not worth it. But people differ. There's certainly no harm in trying, providing you don't find yourself eating more fat.

If I decide to go on a low-sodium diet, how do I go about it? Which foods can I eat, and which should I avoid?

The first step is to stop adding salt to your food at the table and then gradually to reduce the amount you use in cooking. When you've done this, you next go on to consider the foods you normally eat and work out which you should eat more of and which you should avoid. Foods can be divided into three groups: low sodium foods which you can eat as often as you like; 'middling' sodium foods which you can eat sparingly; and high sodium foods which you should avoid altogether. Examples of foods from these groups are given here: a dietitian would be able to give you more detailed information.

Low sodium foods
- All fresh fruit

- All fresh or home-cooked vegetables (but NOT cooked in sodium bicarbonate)
- Rice and pasta
- Fresh meat, fish and poultry

'Middling' sodium foods

- Some breakfast cereals (unsalted porridge; muesli; Shredded Wheat; Sugar Puffs; puffed rice, wheat or oats)
- Some milk and milk products (up to half a pint of skimmed or semi-skimmed milk a day; yoghurt; ice cream; cottage cheese)
- Eggs (not more than two a week)
- Unsalted butter, margarine or spreads
- Unsalted nuts

High sodium foods

- Smoked and tinned fish
- Most breakfast cereals (all except those listed as 'middling' sodium foods)
- Most snacks and fast foods (eg salted nuts; pork scratchings; Bombay mix; pasties; pizzas; samosas and bhajias; pork pies; peanut butter; takeaway burgers and fried chicken)
- Most milk products (eg evaporated or condensed milk; salted butters and spreads; all cheeses except cottage cheese)
- Soups (especially canned or packet soups)
- Curries
- Savoury biscuits and pastries
- Self-raising flour and baking powder
- Preserved meats (this includes bacon, ham, luncheon meat and sausages) and pâtés
- Tinned vegetables (including baked beans and tomatoes)
- Ready-made sauces, stock cubes, savoury spreads and drinks (eg Marmite, Bovril)
- Dried fruits
- Golden syrup, chocolate and toffees
- Saccharin
- Ordinary bread (of any kind) and French white bread
- Chinese food

This sounds a tall order. How do I succeed in keeping to this diet?

There are three secrets of successful reduction of dietary sodium. The first is to reduce salt intake slowly, taking three months or more to reach your target. Through an excellent but unpublicised agreement between the the Health Education Council (now the Health Education Authority) and the big bakers, salt content of bread was reduced by 12.5% in 1986, but hardly anyone noticed. After a few months you find that your sense of taste has more or less permanently changed, and normally salted foods become quite unpleasant. Although there will still be many delicious foods you cannot eat, what you can eat will (eventually) start to taste good again.

The second secret is to include the whole family, so that the whole meal can be cooked in the same way. As high blood pressure runs so strongly in families, this is a good idea anyway. If you enjoy cooking you will be able to devise low-salt substitutes for some high sodium foods. For example, you could replace take-away burgers with home made (made from low-fat mince and chopped onion, seasoned with herbs and spices) or have home made soups (where you can replace the salt with other seasonings) instead of the tinned or packet varieties.

The third secret is to measure your sodium intake (as described later in this section) before starting your reduced-sodium diet (so that you know rather than guess where you're starting from) and perhaps once every six months thereafter (to know what results you've achieved).

Are salt substitutes helpful if you want to use less salt?

Not really. And there's no advantage in using sea salt – it's still salt. Even 'low salt' sprinkles have some sodium in them. The best way is to cut down gradually and so lose your taste for salt, as using substitutes won't help you to change your 'salt appetite'. You could try seasoning your food with herbs and spices instead: vinegar, mint and other herbs, mustard, pepper, paprika and other spices, and lemon juice can all be used on a low-sodium diet.

I did stop adding salt to my cooking but missed the taste, so now I sprinkle a little onto the cooked meal. Is this OK?

No, as you've approached the problem the wrong way around. It's better to start by cutting down on what you put directly on your plate, and then to tackle what you use in cooking (perhaps by replacing it by some of the herbs or spices suggested in the answer to the previous question).

Why can't I put bicarbonate of soda in my vegetables? It keeps them green.

Because the 'soda' part is sodium. Cutting out the bicarbonate would be an easy way to cut down your sodium intake, as it has no effect on the taste of the vegetables. And using bicarbonate when cooking vegetables destroys their vitamin C content, which is another good reason for leaving it out. A better way to keep greens green would be either to steam or microwave them or to boil them in the minimum amount of water for the shortest possible time.

How do I go about measuring my sodium intake?

The standard way to measure your sodium intake is not to measure how much you take in but how much you put out (in your urine) as in our temperate climate the two figures are roughly the same (you do lose some sodium from your body in sweat, but the amount is only significant in very hot weather).

The most accurate results are obtained by collecting all the urine you pass over seven days (you need a seven day collection because sodium output varies so much from day to day), and then having samples from this collection analysed in a laboratory. You will obviously need your doctor's cooperation, both to provide you with suitable containers for collecting your urine and to arrange for the analysis.

Your doctor will explain exactly what you need to do, but in broad terms the procedure is as follows. You will be provided with a large graduated bottle, and it is then up to you to ensure that all the urine you pass over the seven days of the trial (day or night, at home or at work or wherever) gets into that bottle - you may need several discreet containers with tight fitting caps to use when you are away from home, and probably a notice stuck to the toilet to remind you not to use it. At the end of each day you make a note of the total volume of urine in the container. You then shake the container to mix all the urine, and pour out 10 ml into another container (called a universal container and also supplied by your doctor). At the end of the trial you take the seven 10 ml containers and your records of the seven daily urine volumes to your doctor, and they are then sent off for analysis. Then all you have to do is wait for the results.

Exercise

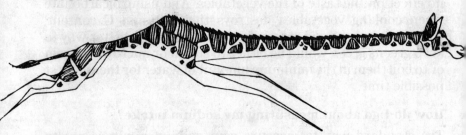

We're always being told that exercise is good for us. Is this true for people with high blood pressure?

Yes. The long-term effect of regular exercise is to reduce diastolic blood pressure by about 10 mmHg, about the same fall as you get with most BP-lowering drugs.

Regular exercise also reduces a wide range of important risk factors for coronary heart disease and stroke. For example, it reduces harmful LDL and VLDL blood cholesterol levels but raises protective HDL blood cholesterol (there is more information about all these types of cholesterol in the section on **High blood cholesterol** in Chapter 6), and it also reduces levels of the blood clotting factor fibrinogen. It helps you control your weight by increasing your energy output (by using up calories) and also by raising your morale (which makes it more likely that you will keep to a sensible diet). In the same way the 'feel-good' effect produced by regular exercise often helps people to stop smoking.

But I thought that vigorous exercise put your blood pressure up?

Yes, the immediate effect of vigorous exercise is to raise blood pressure. The rise is part of your body's process for preparing you for and sustaining you through exercise, because when you exercise you need an increase in the blood flow to the large muscles in your body. But the rise only lasts for a short time, while it is needed – it is not the same as the high blood pressure which continues over long periods of time, which is the type with which we are concerned in this book.

How much exercise do I have to take to get these effects?

Less than you might think. For many years researchers told us that the most important effects on coronary risk factors could be obtained only by taking very vigorous exercise (enough to make you sweaty and short of breath) for a couple of hours at least twice a week. Unless you took exercise really seriously, they said, you might as well not bother, for all the good it did you. The message was 'no gain without pain'.

More recent research shows that this is simply not true. As with everything else in life, you get out of it what you put into it, but even very moderate regular exercise reduces all measurable risk factors for coronary disease, stroke, and heart failure (which are the most serious consequences of high blood pressure). The reason we thought otherwise was that most earlier research used contrasting groups of people who were taking either a great deal of exercise or none at all, so that the effects of moderate exercise were not included.

So moderate exercise works – for example, if you usually take the car everywhere, even on short journeys, then simply walking rather than driving will be good for your blood pressure and for your general health. And it doesn't matter how unwell or unfit you are now: the trick is to do just as much as you can and then, when that amount of exercise begins to seem easy, to do a little bit more, and to keep building it up slowly and steadily. Even a little exercise is better than none at all.

Just how much exercise you will personally need to bring down your blood pressure and improve your general health will depend on many factors - your age, how fit you are and how much exercise you already take, whether you have any problems in addition to high blood pressure, and so on. As a rough rule of thumb, most people will need to aim for about 20-30 minutes of moderate exercise (the equivalent of a brisk walk) about three times a week. There are plenty of books and leaflets available which will give you suggestions for how much exercise you need for your particular circumstances and how to gradually work up to that level, and your doctor should also be able to offer you advice.

I've always hated the very idea of exercise, but (reluctantly) I see that I'm going to have to do something. What sort of exercise should I go in for?

The first rule for all successful exercise programmes is for people to do what they want, what interests them. A serious problem for many people (and it sounds as if you are one of them) is that many forms of sustained exercise are boring. You are far more likely to establish regular new habits and stick to them if you enjoy what you are doing.

People with high blood pressure need to choose a form of exercise which is dynamic (ie you keep moving during exercise) and aerobic (which literally means 'with air' - in aerobic exercise you have to breathe in enough air to supply your working muscles with oxygen). This gives you plenty to choose from: walking, cycling, swimming, running and dancing are all suitable, or you could join an exercise class.

- Walking is simple (we all know how to do it), cheap (all you need is some comfortable shoes) and easy to introduce into your daily routine. It's not essential to take long hikes through the countryside (unless you want to) - you will get as much benefit walking briskly around your local town or in your local parks.
- Cycling is excellent exercise for everyone except people with back problems, although even most of them can manage if they get a really wide, well-sprung seat, and high handlebars. Cycling in heavy traffic can be unpleasant, but some areas

How to help yourself

now have networks of cycle paths that keep you away from the cars, and it is also a good way to explore the countryside.
- Swimming is an ideal form of exercise for older people or people with arthritis, because your body is weightless (the water supports your weight) and your movements may become almost painless when you are immersed in water. If you don't know how to swim, all pools have beginners' classes for all ages, with friendly people you will be glad to meet.
- Running or jogging seems to appeal most to people who like their own company, judging by the number of solitary joggers we see on the roads. Wearing proper running shoes is important, as you may otherwise damage your feet, ankles or knees - a good sports shop will be able to advise you.
- Dancing appeals to people who enjoy exercising to music, and the sort of music you like may be a guide to the type of dancing you will enjoy, be it ballroom, jazz, rock 'n' roll, country dancing or whatever. Your local library should have information on the dance classes and groups available in your area.
- Exercise classes vary widely in the types of exercise they include, the level of fitness you need to take part and the skills of the teacher. Make sure that the teacher is properly qualified, and ask if you can watch a session without joining in - you will then be able to see if it will suit you and if you think you will enjoy it.

A final rule: whatever type of exercise you choose, start slowly, train up gradually, and generally use some common sense (if you don't have this, ask your best friend and listen to what she or he says). If you are concerned about how exercise may affect you, then you could have a word with your GP.

Are there any forms of exercise I should avoid?

If you have established high blood pressure you should avoid extremely vigorous or competitive sports such as squash, and also static exercises such as weightlifting and push-ups, all of which may briefly raise your blood pressure to dangerous extremes.

Stopping smoking

Which is most important for me to do – to stop smoking or to control my high blood pressure?

If you really must choose which of these to tackle first, smoking is almost always a bigger and more completely reversible risk than high blood pressure.

Smoking is not a cause of high blood pressure, but it greatly increases the risks that go with having high BP. For example, if you have high blood pressure already, your risk of a heart attack is increased three times by smoking up to about 50 years of age, and doubled after that age. Heart attacks in people under 45 happen almost entirely in smokers.

Smoking is a very powerful risk factor in its own right, not only for coronary heart disease and stroke, but also for cancer of the mouth, nose, throat, larynx, lung, bladder and pancreas, for asthma and other obstructive lung diseases (eg chronic bronchitis), and for obstructed leg arteries. Unlike all other risk factors, it also affects your family and friends, through passive smoking and the example you set to children.

Does stopping smoking reduce blood pressure?

No. However, the aim of treating high blood pressure is not to reduce the pressure for its own sake, but to reduce the risks of the likely and unpleasant consequences of having high blood pressure. Smoking increases your risks of suffering these consequences; stopping smoking reduces them. For example, for most people with high blood pressure who smoke, stopping smoking reduces the risk of coronary heart attacks more than reducing blood pressure itself, particularly in younger people. Stopping smoking also reduces your risk of many other serious problems, as listed in the answer to the previous question.

If I can't stop smoking, will that make my treatment for high blood pressure ineffective?

Generally, no. Benefit from treatment is greatest in people at highest risk. As people who continue smoking are at much higher risk than those who stop (or who never started) they actually benefit more from treatment, a statistical paradox which is confusing to everyone. However, you will obviously achieve the greatest health gains if you can both stop smoking and reduce blood pressure.

There is one exception to this generalisation. Beta-blocker drugs, which are often used to reduce blood pressure, seem to be less effective in people who continue to smoke. They still reduce blood pressure, but fail to reduce the risks of heart disease.

If I do decide that I want to give up smoking, what sort of help can I get?

The help you need is first of all more information about smoking and how to stop it, and secondly specific individual help for you personally, taking into account your own needs and difficulties.

Information about smoking and how to stop is readily available, usually in the form of leaflets or books (you will find a list of some of the titles available in Appendix 3). Your local library is an obvious source for these, or your GP's surgery may have leaflets available. If you can't find what you want locally, try writing to either Quit (the National Society for Non-Smokers) or the Health Education Authority – the addresses are in Appendix 2.

People start smoking for many reasons, and continue smoking for equally many reasons (the reasons for starting are often different from the reasons for continuing). It's worth discussing your own reasons with someone who is experienced in helping people to stop smoking so that together you can work out a personal stop-smoking plan.

The first place to ask for such help is at your GP's surgery. There is often someone there (not necessarily a doctor) with a special interest in helping people to stop smoking (if there isn't, then I think there should be). Ask the receptionist who that person is, and arrange an appointment with them. Some practices run group sessions rather than arranging individual consultations, and these can be just as useful.

Evidence about the harm smoking has already done to you can help you to stop. At your consultation, ask if you can have your peak flow rate measured. This is a very simple procedure - all you have to do is to blow into a small device called a peak flow meter. See how the result compares with the expected value for your age, sex, and height. Most smokers show an improved peak flow rate (although rarely normal) soon after they stop. Many GPs now have gadgets that measure the amount of carbon monoxide (CO) in your breath, which accurately reflects the proportion of red cells in your blood that have been poisoned by this component of tobacco smoke. This information can often provide you with powerful motivation to stop (even if in the past you have been on of those smokers impervious to advice), particularly when you can see your figures improve once you've given up.

For people with a true addiction to nicotine, temporary substitution of nicotine by another less dangerous route can be a big help in stopping. This can be done with traditional snuff or chewing tobacco (although chewed nicotine introduces new risks of cancer of the mouth) or, more elegantly, by using nicotine chewing gum or skin patches, which are now heavily promoted. Alhough all these techniques are often effective, you need to remember that your ultimate aim is to stop taking nicotine altogether. If you go on taking more or less the same amount of nicotine by these other routes, you will not reduce your risk of coronary heart disease, although you will reduce your risk of lung cancer and stop progression of any airways obstruction you already have.

There is good evidence that all methods of stopping (including nicotine substitutes) work better if reinforced by continuing support from another concerned and informed person. This may be your doctor or someone else at your GP's surgery, in which case you may be able to arrange a telephone 'helpline' to use if you think you are about to weaken. Quit, the National Society for Non-Smokers, also runs a telephone helpline (the phone number is in Appendix 2). An alternative is a friend, a relative or your partner. If they have also read the written material and you have agreed to listen to their advice, you probably have the best support available.

I've tried to stop smoking but I haven't succeeded. Would it be better if I switched to smoking cigars or a pipe? Are they safer substitutes for cigarettes?

Generally speaking, no. People who have smoked cigars or a pipe all their lives, and who have never smoked cigarettes, rarely inhale tobacco smoke and are therefore at much lower risk of all the consequences of smoking (other than cancer of the mouth and throat) but very few such people exist. Virtually all cigarette smokers inhale, whether consciously or unconsciously. If they change to pipe or cigar smoking, they continue to do so (often unconsciously and with furious denials, refuted by tests for carbon monoxide levels). The amounts of both nicotine and carbon monoxide (the main reasons why smoking increases the risks of heart disease) and of tobacco tar (the main reason why smoking increases the risks of lung cancer) in their bodies are even greater than they were when they were cigarette smokers. The only safe alternative to smoking cigarettes is not smoking at all.

Complementary therapies

Do doctors disapprove of complementary or alternative medicines?

Before I answer this question, I want to make a distinction between medicines or therapies which claim to be 'alternatives' to the treatment offered by the medical profession, and those which claim to be 'complementary', which their practitioners intend to be used alongside conventional treatments. Many doctors do not approve of 'alternative' therapies, and in any case no one should stop taking their normal drugs without discussing this with their doctor.

The position on 'complementary' therapies is more complicated, and there are various things here that we need to consider. The first is that when measured repeatedly before treatment starts, blood pressure appears to fall steadily over about three months, and then stabilises at a lower value, often about 10 mmHg less than its first value. This is simply because you become less afraid of the measurement. As some people with borderline high blood pressure are started on medication on inadequate evidence (ie not enough measurements have been taken), many of them would do at least as well on 'complementary' treatments, simply because no active medication was justified in the first place.

A second point is that most complementary therapists take an holistic approach to treatment, that is they aim to treat the whole person rather than just the illness or problem. A complementary practitioner may well recommend that, in addition to your therapy sessions, you alter your diet, give up smoking, take more exercise and so on – and these recommendations will probably be very similar to those given in this book. As mentioned in the section on **Treatment without drugs** in Chapter 4, such changes can reduce your blood pressure by about 10 mmHg. So is it the therapy that is reducing your blood pressure, or the changes you have made to your lifestyle?

We also have to take account of something called the 'placebo effect'. This is discussed in greater detail in Chapter 10, but basically it means that anyone with an illness or problem tends to feel better after they have consulted a professional carer and started some plan of treatment (with or without medication). This effect is real, not illusory. (However, it's worth remembering that even the placebo effect cannot be achieved by hard-nosed clinicians who treat people as though they were brainless machines requiring only adjustments or repairs.) I have not found any convincing evidence that any of the standard 'complementary' treatments have any more than this placebo effect, but it can be substantial. They are without exception based at best on prescientific theories of how the body works. Having said that, for borderline high blood pressure, when the need for any active medication is arguable either way, many people will not only feel better but actually be better off using harmless complementary therapies than potentially harmful pseudoscience.

Very few of the complementary therapies have been subjected to properly controlled trials (see Chapter 10 for more information about what is involved in such trials). This means that there is little hard evidence that the treatments really work. The great merit of scientific medicine is that it recognises how much remains unknown, and that asking appropriate questions is often more difficult than finding the answers. With all its limitations, it's the best we have.

Doctors get upset about complementary therapies if people are tempted to stop their medical treatment, or if they feel that their patients are being misinformed and persuaded to spend large sums of money which they can ill afford. If these features are not present, most practising doctors will take a neutral or encouraging view of these therapies and appreciate that, even if the scientific evidence for them is elusive or nonexistent, they may do some good. This is especially likely if the people concerned feel enthusiastic about them. They may give people a sense of doing something for themselves which can be valuable.

Why don't mainstream doctors and nurses use the holistic approach favoured by complementary therapists?

Most either do so, or try to do so, but often fail because of pressure of work. Good GPs and other medical professionals have always taken this approach, although they may not have bothered to give it a formal name – they have listened to people's problems, provided advice and education on diet and so on, encouraged people to take responsibility for their own health, and only prescribed drugs when they were really needed. Some will be members of the British Holistic Medical Association, whose address is in Appendix 2.

I think that I would like to try using one of the complementary therapies, but I don't know how to go about finding someone to consult. Where do I start?

Whichever therapy you choose to try, the most important thing is to find someone who is adequately qualified. At the moment, there is little to prevent someone with minimal training – or even no training at all – setting themselves up in business as a practitioner and treating clients. In untrained hands, complementary therapies can do harm.

However, reputable practitioners of the various therapies are trying harder to improve their own practices and to give the public more information about their qualifications and training. The British Complementary Medicine Association, the Council for Complementary and Alternative Medicine, the Institute for Complementary Medicine and the Health Education Authority (see Appendix 2 for addresses) are useful sources of further information, or you could ask at your own GP's surgery or health centre for the names of reputable local practitioners. Some practices now offer some complementary therapies themselves.

Cost may be another factor that you want to take into account. These therapies are not often available on the NHS, and they can prove expensive.

I have a very stressful job and wonder if there are ways I could learn to relax. Would this help my high blood pressure? Are there any complementary therapies that would help me relax?

Stress management was discussed in the section on *Treatment without drugs* in Chapter 4. It may work for some people, but as stress (however defined) is not the only or the main cause of high blood pressure in most people, management of it is not likely to provide a successful treatment. Having said that, there are obviously many other good reasons for reducing the amount of stress in your life, regardless of any possible effects this may have on your blood pressure. Being less stressed will certainly help you cope with your BP-lowering treatment. For example, an excuse often given by people who have not given up smoking is that a cigarette helps them when they feel stressed.

If you want to learn to relax, you may find that there are local evening classes in relaxation techniques. Sometimes these are combined with exercise classes, when they are called 'stretch and relax classes' or something similar. Some firms offer their employees stress management courses (although you may find that the offer is only open to members of management – for some reason, firms often feel that their managers and executives suffer stress more than the rest of their staff) or similar courses are available (usually at considerable cost) from various independent training companies. There are also various books and cassettes on relaxation available – your GP or local library may have some that you can borrow, or you can buy them from organisations such as the British Holistic Medical Association (address in Appendix 2).

The complementary therapies which can aid relaxation are meditation, yoga, the various forms of massage, and aromatherapy.

Meditation and yoga (in which stretching and breathing exercises are performed slowly and deliberately – itself a form of meditation) are more a way of life than occasional activities and require considerable commitment and self-discipline. If you want to try them, you may find meditation classes advertised locally, and you can find out about local yoga classes from the British Wheel of Yoga or the Yoga for Health Foundation (addresses in Appendix 2).

There are many different forms of massage, varying from the very gentle to the positively painful. The level of training varies enormously, and people can (and do) set themselves up as massage practitioners after only a few days training. Follow the suggestions given earlier in this section for finding a reputable practitioner, or look for someone with an ITEC (International Therapy Examinations Council) qualification.

Aromatherapy is treatment with essential oils (scented oils extracted from the roots, flowers or leaves of plants by distillation). It often involves massage, but the oils can also be inhaled or added to baths. The Aromatherapy Organisations Council, the International Federation of Aromatherapists, or the International Society of Professional Aromatherapists (all addresses in Appendix 2) can give you the names of properly qualified practitioners in your area. Aromatherapists would recommend that people with high blood pressure avoid buying the essential oils available over the counter in health food shops without taking proper advice first. Not only do they vary in quality, but some of the most commonly available oils (eg clary sage) can act to raise blood pressure.

What about herbal medicine? Are there any treatments

which would be suitable alternatives to my BP-lowering drugs?

The temptation with herbal medicines is to think that because they are natural substances they must therefore be safe. It is easy to forget that plants can do harm. Some herbal remedies may raise blood pressure or may interfere with the effect of conventional drugs. Liquorice and many other herbal remedies used as diuretics promote sodium and water retention and thus raise blood pressure. Long-term use of ginseng often causes high blood pressure. Lily of the valley resembles digitalis (foxglove) – too high a dose can cause heart failure. Horse chestnut taken together with anticoagulant drugs may cause bleeding. As well as often unidentifiable plant alkaloids, traditional oriental herbal remedies often contain heavy metal salts, which may be very dangerous if taken over long periods.

Obviously no reputable herbalist is going to offer you treatments which they know will do you harm, but the risks can be considerable if you consult someone who is inadequately trained or if you try to treat yourself after gleaning some basic information from a book. You should also remember that the pharmaceutical industry is extremely efficient at exploiting any active substances found in plants and in synthesising and testing them for use as drugs. As with the other complementary therapies, there is little published scientific evidence that herbal treatments are effective.

If you have borderline high blood pressure, where the need for any active medication is arguable either way, some of the simpler herbal infusions (drinks made in a similar way to ordinary tea, but probably not tasting as pleasant) suggested by herbalists will probably not do you any harm (although if your doctor has prescribed BP-lowering drugs for you, you should continue to take them). Herbs which can be used in this way include hawthorn, guelder rose, linden and yarrow.

Are there any other complementary therapies reputed to help in high blood pressure?

Homeopathy and acupuncture are both reputed to help in high blood pressure.

Homeopathy is completely safe, because the remedies used are so dilute. It is based on the principle that 'like can be cured by like' (the word homeopathy comes from two Greek words that mean 'similar' and 'suffering'). The remedies contain very dilute amounts of a substance which in larger quantities would produce similar symptoms to the illness being treated. The problem here is that we have no scientific explanation for what (if anything other than the placebo effect) is going on. However, it is available through the NHS, although the provision is limited, and you can obtain information on homeopathic doctors from the British Homeopathic Association (address in Appendix 2). There are no specific homeopathic remedies recommended for high blood pressure – the treatments a practitioner would suggest would simply be those thought to have a general strengthening effect on your constitution. Homeopathic doctors are all trained in orthodox medicine, and so usually reserve their complementary treatments for minor, self-limiting, or emotional illnesses.

Acupuncture, which involves inserting needles into the skin at particular sites on the body, has been a standard form of medical treatment in China for 5000 years. In the last 20 years it has become more widely used in this country, usually for conditions such as a painful back where orthodox medicine often fails to help. We should know fairly soon whether or not it is effective as a treatment for high blood pressure, as a properly controlled trial is currently being carried out and the results are due to be published shortly. In the meantime, a course of acupuncture treatments will certainly do you no harm, and you may find it a helpful aid to relaxation.

6
High blood pressure plus...

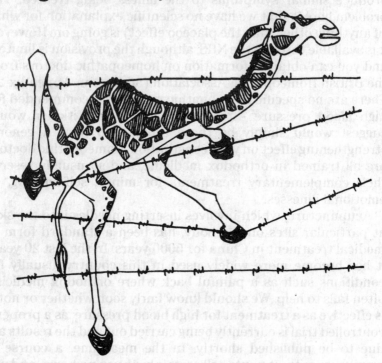

Other problems in general

I've been on pills for high blood pressure for 20 years. For the past five years, most days I have a troublesome cough, a lot of back pain, and sometimes I feel so miserable I wish I could pack it in altogether. I go to our medical centre every three months for a repeat prescription, and either the practice nurse or one of the five doctors checks my blood pressure. Should I talk to them about these other problems? I mean, do

they remember I have these other problems, and the other pills I'm taking for them?

No matter where you have your check-ups - at a special high blood pressure clinic, at your medical centre or a hospital outpatient clinic - you should mention these other problems, and make sure whoever sees you does know about your other medication. The best way to do this is to bring along all your medication, in the original containers, so they can see what they are.

No doctor or nurse, however friendly and interested, can possibly remember the whole story about everyone, including the full range of their problems and all the medication they take. All health professionals, both in general practice and in hospitals, have to depend on what is in people's medical records - they simply can't remember everything about everyone. Even if all the information is fully recorded in these, it may be difficult to find. Because the whole NHS is understaffed and overworked, most doctors and nurses are permanently in a hurry, and therefore keen to simplify the care of the people they see as much as they can, so they can make a bit more time for the next person. You are the person who has the most serious and personal interest in remembering the real complexity of your situation. Help your doctors and nurses by making sure they don't forget.

Don't most people attending a high blood pressure clinic have pretty straightforward problems?

In my experience, straightforward problems seem to be exceptional. In my own practice in a working class area near Swansea, over a period of 26 years we treated 344 people for high blood pressure. We searched their records for 12 other problems, all of which modify the medical management of high blood pressure: high blood cholesterol, evidence of damage to heart or arteries, chronic joint pain, chronic bronchitis or asthma, severe overweight, recurrent suicidal depression or other major psychiatric problems, alcohol problems, kidney impairment, gastric or duodenal ulcers, diabetes, gout and impotence (all of these problems are discussed somewhere in this book, many in later sections of this chapter). Only 3% of the men and 7% of the women in our study had none of these other recurrent or continuing problems. Studies in more affluent areas in Holland show a much higher proportion of people needing treatment only for high blood pressure, and these may be more typical of middle class areas of Britain.

But however you look at it, management of high blood pressure is seldom the only issue, and there are usually other problems which must modify a doctor's decision about the best treatment. This is one of the main reasons why most people should be treated for high blood pressure by GPs rather than in hospitals, that is seeing generalists rather than specialists.

High blood cholesterol

What is cholesterol and why is it important?

The first thing to say is that despite all the bad press it receives, cholesterol is not some sort of poison. It is an essential component of all body cells and of many important circulating chemicals in the blood.

The concentration of cholesterol in your blood matters because the higher it is, the more of it is deposited as waxy plaques on the walls of your arteries - the coronary arteries supplying blood to the heart, the brain arteries, and the aorta and leg arteries. The plaque causes the arteries to narrow, which means dangerous blood clots are more likely to form, and all this can lead to partial or complete destruction of the organs supplied by these arteries.

Many scientific studies in many countries over many years have confirmed a close connection between the average levels of blood cholesterol in large groups of people and their chances of developing coronary heart disease under the age of 65, and a similar but somewhat less close connection for individuals. There is no doubt whatever that in all societies where average blood cholesterol is low then coronary heart disease is rare, or that in all societies where average blood cholesterol is high then coronary heart disease is common. This remains true even if other risk factors for coronary heart disease are common in the low-cholesterol societies, or low in the high-cholesterol societies. For example, although high blood pressure and heavy smoking are extremely common in China (resulting in a high number of strokes) coronary heart disease remains rare; whereas in Western countries (such as Sweden) where both smoking and uncontrolled high blood pressure have become much less common, average blood cholesterol has not fallen, and coronary heart disease remains common.

When it comes to individuals, there is consistent evidence that your personal level of blood cholesterol is linked to and mirrors your personal risk for coronary heart disease (although very inaccurately if considered in isolation from other major risk factors such as smoking, blood pressure, and your family history). There is also some evidence that if people at very high risk of coronary heart disease (ie with a greater than 3% risk of a fatal heart attack during the next 12 months) reduce their blood cholesterol by reducing their fat intake and/or taking cholesterol-lowering medication, about 17 fatal heart attacks can be prevented per 1000 people treated over one year. People at medium risk have not been shown to benefit from such treatment, and those at low risk can be expected to have a bit more than one additional death per 1000 treated over one year. These extra deaths seem to occur only in people on medication, not those treated by diet alone.

There are still a few doctors who refuse to believe there is any connection between blood cholesterol and coronary heart disease, just as there are still one or two who deny any causal link between smoking and lung cancer.

Where does the cholesterol in my blood come from?

Cholesterol itself can be found in food (it is present in large quantities in some foods such as egg yolks, liver, kidneys, other meat offal and pâtés, and fish roes) but most of it is formed in your body from the many different sorts of fats and oils found in what you eat. It is then distributed where it is needed in the body. If there is a surplus, most of this is stored in the liver, but some remains circulating in the blood.

Is all cholesterol the same, or are there good and bad kinds?

Indeed there are. When doctors talk loosely about 'blood cholesterol' they normally mean total cholesterol, but this is actually made up of three different cholesterol-containing substances.

If you leave about 10 ml of blood standing in a glass tube until it has clotted, the cholesterol it contains becomes easily visible as a cloudy yellowish substance, occupying the top quarter or so of the tube. It looks like what it is, a sort of fat. If you put this in a high speed centrifuge, the yellow stuff separates into three fractions. These are called High Density Lipoprotein (HDL), Low Density Lipoprotein (LDL), and Very Low Density Lipoprotein (VLDL) cholesterol.

LDL and VLDL cholesterol are 'bad' cholesterol, the source of waxy plaques on the walls of the aorta, coronary arteries, brain arteries and leg arteries that ultimately weaken or block these vessels, and cause organ damage by clotting or bleeding. HDL cholesterol, on the other hand, is 'good'. Many studies have shown that concentrations of HDL cholesterol above about 1.5 mmol make coronary heart disease less likely, and low levels (below 1 mmol) make it more likely. This is probably because HDL is the form in which cholesterol is transported in the blood before storage in the liver or excretion in bile. LDL and VLDL are thus measures of a tendency to deposit harmful cholesterol in artery walls, whereas HDL is a measure of beneficial transport of cholesterol to the liver or to be excreted in bile.

How is blood cholesterol measured, and what are the normal levels?

From a sample of your blood – either from a finger-prick or ear-lobe prick sample using a desk-top machine, or from a sample taken from a vein sent to a hospital laboratory.

Blood cholesterol concentration is measured in millimoles per litre (abbreviated to mmol). The 'normal' value varies between countries (mainly because of differences in fat intake) from an average below 4 mmol in China to nearly 6 mmol in the UK For individuals, blood cholesterol levels can vary from about 3.5 mmol to about 15 mmol, and they can also vary from hour to hour and day to day. Levels under 5.2 mmol are usually regarded as desirable, and over about 6 mmol are usually regarded as being high.

As LDL and VLDL together usually account for about 80% of total blood cholesterol, total blood cholesterol can generally be accepted as a valid though approximate measure of 'bad' cholesterol, while ignoring the contribution from 'good' cholesterol. This is normal practice, which I have followed throughout this book.

Sophisticated measurements of blood fats (lipids) often also include triglyceride, the form in which fat is first absorbed from the gut. Measurement of triglyceride is rarely of practical value except in diabetes and in a special case called inherited familial hypercholesterolaemia (discussed in a later answer in this section). High values are commonly associated with being fat, or with high alcohol consumption, or both. Once these are taken into account, high triglyceride is a poor independent predictor of the risk of coronary heart disease.

Measurements of cholesterol fractions and triglyceride are obviously more complex and costly for the laboratory, but they are also more bother for the person being tested. While total cholesterol and HDL cholesterol can be measured accurately on any blood sample, LDL and VLDL cholesterol and triglyceride can only be measured accurately after a minimum fasting period of 12 hours, during which no food or drinks other than water can be taken.

Should blood cholesterol be measured routinely in everyone?

In my opinion, no – and there is probably majority professional agreement in the UK that universal adult screening for blood cholesterol level would not only be uneconomic but also counter-productive. This conflicts with the professional consensus in the USA, where there have been professionally supported campaigns encouraging everyone to 'know your own number' for blood cholesterol.

Screening for blood cholesterol level in isolation from other risks for coronary heart disease (or screening for multiple risks where the results are not brought together and intelligently interpreted for each individual case) can result in many people being told that they are at much higher risk than they actually are. In consequence they may be frightened into accepting overtreatment on extremely doubtful evidence.

Blood cholesterol levels should be measured routinely only in people with other risk factors for coronary heart disease: people with blood pressure high enough to consider treatment; people with diabetes or glucose intolerance; people who continue to smoke; and people with a family history of coronary heart disease affecting a parent, brother or sister before they reached 60 years of age. In these people, screening is not only justified, but should be done thoroughly, using two or three measurements to give a really accurate measure of blood cholesterol level before considering any action.

I'm having treatment for high blood pressure. Should I have my blood cholesterol measured?

Yes, because as explained in the answer to the previous question you are already at increased risk from coronary heart disease because of your high blood pressure.

How reliable are these measurements of blood cholesterol? Do doctors measure it more accurately than the machines in chemists' shops? Or is it worth me buying a home testing kit?

The measurements are not very reliable. According to accepted laboratory standards, measurement errors over 3% either side of the true value result in significant misclassification of risk. Even in NHS hospital laboratories (which are generally better than private laboratories, and much better than desk-top machines), independent audits in Scotland and Northern Ireland have shown that measurements around a cut-off point of 7.8 mmol were over-estimated by over 4%, resulting in a 50% increase in people apparently needing cholesterol-lowering medication. NHS hospital standards are improving, but the common assumption that laboratory figures cannot lie is wrong.

A common source of substantial error in desk-top machines (whether at your doctor's surgery or in the chemist's shop) is that blood samples taken from a cold finger or ear may grossly underestimate the true value, so beware of surprising results obtained in winter. A more serious source of error is failure to calibrate or maintain desk-top machines regularly. NHS hospital laboratories are all checked regularly and randomly by independent laboratories for faults in equipment or laboratory technique. The same cannot be said for many of the commercial laboratories or the desk-top machines now in use. Three separate studies of desk-top machines as routinely used by general practitioners showed errors of 5.5%, 7.5%, and 8%. Errors of this size cannot consistently tell the difference between a blood cholesterol of 5.3 mmol ('normal') and 7.2 mmol ('high').

Another inescapable source of error is the true variability of blood cholesterol in individual people from hour to hour and day to day. This often amounts to 5% or more.

Just as we should be critical of decisions taken to embark on a lifetime of treatment for high blood pressure based on one or two careless sphygmomanometer readings, we should be equally critical of careless or inadequate measurements of blood cholesterol. As with high blood pressure, to assess your cholesterol level properly you need at least three measurements taken on separate days, with long-term treatment decisions based on the resulting average. Desk-top machines may be satisfactory for follow-up if they are used by trained staff, are regularly maintained, and are regularly checked by an independent laboratory, but at present these conditions are rarely fulfilled. Exactly the same reservations apply to desk-top machines in chemists' shops. As these machines cost a lot, and can only be paid for by using them, those who have bought them naturally have to believe in them, but you should be less credulous.

Home test-kits for measuring blood cholesterol have been marketed for several years. Don't waste your money.

Is high blood cholesterol inherited?

Yes, very much so. Regardless of inheritance, people on an extremely low-fat diet (for example the poorest people in China) cannot have high blood cholesterol levels. However, once people are rich enough to eat as much as they want of the cheaper foods available, then what mainly determines individual blood cholesterol levels is not what you eat but your personal chemistry, and this is strongly inherited. Some people can eat a lot of fats and oils without getting either a high blood cholesterol or cholesterol plaques in their arteries; others are not so lucky, and the main difference lies in their genes.

A very few people (fewer than one in every 500) have inherited genes for very high blood cholesterol – a condition called inherited familial hypercholesterolaemia. These people have total blood cholesterol levels around 9–15 mmol, with very high LDL and VLDL ('bad') cholesterol levels, very low HDL ('good') cholesterol levels, and usually very high triglyceride levels. They all deserve specialist investigation and initial counselling and treatment at a special lipid clinic. As well as skilled dietary advice, almost all of them need medication with cholesterol-lowering drugs. Anyone with a close relative who has had a heart attack under the age of 50 should tell their doctor so that they can be investigated for this condition.

The majority of people with 'high blood cholesterol' are not in this category. They simply eat what most of us eat, and suffer the consequences of any diet in which 40% or more of all energy is consumed as fat – an increased risk of coronary heart disease.

Can I do anything to increase my levels of 'good' HDL blood cholesterol?

Yes. HDL is substantially increased by exercise, by stopping smoking, and by drinking alcohol in moderation. The latter is probably the main reason for low death rates from premature coronary heart disease in France, but correspondingly high death rates for cirrhosis of the liver more than make up for this. That drinking alcohol is good for your HDL cholesterol levels is NOT a licence for heavy drinking – heavy drinking raises blood pressure, apart from the other problems it can cause. Keep within the recommended limits, which are not more than 4 units of alcohol A DAY for a man or 3 units A DAY for a woman (a unit of alcohol is one glass of wine OR one single measure of spirits OR half a pint of average strength beer or lager).

Can I really reduce my high blood cholesterol by changing what I eat?

There is no doubt at all that the big differences in average blood cholesterol levels (and consequent differences in premature coronary death rates) between different countries depend on differences in what people eat, and that when nations as a whole eat less fat or take more exercise (for example, the USA and Finland), average blood cholesterol levels fall, and so do coronary death rates.

Unfortunately, efforts put into the same changes in personal diets have less effect, essentially for two reasons.

First, it is often easier to change group habits than personal habits. Anyone seen wearing platform shoes in the 1950s would have been considered eccentric, if not completely mad, but in the 1970s, in some age-groups, nobody who was fashion-conscious and concerned to stay in with their own crowd could afford not to wear them. So it is with what we eat. We do not in fact eat just what we like; we tend to eat what everyone else seems to like, the foods that are in fashion. Healthy living has now become so fashionable among affluent North Americans that some aspects of it (over-medication for high blood pressure or high blood cholesterol, for example) have become a threat to health. This may be beginning to happen in the UK, but only just. On the whole, people here who are determined to eat less dangerously are still pretty much on their own. You can start to overcome this by persuading your whole family to change how they eat.

Secondly, there are huge personal differences in the response of blood cholesterol to changes in fat intake. These differences are inherited, and depend on differences in the way people's bodies handle fat chemically. Some people get a large fall in blood cholesterol after fairly small, easy reductions in fat intake and/or increases in exercise, others get very small changes despite heroic efforts. The only way to know how easy or difficult this is for you is to try, with several accurate measurements of your blood cholesterol as a baseline before you start, and several accurate measurements from time to time afterwards.

When scientists have carried out randomised controlled trials of relatively simple cholesterol-lowering diets, the results have been disappointing, with an average reduction of only about 5% in blood cholesterol levels. However, there are huge personal differences in response, so that some people get big reductions in blood cholesterol from relatively small shifts in their eating habits, so it's always worth trying.

If other countries have lower-cholesterol diets than we do, why don't we all just switch to one of those?

Average blood cholesterol levels are much lower in some countries than others, and these differences are caused almost entirely by what peole eat and how much exercise they take, not by genetic differences in cholesterol metabolism. Adopting these cholesterol-lowering diets would therefore certainly be possible, if cultural barriers could be overcome. As fast-food companies move into Asia and the Mediterranean, cholesterol-raising diets are rapidly displacing the traditional low-cholesterol diets, showing that cultural barriers can certainly be crossed, probably in both directions.

Unfortunately some of the traditional cholesterol-lowering diets are unhealthy in other ways. For example, although the low fat content of traditional Chinese and Japanese cuisine keeps blood cholesterol levels low, so that they have low death rates from premature coronary heart disease, their very high sodium content raises average blood pressure and causes high rates for stroke. An average portion of Chinese take-away food contains about twice as much sodium as the daily intake recommended for the general population, and four times as much as the allowance on a low-sodium diet.

A traditional Mediterranean diet, with a lot of olive oil, garlic and pasta, no butter, and a little wine with meals, seems to be an effective way to keep average blood cholesterol and premature coronary mortality low. Exactly how this traditional diet compares with the versions we see in cookery books or eat in Spanish, Greek and Italian restaurants in this country, nobody seems exactly to know, but it all sounds like a good idea, and certainly better for us than what's on offer from the local hamburger chain. It's interesting that this type of diet is currently becoming more fashionable in this country.

I can't see me persuading the rest of my family to eat what they call 'foreign food' at every meal. How do I reduce the amount of cholesterol in my diet without them noticing too much?

You'll find suggestions in Chapter 5, particularly in the section on *Fats and oils*. Reducing your fat intake will automatically reduce your cholesterol intake.

Are cholesterol-lowering drugs an easier alternative than cholesterol-lowering diets?

At first sight yes, but after serious thought, usually no.

It's certainly easier to remember to take pills than to change what and how much you eat, and how much exercise you take. In fact that's really the trouble: although all the pharmaceutical companies which promote cholesterol-lowering drugs advise people to use them only if diet alone has failed, we all know this rule is rarely observed.

Although taking pills may be easier than living differently, you also have to consider possible unwanted side-effects from drugs which will probably have to be taken for many years, and may have to be taken for the rest of your life. As there are still no results from long-term controlled trials of this medication in large numbers of people, such unwanted side-effects have been measured only for relatively short periods of five years or so, not for the 30 or 40 years for which many people would be likely to take them. The jury is therefore still out on this, and there is a real possibility that below a threshold of about 7 mmol total cholesterol for men, some or all of the cholesterol-lowering drugs may increase deaths from some other causes more than they reduce deaths from coronary heart disease. Most doctors in the UK think that until we have real evidence that these drugs can reduce deaths from all causes put together, they should be prescribed only for men with cholesterol levels above 7 mmol. We still have no good evidence for women, who are certainly at lower risk.

Who should have cholesterol-lowering medication?

The short answer is only someone who either has familial hypercholesterolaemia or who otherwise is at very high risk of coronary heart disease, and whose total blood cholesterol has not been reduced to a reasonable level by a really serious attempt to follow a cholesterol-lowering diet. In practice, 'very high risk' means men who already have good evidence of established coronary heart disease, or with cholesterol levels over 7 mmol.

As I mentioned in the answer to the previous question, we still do not have enough evidence to know that taking cholesterol-lowering medication is worth the still unmeasured risks for most men and nearly all women. Although expert bodies have suggested guidelines, they are mostly based on informed guesswork and experience with the minority of people referred to hospital specialists rather than the general population. My recommendations follow those that the Royal College of Physicians Research Unit made in 1993, and they estimate that this would mean about 1% of the population of this country taking cholesterol-lowering medication. On the other hand we have the Royal College of General Practitioners' guidelines which were produced in 1992: if we followed these, everyone in the country aged between 20 and 75 would have to have their blood cholesterol levels measured at least once, about two-thirds of these people would then need to be encouraged to go on a cholesterol-lowering diet, and about 3.5% of the population would be taking cholesterol-lowering medication. Attitudes to treatment in the USA are much more aggressive, with about 12% of all adults already on cholesterol-lowering medication, and one committee of experts recommending that this should be increased to 36%. Most practising family doctors in the UK remain deeply suspicious of policies of this sort.

As with medication for high blood pressure, a decision for or against medication for high blood cholesterol should be based on careful assessment of the probable benefits and possible penalties either way, which vary from one person to another. It should be a joint decision by the person concerned and their own doctor after proper discussion of all the pros and cons.

Reduction of blood cholesterol by diet alone may be a nuisance, but has no important side-effects. A large majority of people would undoubtedly benefit from a better balance between energy intake and energy output (ie fewer calories in and more exercise), and by substantial reduction in their intake of fats and oils. This has been discussed in more detail in Chapter 5.

What cholesterol-lowering drugs are available? How do they work? What are their side-effects?

There are five main groups of cholesterol-lowering drugs. The first four groups consist of the most widely-used and older cholesterol-lowering drugs on which most of our present information is based. All commonly cause minor side-effects which are uncomfortable, and a few are occasionally dangerous. The fifth group, the Co-A inhibitors, are a newer class of very effective and much better tolerated cholesterol- lowering drugs, first introduced in 1989.

- **Group 1: Bile-acid binding resins**
  Drug names: cholestyramine (Questran); colestipol (Colestid)

  These reduce the level of blood LDL and VLDL ('bad') cholesterol by blocking absorption of fat from the gut, and may raise HDL ('good') cholesterol. They are difficult to take, with a vile taste. They are available only as powders with the consistency of sand, usually taken mixed in fruit juice. They often cause a wide variety of gut symptoms – nausea, vomiting, constipation or diarrhoea, acid risings and heartburn, and eruptions of gas both ends. However, these symptoms may last for only a short time in some people, and in many they never occur. These drugs interfere with the digestion of fat-soluble vitamins, and this can have serious consequences in childhood, in pregnancy and during breast feeding, and for people who have to take other drugs to stop their blood clotting too easily. Because they may interfere with absorption of other drugs, BP-lowering medication must be taken at least an hour before or after these drugs.

- **Group 2: Fibrates**
  Drug names: clofibrate (Atromid-S); bezafibrate (Bezalip); ciprofibrate (Modalim); fenofibrate (Lipantil); gemfibrozil (Lopid)
  Their main effect is to reduce triglyceride, a different form of blood fat which is usually less important for preventing heart disease, but they do also reduce LDL and VLDL and raise HDL blood cholesterol, although less than drugs in Group 1.
  Clofibrate, the first of these drugs to be widely used and the subject of several large randomised controlled trials, commonly causes gallstones, and should be used only in people whose gallbladders have already been removed. Gemfibrozil also causes gallstones, although possibly less than clofibrate, and all the drugs in this group are suspect in this respect. All of them can also cause an inflammatory disorder of muscle cells, particularly in people with kidney problems.

- **Group 3: Anti-oxidants**
  Drug name: probucol (Lurselle)
  Probucol reduces all types of blood cholesterol, including HDL ('good') cholesterol. Its promoters hope that its anti-oxidant action may prevent cholesterol plaque forming on artery walls. It often causes diarrhoea but is otherwise well tolerated.

- **Group 4: Nicotinic acid (niacin) and related substances**
  Drug name: acipimox (Olbetam)
  Nicotonic acid (also called niacin) is a water-soluble vitamin of the B vitamin group, and is not marketed under any brand name. Acipimox (Olbetam) resembles nicotinic acid but its effectiveness is less certain.
  Drugs in this group reduce LDL and VLDL ('bad') blood cholesterol by preventing them being made in the body, and also raise HDL ('good') blood cholesterol.
  Initially they cause an unpleasant sensation of blushing and prickly heat around the face and neck (less so with acipimox than with nicotinic acid, but it also has less of a

cholesterol-lowering effect), but in most people this side-effect wears off after 3–4 days and then does not return. (It can also be prevented by taking an aspirin tablet half an hour before the nicotinic acid.) Nicotinic acid can cause liver damage in overdosage, which may occur in people who switch from an ordinary to a long-acting tablet without realising that this will increase absorption of the drug.

Paradoxically, although nicotinic acid is the first cholesterol-lowering drug shown to reduce deaths from all causes in a major drugs trial, it is probably prescribed less than any other cholesterol-lowering agent. Apart from the initial incovenience of flushing, the only obvious reason for this (to my mind) is that it is an old drug which long ago ran out of patent protection and is therefore less profitable – so no one bothers to advertise and promote it.

- **Group 5: Co-A (Coenzyme-A reductase) inhibitors**
  Drug names: fluvastatin (Lescol); pravastatin (Lipostat); simvastatin (Zocor).

  They are very effective in reducing LDL and VLDL ('bad') blood cholesterol, especially if combined with nicotinic acid or fibrates (the drugs in Group 2).

  Inflammation of muscle cells (myositis) has occured in about 1 per 200 people treated, presenting as muscle pain, weakness, or unexplained fever. Other possible side-effects are headache and liver damage (regular checks on liver function are recommended). They are now the fastest-growing cholesterol-lowering drugs on the market.

Heart and circulation problems

I've now got angina, but my GP says that I don't need to take any more tablets, just go on with the beta-blockers that I take for my high blood pressure. Please can you explain why?

Many people with high blood pressure get angina (pain over the front of the chest on exertion), and many people with angina are eventually found to have high blood pressure. Bringing down BP, by whatever means, nearly always reduces the frequency of anginal pain, probably because with a lower BP, your heart has less work to do. Beta-blockers and calcium-channel blockers (discussed in more detail in Appendix 1) are both usually very effective treatments for angina, as well as for high blood pressure. Beta-blockers are also very effective in preventing attacks of angina, so you can see that they are particularly useful as a treatment that kills two birds with one stone. If for any reason you have to stop taking them suddenly, your angina may become much worse for a while.

All the drugs commonly used to treat or prevent angina also reduce blood pressure, although nitroglycerin (as tablets or sprays to be used under the tongue) only has this effect for a short time.

There is a section on *Angina* in Chapter 9.

Because of disease in my arteries, I get severe leg pains when I walk any distance. I'm on beta-blockers for my high blood pressure. Is it true that these tablets can make the pain worse?

In many ways this leg pain (claudication) resembles angina: it is pain from a muscle when the demand for blood exceeds the supply. As with angina, when your blood pressure falls, this demand is reduced, the blood supply increases, and the amount of exercise you can take before the pain makes you stop increases.

One of the side-effects of beta-blockers is less good circulation in the feet and hands (many people who take them find that they get cold hands and feet in the winter and always need gloves or thick socks). Because of this it was once thought that they were bound to make claudication worse, but we now know that this is not so. All studies show that the opposite occurs (except in a few unusual instances), probably because beta-blockers only affect the superficial, and not the deeper, blood flow. Bringing your BP down, whatever the drug used, helps improve the circulation in your legs and reduce the pain.

My father has been on treatment for high blood pressure for a long time, but his doctor changed his tablets last year after he had a minor heart attack. Why?

Evidence that damage has already occurred to the heart or arteries (usually the aorta, neck arteries or leg arteries) makes control of high blood pressure more urgent, and occasionally narrows the choice of BP-lowering drugs. Your father's heart attack was evidently of this sort, so his doctor wisely decided to review his treatment, perhaps for one of the following reasons.

For people who have already had a heart attack (coronary thrombosis), some beta-blockers (metoprolol, propranolol and timolol) have been shown to reduce the risk of a fatal disturbance of heart rhythm during the next two or three years.

In people who already have extensive heart damage, usually survivors of repeated or severe coronary heart attacks, beta-blockers reduce heart output and may precipitate heart failure (discussed in the answer to the next two questions). This does not mean they should never be used, but they must be used cautiously, particularly in elderly people, with a sharp look-out for evidence of increasing heart failure (mainly increasing shortness of breath, often with a dry cough).

At one time it was thought that calcium channel blockers were likely to worsen claudication (leg pain from hardening of the leg arteries). We now know this is not so, but if there is also evidence of heart damage, calcium channel blockers taken in combination with beta-blockers may precipitate heart failure.

You will find more information about beta-blockers and calcium channel blockers in Appendix 1, and there is a section on *Heart attacks* in Chapter 9.

What is heart failure? Does having it change your treatment for high blood pressure?

Heart failure means that the heart has difficulty in keeping up with its work of pumping blood around the body. It does NOT mean that the heart will fail to beat or is about to stop. The main symptoms are tiredness, shortness of breath on slight exertion, and often a dry cough with or without wheezing. One of the commonest causes of heart failure is uncontrolled high blood pressure over many years. Whether having it changes your treatment will obviously depend on what treatment you are on.

People who already have heart failure have a low output of blood from the heart. This will be lower still if they take beta-blockers (see Appendix 1 for more information about these drugs). However, heart failure brought on by beta-blockers rarely occurs in people with high BP treated by GPs, probably because as heart failure advances so blood pressure falls, meaning that few people in this state will start beta-blockers as a treatment for their high BP. Many start them as a treatment for angina, but even for these people, very few seem to get problems from worsening heart failure. For the large majority of people treated for high BP before it has caused heart failure, beta-blockers seem to be as effective as other BP-lowering drugs in preventing this complication.

Patients with severe heart failure treated with diuretics (again there is more information about these drugs in Appendix 1) are at risk of low blood potassium. The main symptom of this is extreme tiredness and muscular weakness. Most of these people will be seen regularly in hospital outpatient departments, which usually do occasional checks of blood potassium. This can be done by a GP, providing the blood sample can either be transported to a laboratory in under three hours or the red cells separated from the plasma in a centrifuge.

I have an irregular heartbeat which my doctor says is caused by fibrillation. Could you please explain what this means, and if it affects my treatment for my high blood pressure?

Fibrillation means independent, irregular and unco-ordinated movement of the fibres of the heart muscle, so that instead of acting effectively together to squeeze blood through the heart, they tremble or flutter ineffectively, producing shallow, irregular, rapid heartbeats.

There are two types of fibrillation, one more serious than the other. When fibrillation happens in the ventricles (the main chambers of the heart), the result is a cardiac arrest from which you will die within seven minutes, unless someone can stop this process and restart normal rhythm by giving your heart an electric shock. As you have not had a heart attack, what you have is the other kind, fibrillation of the two upper and less important chambers of the heart (called the auricles or atria) – you have atrial fibrillation.

Atrial fibrillation is very common, usually but not always in people with heart failure. Normal heart rhythm can be restored, either by using drugs or by giving a controlled electric shock, sometimes followed by insertion of a pacemaker to maintain the heart's normal rhythm. This is rarely necessary. Most people with atrial fibrillation manage well with treatment for heart failure by ACE-inhibitors or diuretics (there is more information about these drugs in Appendix 1) and sometimes digoxin to slow their heart rate and raise their heart output (the amount of blood the heart pumps out to the rest of the body).

Your high blood pressure is likely to have been one of the main causes of your heart failure. Paradoxically, your blood pressure will tend to fall as your heart fails, and to rise when your heart failure is controlled and your heart output rises. The main consequence for your treatment is that you will need very carefully balanced medication to treat your heart failure, to make sure your BP doesn't go too high again, and usually also to prevent clots forming in the flabby parts of your heart by using anticoagulants (drugs which stop your blood clotting too quickly) such as warfarin, or warfarin + aspirin, which is twice as effective.

Another important problem is that blood pressure is difficult, often impossible, to measure accurately in people with atrial fibrillation, because each heartbeat is so different, some giving a high pressure, others such a low pressure that no pulse wave can be felt. Usually all that is possible is a rough estimate of BP, but this is usually all one needs, because control of blood pressure is seldom the main difficulty in this situation.

Pain, particularly joint pain and arthritis

I'm on tablets for my high blood pressure, but I've also got

arthritis, so I often need painkillers. How do I know which ones to ask for?

You don't say what kind of arthritis you have, or which of your joints are affected. Basically there are two kinds of arthritis – non-inflammatory and inflammatory. Non-inflammatory arthritis, otherwise known as osteoarthritis, osteoarthrosis or degenerative arthritis, usually affects the large joints in the shoulder, hip, knee or ankle and is caused by wear and tear damage to these joints. As we get older, we nearly all have some arthritis of this type, but how severe it is and how much pain it causes varies from person to person. Inflammatory forms of arthritis (rheumatoid arthritis, ankylosing spondylitis and some other rare disorders) can affect almost any joint. As the name implies, the problem here is inflammation and swelling of the joints, rather than one of injury or wear and tear. (Rheumatoid arthritis and ankylosing spondylitis are dealt with in more detail later on in this section.)

Both of these forms of arthritis can be treated with so-called 'painkillers', an odd name, as everyone who has ever suffered from them knows that these pains seldom die. The three main types of painkillers are NSAIDs (which stands for non-steroidal anti-inflammatory drugs), paracetamol and aspirin. Both paracetamol and aspirin are sold under a wide variety of brand names, but you needn't worry about those – it's the same drug underneath all the packaging, and the non-branded versions are just as effective (and much cheaper).

All the following comments apply to anyone needing painkillers for whatever reason (back pain, injuries, period pains and so on), not just to those with arthritis.

- **NSAIDs**
  There are dozens of different NSAIDs available on prescription, far too many to list here. The most widely used is ibuprofen (brand names include Brufen, Cuprofen and Nurofen) which can now be bought across the counter at chemists without a prescription.

  All the NSAIDs raise blood pressure by an average 5-10 mmHg, roughly the same as the reduction produced by most

BP-lowering drugs. There is no doubt at all about this effect, but it is still very generally ignored. At least some of the pharmaceutical companies which market these drugs are well aware of this, because they promote some of them in Germany for treatment of 'low blood pressure'. Doctors generally (specialists as well as GPs) are rarely aware of this important side-effect, although other common side-effects (usually on your digestive system) are well known. It's therefore important that you remind your doctor or pharmacist about your high BP when you need painkillers, so that they can avoid giving you NSAIDs if possible.

NSAIDs rarely have much effect on 'wear and tear' osteoarthritis, or on minor aches and pains from overused or strained muscles. They are all effective for period pains and one - mefenamic acid (Ponstan) - has been particularly promoted for this. They are certainly useful, and often indispensable, for proven inflammatory arthritis, such as rheumatoid arthritis and ankylosing spondylitis. However, most 'rheumatic' disorders causing joint and back pain are not inflammatory and respond poorly if at all to NSAIDs. Some people with mild inflammatory arthritis, and nearly all people with non-inflammatory arthritis, sciatica, and shoulder-arm pain will get as least as much if not more relief from pain with the simpler alternatives - aspirin and paracetamol.

Having said all that, roughly 40% of all people needing BP-lowering drugs also suffer from chronic rheumatic pains for which NSAIDs are often prescribed. If you have severe pain, and if you have found from experience that this can only be relieved by one of these NSAIDs, obviously you may need to use them, even though they may undo any good your BP-lowering medication may be doing. You should at least be aware of this contradiction, stop using them as soon as possible, and make sure your BP doesn't go right out of control.

- **Paracetamol**
Taken as two 500mg tablets every four hours, not more than

three times a day, paracetamol is a safe and effective drug which will take the edge off severe pain for about three hours. It has no harmful interactions with any drugs used to reduce BP, and can be used safely in kidney failure, pregnancy, and during breast feeding, and has no harmful effects on stomach or gut. It has no anti-inflammatory effect, so although it will reduce the perception of pain in inflammatory arthritis, it will not help to control its cause.

- **Aspirin**
Aspirin controls pain about as effectively as paracetamol but works in a different way, which makes it possible for the two drugs to be combined to give a slightly stronger effect. Unlike paracetamol, aspirin has some anti-inflammatory effect, so it is more effective than paracetamol for inflammatory arthritis.

Aspirin does have a major and very prolonged effect on the blood, making it less 'sticky' and so less liable to clot. Because of this, aspirin is therefore very widely (and correctly) used to prevent coronary heart attacks and strokes in people at high risk, especialy those who have already had one heart attack, small stroke, or transient ischaemic attack (TIA). There is no evidence that it does more good than harm for other people at lower risk. This effect on clotting seems to be greater in small doses, that is at less than half the usual dose needed for pain relief and taken only once a day. Even very small doses of aspirin often cause minor bleeding from the stomach or gut, particularly if taken regularly, and (rarely) this may cause severe and dangerous bleeding requiring urgent hospital admission. This effect means that it cannot be used safely in people who have ever had a gastric or duodenal ulcer, or in the last three months of pregnancy.

Aspirin has no effect on BP, no significant interaction with BP-lowering drugs, and is safe in all but severe kidney failure.

There is also a bewildering variety of more powerful pain-relieving drugs available on prescription, all related more or less closely to morphine, but less powerful and less addictive. These range from codeine through dextropropoxyphene to buprenorphine (Temgesic). The nearer these are chemically to morphine, the more likely they are to relieve severe pain but, like morphine, they tend to cause nausea and vomiting, particularly in people who are up and about and try to keep going. Combinations of the least morphine-like of these with paracetamol are very widely prescribed, for example paracetamol + codeine (Cocodamol, Tylex), paracetamol + dihydrocodeine (Codydramol), and paracetamol + dextropropoxyphene (Coproxamol, Distalgesic). None of these has any effect on blood pressure, nor any significant interaction with BP-lowering drugs, but they often cause other unpleasant minor side-effects such as constipation, nausea, and minor depression, which may make them unsatisfactory for regular daily use.

I have severe rheumatoid arthritis treated with steroid tablets (prednisolone). Does this affect my treatment for high blood pressure?

The steroid tablets we are talking about here are the corticosteroids, NOT the anabolic steroids which we often hear about being abused by athletes. Corticosteroids include prednisolone, prednisone and adrenocorticotrophic hormone (ACTH). They are necessary and effective for severe, acute attacks of rheumatoid arthritis, particularly in the first few months after onset of the disease, if this is very severe. In these circumstances they may not only relieve pain, but also reduce long-term joint damage. Although they raise BP by causing sodium and water retention, and thus increasing the volume of blood in the body, this is almost always a price worth paying, even for people with severe high blood pressure. In any case, people whose problems are so severe will usually be under the care of a hospital specialist, whose job it is to make a balanced decision on their treatment in the light of all the available evidence.

Prescription of corticosteroids for the more usual gradual onset of rheumatoid arthritis is another matter, as there are other more serious side-effects to be considered as well as a rise in blood pressure. Raised BP, even in people with high blood pressure, is one of the smaller risks of their long-term use. As usual, the risks from these side-effects have to be balanced against the benefits you get from taking them, something which your doctor will have taken into account before prescribing them for you.

Long-term use of NSAIDs is almost always necessary for all but the mildest cases of rheumatoid arthritis. There seems to be little difference between the many varieties available, in their tendency to raise BP. They have been discussed in greater detail in the answer to the first question in this section.

I have severe chronic back pain, which I have been told is caused by ankylosing spondylitis. I am told that my painkillers (which I can't do without) are a type of NSAID and that these will actually have the effect of raising my (already high) blood pressure. Are there any alternatives?

Spondylitis means inflammation of the small joints connecting the 'wings' either side of the vertebrae. Most back pain probably originates either from these joints, or from pressure on nerve roots as they emerge from the spinal cord between the vertebrae. It has two entirely different causes – simple spondylitis and ankylosing spondylitis.

Joint changes caused by simple spondylitis are common and can be seen on X-rays. Simple spondylitis is mainly wear-and-tear damage to the spondylar joints, similar to osteoarthritis (or osteoarthrosis) in other joints. Inflammation plays little or no part in causing the pain, so NSAIDs (discussed in more detail in the answer to the first question in this section) are seldom effective in relieving it and, for people who also have high blood pressure, they seldom give enough relief to justify their harmful effect in raising BP.

However, you know that you have ankylosing spondylitis rather than simple spondylitis. Ankylosing spondylitis is an eventually serious disorder that runs strongly in families (usually with other people in the family being affected with rheumatoid arthritis, or sometimes with inflammatory gut disorders such as ulcerative colitis). It usually starts in young people in their 20s or 30s, and it may not be properly diagnosed for a long time. People with ankylosing spondylitis generally have severe back pain, typically relieved by movement and worse when they are at rest, often dramatically relieved by NSAIDs. Joints tend eventually to fuse together by bridges of bone, producing the typical 'bamboo spine', and sometimes (usually in neglected cases), forward curvature of the upper spine like a question mark. People with ankylosing spondylitis absolutely depend on NSAIDs. If, like you, they also need treatment for high blood pressure, this contradiction must simply be accepted as inevitable: at present there is unfortunately no alternative.

What about gout?

Gout happens when your body fails to get rid of one of its waste products, a substance called uric acid. Usually the kidneys remove uric acid from your blood (you then get rid of it in your urine) but in those people who produce too much of it, it can accumulate as crystals in the joints. The result is an attack of gout, with very severe pain, swelling, redness and tenderness in one or more joints. Untreated, this can last for several days and is very disabling. It usually affects the small joints, most commonly but not always in the big toe. It is a very common problem and often runs in families.

The level of uric acid in your body is raised by alcohol, by some foods (liver, sweetbreads and other offal, and fish roes) and by the thiazide diuretics used for treating high BP (there is more information about these drugs in Appendix 1).

Acute attacks of gout cause severe pain, which can usually be brought to an end quickly (sometimes dramatically quickly) with one or two day's treatment with one of the NSAIDs, usually indomethacin (there is more about NSAIDs in the answer to the first question in this section). These courses of NSAID treatment are too short to have any significant effect on control of blood pressure. Probenecid (Benemid) is an alternative and equally effective treatment for acute gout which has no effect on blood pressure. Both indomethacin and probenecid help the kidneys to get rid of uric acid.

Allopurinol (Hamarin, Zyloric), taken regularly to prevent attacks of gout rather than to treat them, has no effect on blood pressure. People who get repeated attacks of gout even on low doses of thiazide diuretics often need to take allopurinol regularly to prevent them. Thiazides are so effective for controlling high blood pressure, both by their own effect and by increasing the effect of other BP-lowering drugs, that it is often difficult to stop taking them without loss of control.

Though many total abstainers suffer from gout, and it is not a reliable indicator of alcohol problems, there is no doubt at all that in people who are prone to it a skinful of beer or spirits is a common cause of acute attacks. So if you like a drop more than you should, don't fool yourself: when you get agonising pain in your toe, someone may be trying to tell you something.

Asthma and other breathing problems

Before my doctor prescribed me some drugs called beta-blockers for my high blood pressure, he asked me about my breathing and gave me a test to see if I had asthma. I didn't, but I wondered why he wanted to know – shouldn't people with asthma take beta-blockers?

They shouldn't, because a serious side-effect of beta-blockers is narrowed lung airways in people with asthma (and they already have some narrowing in their airways because of their asthma). Some people with asthma have a clear history of recurrent wheezing attacks (usually beginning in childhood) but some have asthma without knowing it (perhaps because they have none of the typical symptoms and so have not consulted a doctor – and doctors cannot diagnose asthma in people that they have not seen). Any use of beta-blockers can be very dangerous for any of these people, however mild their asthma may appear, as even a single dose can cause very severe tightening of the airways (which could be fatal).

Doctors will suspect asthma in anyone who has recurrent episodes of coughing, wheezing, shortness of breath, or chest tightness (all typical symptoms of asthma). Other clues are a history of allergies, and asthma affecting other members of the family. Anyone with these symptoms should have their lung function checked to see if they have asthma. This usually involves taking a series of peak flow measurements over a week or so. Taking these measurements is very simple – all you have to do is to blow as hard and as fast as possible into a small device called a peak flow meter, and the result (your peak flow measurement or peak flow rate) can then be read off its scale. Sometimes your doctor may want you to take these measurements both before and after taking some asthma treatment – if the treatment improves your readings, then you definitely have asthma.

In my opinion, it is wise for everyone to have at least one peak flow reading before starting on beta-blockers. The results can then be compared with the expected value for your age, sex and height – if your reading is 25% or more below the expected value, then you should definitely avoid beta-blockers, and perhaps have more readings to see if you have asthma.

I have severe asthma, for which I use inhalers all the time, and I have steroid tablets for acute attacks. Will any of these drugs interfere with my treatment for my high blood pressure?

There are two ways in which asthma narrows your airways and causes you difficulty with your breathing, and you probably have two different sorts of inhaler to help you deal with them. The underlying reason is inflammation of the linings of your airways, so that they become swollen and produce too much mucus: the inhalers to help you deal with this contain drugs known as preventers. The inflammation makes your airways very twitchy and irritable, which means that the spiral muscles that surround them tighten up (spasm) and narrow them still further when you come across anything that starts you coughing or wheezing (ie when you have an asthma attack). The inhalers you use during an attack contain drugs known as relievers. (Some people with milder forms of asthma only have one type of inhaler, which will be one of these relievers).

There are many different reliever inhalers, but perhaps the best known are salbutamol (Aerolin, Ventolin) and terbutaline (Bricanyl). Whatever the name, they work by relaxing the spiral muscles, which in turn allows the tightened airways to open up. They generally have a very rapid and easily recognised effect, so people with severe asthma are often tempted to overuse them.

Relievers have little or no effect on your blood pressure. However, if you take too much of them then they can cause disturbances of heart rhythm which can be serious, particularly in people who already have high blood pressure. They are only intended to be used to relieve your asthma symptoms, so you should only use them when your asthma is causing you problems – if you have no symptoms, then don't use your reliever inhaler (and if you keep having symptoms, then you should go back to your doctor or asthma clinic for further advice). On the other hand, if you have a very bad attack of asthma, then this is an emergency and you should take a high dose of your reliever (in these circumstances it is much more important to get your asthma under control than to worry about your blood pressure).

You can also take some relievers as tablets, but this is much less effective because the dose is not concentrated in your lungs, and side-effects such as disturbed heart rhythm can occur more easily.

Preventer inhalers are designed to be taken regularly, as their purpose is to reduce the underlying inflammation in your airways. Once again there are many different types, but the best known contain corticosteroids such as beclomethasone dipropionate (Aerobec, Becotide, Filair), budesonide (Pulmicort) and fluticasone propionate (Flixotide). Because each dose is concentrated in the lung, preventer inhalers rarely cause significant sodium retention, which in turn means that they rarely cause a rise in blood pressure. This means that there is no reason why you should not take your preventer inhalers regularly as prescribed.

The steroid tablets you have been given for very severe asthma attacks are also corticosteroids, usually prednisolone. They may cause some rise in your blood pressure after a few days, but even for people with high blood pressure, the risks of this are trivial compared with the risks of severe uncontrolled asthma. As you should only need to take an occasional short course of these tablets you should not need to worry about their longer term side-effects (discussed in the answer to the question about rheumatoid arthritis in the section on *Pain, particularly joint pain and arthritis* earlier in this chapter).

My husband and I are both on treatment for high blood pressure. Our daughter aged 15 has severe asthma, for which she has regularly to use a steroid inhaler. Could this combination of inheritance and use of steroids give her high blood pressure later on?

Regular inhaled steroids and occasional courses of steroid tablets may often be life-saving for children with severe asthma. Compared with this very real benefit, worries that these treatments may perhaps cause possible high blood pressure sometime in the future will probably seem trivial to you. It is also very unlikely that her current blood pressure has been significantly raised by her inhalers.

Your daughter is in any case likely to have a higher than average blood pressure when she grows up because of her inheritance, as it does tend to run in families. Likely does not mean inevitably, but it is important for you all to realise that the possibility is there so that she can avoid, for example, becoming overweight in her 20s and 30s. You will find more information about the inheritance of high blood pressure in the section on *Causes* in Chapter 2.

I've got a very wheezy chest, I think it's bronchitis, and I've also got high blood pressure. Should I tell my doctor about my wheezing?

You should. Wheeziness has many causes, including bronchitis, but asthma is probably the commonest of them. Your doctor will be able to tell you exactly what is wrong.

Problems arise with people with chronic coughs or wheezy chests, with chronic bronchitis, emphysema, pneumoconiosis, or a mixture of all these, and who may or may not have asthma as well. Among industrial workers and their families, this includes about one-third of the men and a quarter of the women needing medication for high blood pressure. It is probably best for all of these people to avoid beta-blockers, as explained in the answers to earlier questions in this section. If you are one of these people, you may have been prescribed one of the reliever inhalers usually used for asthma (and discussed in more detail earlier in this section): if so, you should discuss with your doctor how often and under what conditions you should use it.

If you have a chronic bad chest, the most important question is whether you still smoke. Very few people with chronic bad chests are not either smokers or ex-smokers, and most of those few have unrecognised asthma. For most people, stopping smoking is more important to both life and health than reducing blood pressure. There is a section on **Stopping smoking** in Chapter 5.

Diabetes

I've got diabetes. Will I automatically also get high blood pressure?

No, but people with high blood pressure are perhaps more likely to develop diabetes than other people, possibly because they share common underlying causes.

Rigorous control of high blood pressure is however very important for people with diabetes. Having diabetes means that you have one risk factor for problems such as kidney damage or kidney failure, coronary heart disease, artery problems and stroke. Having high blood pressure as well adds in another risk factor for these problems. This is true even if your BP is only moderately raised (diastolic pressure over 90 mmHg).

This rigorous control of BP must go hand-in-hand with equally rigorous control of your diabetes, which means accurate home monitoring plus regular checks of your longer-term average blood sugar levels at your diabetes clinic. Good weight control, by a combination of sensible eating and a regular exercise programme, improves control both of diabetes and of high blood pressure.

High blood pressure plus . . .

I've heard that some BP-lowering drugs can interfere with hypo warning signs. Is this true, and is there any other way they could interfere with my diabetes treatment?

Hypo is short for hypoglycaemia, which means low blood sugar. Hypos come on quickly, can lead to unconsciousness (but this is rare), and the usual warning signs include dizziness, sweating, mental confusion and so on. In a few people beta-blocker drugs suppress these usual warning symptoms: as this could obviously be dangerous they should be avoided if there is any reason to suspect that this is happening.

Thiazide diuretics tend to reduce even further your body's ability to deal with glucose (the reason why you have diabetes in the first place). However, people with diabetes who cannot get good control of their blood pressure without them are likely to gain much more than they will lose by using them. It is important to stick to the lowest possible dose.

ACE-inhibitor drugs are probably more effective in delaying kidney damage than other BP-lowering drugs, and for most people with diabetes these are probably the best first choice.

You will find more information about all these BP-lowering drugs in Appendix 1.

My elderly mother had a test for diabetes. She turns out not to have it, although the doctor said she did have impaired glucose tolerance but that this might just be due to her blood pressure tablets, and that he would keep an eye on it in the future. If her tablets might lead to her developing diabetes, why doesn't he change them?

Not just sugars, but many other foods are broken down in the gut and transformed into glucose, the main source of energy for all cells throughout the body, and the only source of energy for brain cells. In diabetes, the chemical pathways for both production and use of glucose fail to work properly. Impaired glucose tolerance (or glucose intolerance) describes a halfway state between normal glucose handling and diabetes – in other words the level of glucose in your mother's blood is a bit too high, but not high enough to be diagnosed as diabetes.

You don't say which BP-lowering drugs your mother is taking, but it sounds from your description of her doctor's comments as if they are thiazide diuretics. At all but the lowest possible doses, all thiazide diuretics tend to impair glucose tolerance after two or three years, and this tendency increases with age. Even at low doses, impaired glucose tolerance is twice as common in elderly people taking thiazide diuretics, and at the unnecessarily high doses still commonly used, about 1% a year develop full diabetes. This is important because both impaired glucose tolerance and diabetes may increase her risks of developing coronary heart disease or stroke.

However, this evidence has to be balanced against the results of large trials which consistently show larger net benefit from BP-lowering treatment with thiazides in the elderly than in younger people, even though glucose tolerance falls rapidly with age. Trials in the elderly showed not only big reductions in strokes, heart failure, and coronary heart disease, but in deaths from all causes. Evidently for the average person, particularly for the elderly who are most likely to develop diabetes, the advantages of thiazide diuretics greatly outweigh their disadvantages, and this will be why your mother's doctor has not changed her drugs.

For people with high blood pressure who already have diabetes, or who are at high risk of getting it because they are seriously overweight or have close relatives who have diabetes, thiazide diuretics should be avoided if their blood pressure can be controlled without them. Some authorities believe thiazide diuretics should never be used in these people, but they are so effective and so useful that such advice is often difficult if not impossible to follow.

There are two reasons why people with diabetes may need to take thiazide diuretics. Firstly, in the many cases where other drugs are ineffective unless taken in combination with thiazides, they will probably continue to be used until something better is available (but there seems to be no prospect of this at the present time). Secondly, good BP control is essential for people who already have diabetes in order to prevent kidney damage. If you have both diabetes and high BP, and your BP cannot be controlled properly without thiazide diuretics, then you will still gain more than you lose by taking them, even if they raise your blood glucose levels and so mean you taking more insulin or more 'anti-diabetic' drugs. Their effect on blood glucose levels can be minimised by using the lowest possible doses.

I've heard that both diabetes and high blood pressure can affect your eyes and your kidneys. Is this true, and what can be done about it?

Yes, both uncontrolled diabetes and uncontrolled high blood pressure can affect the small blood vessels in the retina (the back of the eye) and, if this goes undetected and untreated, it can affect your sight. Good control of both your diabetes and your high blood pressure will help to prevent this happening. You should also be sure to take advantage of all the routine eye checks you will be offered (at your diabetes clinic, at your GP's or wherever else you are getting your diabetes and/or blood pressure care) when the backs of your eyes will be examined through an instrument called an ophthalmoscope, and any problems will be detected at an early stage before they have any noticeable effects. Eye tests of this sort are also available free to people with diabetes from any optician.

The small blood vessels in the kidneys can be affected in just the same way as those in the retina, and the same advice applies – keep good control of both conditions and take advantage of all the tests you are offered. The routine test here will be to check if you have protein in your urine (the first sign of kidney damage), done very simply by your doctor or nurse dipping a special test strip into your urine sample.

Digestive system problems

I had an operation for an ulcer a couple of years ago, and still have to take anti-ulcer drugs. My doctor says that if I can't get my blood pressure down on the diet he's given me, then I'll need to take drugs for that as well. Will the two lots of drugs interfere with each other?

It is possible, but your doctor should obviously prescribe drugs for you which don't interfere with each other.

One of the most popular anti-ulcer drugs, cimetidine (Tagamet), is used to suppress acid production in the stomach. It is usually prescribed for four to six weeks to heal gastric and duodenal ulcers, and intermittently thereafter to suppress symptoms if there is a relapse. Cimetidine slows the normal process of breakdown of beta-blockers and calcium-channel blockers, so that blood levels of these BP-lowering drugs rise and you need a lower dose. Ranitidine (Zantac) is an equally effective ulcer treatment, and has no effect on beta-blockers or calcium-channel blockers. (You will find more information about both beta-blockers and calcium-channel blockers in Appendix 1.)

Most people with ulcers are now treated by intensive combined antibiotics. These antibiotics eradicate the underlying cause of ulcers, infection by *Helicobacter pylori* bacteria. This treatment is very effective and has no effect on blood pressure.

I sometimes get heartburn. Is there anything I can get for it in the chemist's which won't upset my BP-lowering drugs?

You would be wise to avoid cimetidine (Tagamet) although it is frequently used to treat heartburn, particularly since it became available over the counter without prescription. As I mentioned in the answer to the previous question, it can interact with some BP-lowering drugs.

Few people with minor heartburn actually need such powerful drugs, and most would in any case be wiser to stick to one of the many simpler and older antacid preparations available to treat 'indigestion'. These have no effect on any BP-lowering drugs. However, some of the most popular antacids on sale contain large amounts of sodium, so you may want to avoid these if you are trying to follow a low-sodium diet (as outlined in the section on ***Sodium and salt*** in Chapter 5).

People with severe heartburn (the technical name for it is 'reflux oesophagitis') and people who frequently get minor heartburn should obviously consult their doctors, as it may be a symptom of a more serious problem, such as an ulcer. The commonest cause of acid reflux is being overweight, and weight reduction is its simplest and most effective treatment.

Constipation causes me to strain when I go to the toilet. Does this raise my blood pressure, and is it important as I have high blood pressure already?

Straining to empty your bowels does cause a temporary rise in blood pressure both in your veins and your arteries, but this has no long term effect either as a cause of high blood pressure in the first place, or on the management of your established high blood pressure. Such brief rises in blood pressure are not dangerous even if you already have high BP.

Kidneys and prostate problems

My doctor says that because I've got some slight problems with my kidneys I need to be extra careful about my blood pressure. Why?

Because if you have some damage in your kidneys then raised blood pressure greatly speeds up its further progress (to kidney failure). This development can be delayed or arrested by good control of high blood pressure. It is therefore very important to maintain really good control of blood pressure in anyone who shows signs of even minimal kidney damage, whatever its cause, and also in anyone who has diabetes. Kidney damage can be a complication of long-standing diabetes (usually combined with high blood pressure), and an occasional cause of (secondary) high blood pressure.

Early kidney damage is signalled by a rise in the blood levels of both urea and creatinine, and usually by protein in urine. I described the tests for these in the section on *Diagnosis and initial investigations* in Chapter 2. If you have some kidney damage then these tests usually need to be done about once a year, so that they can be used to measure any changes that may be taking place.

People with kidney failure and high blood pressure need either to avoid altogether those BP-lowering drugs that are excreted through the kidneys, or greatly reduce the dose they take. All the BP-lowering drugs need to be used cautiously and usually at lower doses, and the ACE-inhibitor drugs and thiazide diuretics are particularly hazardous (there is more information about all these drugs in Appendix 1). Management of high blood pressure complicated by kidney failure is beyond the competence of GPs working alone, and should be shared with specialists in a renal (kidney) unit, who can advise on medication.

Since I've had problems with my prostate, I've also had high blood pressure. Will this problem go away once I've had my prostate operation?

Chronic obstruction of the bladder, usually by enlargement of the prostate, is a common and important cause of sustained high blood pressure. BP falls quickly to its original level after the obstruction is relieved by draining the bladder with a catheter or by operating on the prostate, so your problem may either go away or at least be reduced.

Psychological problems

My husband has been told he has high blood pressure, and he also has just been diagnosed as suffering from depression (I don't simply mean he gets depressed, I mean he is what I think is called clinically depressed). Which is it more important for us to tackle first? And if he needs to take drugs for his depression, will he have to change his BP-lowering drugs?

Your husband's situation is particularly unfortunate, as depression raises blood pressure substantially in many people, and most drugs used to control blood pressure tend to make depression worse. Unless high blood pressure is so severe that it seems to present an immediate risk of organ damage, it is nearly always best to get depression under control first with antidepressant drugs, and leave the question of treating high blood pressure until later (often blood pressure will have fallen by then anyway).

If his high blood pressure is already receiving treatment, then he needs to continue with his BP-lowering drugs. You don't mention which (if any) BP-lowering drugs he is taking, but people with high blood pressure and a history of recurrent depression should avoid treatment with the BP-lowering drugs that act mainly on the brainstem such as methyldopa (Aldomet) or clonidine (Catapres), or with beta-blockers that reach the brain, such as propranolol (Inderal). A good alternative beta-blocker which does not reach the brain is atenolol (Tenormin). (You will find more information about all the BP-lowering drugs mentioned here in Appendix 1.) His BP-lowering drugs are unlikely to have been the main cause of his depression (although they may have contributed a little) unless he has been taking one of the drugs acting mainly on the brainstem.

Should your husband's depression unfortunately turn out to be so severe that antidepressant drugs fail to help, then his doctor may refer him to a psychiatrist, to consider electroconvulsive treatment (ECT). Although nobody yet knows how it works, it certainly does work in most cases, and can be lifesaving. Because blood pressure rises steeply during ECT, steps may have to be taken to bring it under control first. These treatments would involve your husband going into hospital, preferably with responsibility for his care shared equally between a psychiatrist and a skilled physician.

Lithium can be a very effective long-term treatment for recurrent severe depression, but its level in the blood requires frequent close monitoring. Some BP-lowering drugs can affect lithium treatment. Taking thiazide diuretics makes stable control of lithium levels almost impossible, while methyldopa (Aldomet) may suddenly make lithium toxic (poisonous) to nerve cells, so neither can be used. ACE-inhibitors increase excretion of lithium and therefore may require the dose of lithium to be modified, but they can be used safely.

My father has depression, apparently because of his Parkinson's disease. Will any of his BP-lowering drugs make his

depression worse? Or will any of them affect his Parkinson's medication?

Many people with Parkinson's will have some degree of depression at one time or another. It is generally believed to be part of the illness and not only a reaction to it – the chemical changes in the brain which are connected with Parkinson's may lead to a biochemical form of depression.

Your father should avoid BP-lowering drugs which are known to be liable to increase depression such as clonidine (Catapres), and beta-blockers such as propranolol (Inderal) that reach the brain (alternative beta-blockers are available).

Because of his Parkinson's he should avoid methyldopa (Aldomet) as not only does this makes Parkinson's worse, but it also opposes the action of the most frequently used Parkinson's drugs (Sinemet and Madopar). All the other BP-lowering drugs can all be used – you will find more information about all of them in Appendix 1.

Is it true that people with schizophrenia never need treatment for high blood pressure?

Never is perhaps too strong a word, but most people with schizophrenia are on long-term treatment with phenothiazine drugs, given either as tablets or once a month as a slow-release injection. These drugs have a powerful BP-lowering effect, which usually makes any other BP-lowering medication unnecessary.

Long-term treatment with phenothiazines can cause involuntary writhing movements, usually affecting the face and limbs. This effect is increased by methyldopa (Aldomet), which should therefore not be used to treat high blood pressure in people with schizophrenia.

I don't think my father is actually an alcoholic, but he is certainly a very heavy drinker. He says that it can't make any difference to his blood pressure while he continues to take his tablets, but I'm sure it must do. Which of us is right?

You are. Stopping drinking alcohol – or even greatly reducing a heavy alcohol intake – may bring high blood pressure down to normal without any other medication, particularly in people under 40. Many middle-aged and elderly people whose high blood pressures have failed to respond to apparently adequate doses of BP-lowering drugs get good control if they stop or greatly reduce their alcohol intake.

Heavy drinkers are likely to damage their livers and eventually this can lead to liver failure. People with high blood pressure complicated by liver damage may need lower doses of BP-lowering drugs. All diuretics, but particularly the most powerful ones like frusemide (Lasix) must be used very cautiously, because with liver impairment they can cause dangerously low potassium levels. Methyldopa (Aldomet) and labetalol (Trandate) should be avoided altogether because they may bring on liver failure. Management of high blood pressure complicated by advanced liver failure is beyond the competence of GPs working alone, and should be shared with specialists in a gastroenterology unit, who can advise on medication.

7
Living with high blood pressure

Work

I've got high blood pressure, but it's properly controlled by my treatment and I've had no problems at my current work. I've now been offered a new job, but I will probably have to have a medical before they confirm the offer (it's not just me, they make everyone have one). Will they be able to tell that I've got high BP and will it make any difference? If they don't spot it, do I have to tell them about it?

The first thing to say is that (as you've already proved in your current job) people whose originally high blood pressure has been controlled by medication are no more likely to injure themselves or others, to make mistakes, or to lose time at work than other people with lower pressures. Providing BP is well controlled, the original level of pressure is irrelevant, no matter how high it was.

Most firms which ask job applicants to have a pre-employment medical are trying to identify people at increased risk of injury, error, or absenteeism, not for the sake of the workforce, but to help management and shareholders, and perhaps to fulfil conditions for pension funds. A company doctor measuring your BP at a pre-employment medical examination has no way of telling if you are on medication, and is not likely to ask.

The question about what you should do if you are asked about your BP is more problematical, and the same problem occurs when we consider whether you should disclose the information yourself without being asked. There is no legal protection for applicants refused a job on account of their health (even if you could discover that that was the real reason), and almost none for employees dismissed because of their health record. This might make you feel that you would prefer not to tell anyone about your high blood pressure or to be evasive if you are asked a direct question about it. Unfortunately, you can also be dismissed – again apparently quite legally – at any time in the future if you fail to disclose information of this type when you are being considered for the job. It's a Catch-22 situation, and only you can decide (based on your knowledge of yourself and of the company you want to work for) what are the best steps to take.

What help is there if an employer does want to sack you because of your high BP?

Much will depend on whether your employers are prepared to listen to reason – they may simply know nothing about high blood pressure and be over-reacting. If they are open to discussion (and it's always worth trying) you could explain to them that having properly controlled high BP will not affect your job performance (perhaps your GP would write to the company on your behalf explaining this). If you need help presenting your case, and you belong to a union, or to a staff or professional association, then they may be able to provide someone to help.

Are there any kinds of work which people with high blood pressure are not allowed to do?

A few occupations, such as being an airline pilot, a submariner or an undersea diver, unconditionally exclude everyone with an average BP over 140/90 mmHg even if it is fully controlled by treatment. This is reasonable, because all BP-lowering drugs other than thiazide diuretics interfere with normal body responses to the extreme conditions of changes in atmospheric pressure or acceleration which are to be expected in these activities.

Some drugs used to lower BP can make you drowsy, and this could cause problems in some occupations, for example for train drivers, for people who need to drive cars or lorries in their work, or for those who operate dangerous machinery. If your job involves these or similar activities, then discuss it with your doctor before you start on BP-lowering medication, so that any drugs with these side-effects can be avoided.

There is a question about driving cars in the *Miscellaneous* section at the end of this chapter.

Could my high blood pressure have been caused by my work?

This question is difficult to answer, because we still know so little about what the environmental causes of high blood pressure are. Some research suggests that sustained industrial noise, at levels that make it necessary for workers to shout in order to be heard over a distance of one or two feet (30–60 cm), may cause a sustained rise in blood pressure. At these levels ear protectors are essential to prevent damage to your hearing, so even if noise does raise BP, this should prevent it. There is no convincing evidence of any effect from shift work.

Several metals, their soluble salts, or their welding fumes can

Living with high blood pressure

cause high blood pressure either directly, or by damaging the kidneys. These include cadmium and lead. The many workers who handle unknown chemicals of all kinds need to be aware of the possibility that these may cause many different sorts of damage, usually to the liver and/or kidney, and this in turn may show up as high blood pressure. Carbon disulphide, an unstable intermediate product of a now obsolete process for making viscose rayon, was correctly suspected of being a hitherto unknown cause of coronary heart attacks by a vigilant GP in North Wales. Other discoveries of this sort may be made in the future: it is sometimes important to keep an open mind.

Are there any types of employment I should avoid – I have high blood pressure?

Providing your high blood pressure is well controlled, the only kinds of work you cannot do or should absolutely avoid are those discussed in the answer to the previous two questions. Apart from those, the only occupations or working conditions which will affect your health are those which would affect anyone's health, whether or not they had high blood pressure. For example, systematic excessive overtime is now common, and is almost as bad for the health of those who do it as the unemployment it helps to impose on others (in studies of Norwegian shipbuilders, both unemployment itself and the fear of impending unemployment were shown to raise both blood pressure and blood cholesterol). This is not specific to high blood pressure, but can be used as an argument where employers try to make such systematic overtime compulsory.

I'm about to take up a job abroad. What should I do about my BP-lowering drugs and my medical supervision while I'm there?

You don't say where you are going or for how long, both of which will make a difference to what you should do.

Where you are going makes a difference because European customs on management of high blood pressure, particularly in France, all the Mediterranean countries and in Germany and points east are entirely different from ours in the UK and may be very confusing. Customs in Holland, Scandinavia and North America resemble our own, although doctors in the USA tend to prescribe more aggressively than we do in this country. Treatment practices vary equally widely in other parts of the world.

All the commonly prescribed BP-lowering drugs are available in other economically developed countries, although often at very high prices. Brand names in other countries are often different from those used in the UK, so you should make sure you know the generic names of your medication before you go.

In my opinion, if you are getting good regular supervision from your own family doctor in the UK, you should avoid interrupting this by seeking other advice, unless this is absolutely necessary. Discuss this with your GP before you go: he or she may not object to giving you advice over the phone while you are away, providing you remember any differences in time zones. Unless you are going away for more than three months or so, your family doctor will probably prescribe enough of your medication to cover the whole period of your work abroad. If you have to take more than 100 of any tablets for your personal use, it is wise to ask your doctor to write a note confirming what he has prescribed, how much, and that this is necessary for your personal care. Customs officials can be very difficult about this, particularly in Latin America, the Middle East and South-East Asia.

If you are going away for longer periods, then you will need to consider carefully what to do and to get advice from your own GP, from the relevant embassy, from the company you work for, and from any other sources you can think of. For example, you might be able to have your follow-up checks on your visits home. Much will obviously depend on your individual circumstances, so it is impossible for me to give you more specific advice here.

Whatever your circumstances, you still need to be prepared in case you need treatment while you are abroad. Make sure before you go that you know exactly what medication you are taking, generic names as well as brand names, and roughly what your blood pressure was before you started treatment. It may help to have this written down, perhaps in translation into the appropriate language, to prevent possible confusion.

Because local practice varies so much, think carefully before adding any suggested new medication to what was prescribed for you in this country. For example, south and central European countries have strong traditions of multi-medication for everything, which I think you should avoid. Just ask what exactly the new prescription is for, and if in doubt, don't collect it. You are much more likely to suffer from overtreatment than undertreatment.

Insurance and mortgages

My blood pressure was found to be high at an examination for private insurance. What should I do about this?

The main difference between a BP measurement taken by your own doctor, and by a doctor acting for an insurance company, is that your own doctor is more likely to give you the benefit of any doubts. Virtually all insurance companies agree that if a high pressure is found, the examining doctor can let the applicant lie down and rest for about half an hour, repeat the measurement, and use the lower figure if there is one.

Remember that one high measurement does not mean that you have high blood pressure – the single high measurement could have been caused by you rushing to get to your appointment on time, or because you needed to empty your bladder, or for many other reasons. If either the examining doctor or your own GP feels that it might indicate a cause for concern, then the answer is for you to have a series of accurate measurements made on separate days to establish whether or not you really do have a BP high enough to need treatment. I have discussed this in greater detail earlier in this book, eg in the ***Diagnosis and initial investigations*** section in Chapter 2 and the section on ***Accuracy and reliability*** in Chapter 3.

What if I really do turn out to have high blood pressure, or if it was someone who knew they had high BP before they

applied for insurance? Would it make a difference – would it affect my ability to get insurance?

Insurance companies are conservative in their habits. Your BP would have to be very high indeed for insurance to be refused outright, but a weighted premium is likely if you come close to the usual threshold for considering treatment (about 160/90 mmHg). If this happens, you won't be told the reason (although if your own GP did the examination, he may have a good guess). If you were examined by a different doctor, and your own doctor has good evidence of numerous low readings, you could get this sent to the insurance company, asking them to take it into account.

The British Heart Foundation (address in Appendix 2) can supply you with a list of insurance companies and brokers who understand about high blood pressure and who can help you find suitable policies.

Do I need to mention my high blood pressure on the form for my travel insurance?

Yes, because it is what insurance companies regard as a 'pre-existing condition'. This applies to all forms of insurance, not just travel insurance – it is up to you to inform the insurance company about all pre-existing medical conditions, whether or not they specifically ask you questions about them. If you do not mention that you have high blood pressure, then your insurance may turn out to be invalid.

I am 28, and I've been turned down for a mortgage because of high blood pressure, but my GP says my blood pressure is not high enough to need treatment. Can you make sense of this?

This is a not uncommon situation. Mortgage companies (like insurance companies) make their profits by calculating accurately the odds on earlier-than-expected deaths in their customers over the periods of the loans or the associated insurance policies. However, they have to get this right for large groups, not for individuals – hence their tendency to put people into categories and not to consider individual circumstances to the extent that we, the customers, might like. Family doctors also deal in probabilities, but they are concerned with personal predictions for individuals.

Until very recently, high blood pressure was generally considered to mainly affect middle-aged and older people, and it was seldom looked for systematically in those under 40 (except in women, where it was often found during routine antenatal care or when they were thinking of starting on the contraceptive pill). In fact most people found to have high blood pressure in middle age already had high pressures in their 20s or 30s - it was either never measured when they were younger, or it was ignored because although it was considered 'high for age' it still fell below the conventional threshold for diagnosing 'hypertension' as a so-called disease. So as far as groups of people were concerned (and it is groups of people in whom the statisticians are interested), high blood pressure was to be expected and allowed for in older people but not in people of your age. Perhaps the mortgage company that you applied to hadn't updated its statistics, or was not aware that effective treatment for high blood pressure reduces its attendant risks.

What can you do about it? The answer is much the same as for the questions about insurance earlier in this section - first find out whether or not you really have high blood pressure by having a series of accurate readings, then get the appropriate treatment if you need it, and finally go back to the mortgage company with your supporting evidence and try again.

Travel and holidays

Will flying in a pressurised aircraft have any effect on my blood pressure?

No. However, middle-aged and elderly people with problems of obesity or heart failure should make sure they have room for their legs without pressure from luggage, do frequent static leg exercises every half hour (by alternately tightening and relaxing their calf muscles), and should get up and walk around every few hours on long journeys. They have high risks of deep vein thrombosis in the legs if this advice is not followed – and it applies equally well to travelling in cars or trains or coaches, anywhere where they are remaining still in a confined space for a long time.

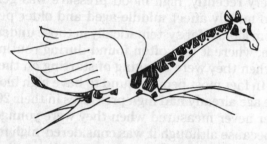

We'd like to go on holiday to a mountain resort, but my wife has high blood pressure and is a bit worried about this because she's heard that living high up affects your blood. Does high altitude have any effect on high blood pressure?

People living long enough at very high altitude (ie above 10,000 feet or 3,000 metres) to become fully acclimatised develop thicker blood because they need more red blood cells to carry the smaller amount of oxygen available. As blood viscosity increases, so does blood pressure and the risk of stroke. A holiday should not really be long enough to cause such changes to occur, but if your wife's high blood pressure has not yet been fully controlled by her medication it might be wise to postpone travel to such areas until her BP has been brought down to normal. Once it is normal then you can enjoy your holiday without worrying.

What happens if I need some sort of treatment when I'm abroad, for example if I lose my tablets and need to get more?

The average 2–3 week holiday need not interrupt your regular pattern of treatment and follow-up, as your GP can give you enough of your tablets to take with you. It would be sensible to keep them in your hand luggage in case your suitcase goes astray. However, make sure you know exactly what they are (generic names as well as brand names, as brand names can vary from country to country) just in case something goes wrong and you do need extra supplies. All the commonly prescribed BP-lowering drugs are available in other economically developed countries, although often at very high prices.

Medical attention is officially free in all European Union countries, provided that you have obtained certificate E111 (from your local Post Office or Department of Social Security office) before you go. In practice it may be difficult, sometimes impossible, to find a public service GP and you have to consult privately in holiday areas. For this reason, anyone going abroad (whether or not they have high blood pressure) should obviously make sure that they have adequate insurance cover (there is a question about travel insurance in the previous section on **Insurance and mortgages**). The Department of Health publishes a booklet called the *Traveller's Guide to Health* which you may find useful (details are in Appendix 3).

If you do happen to need to consult a doctor when you are on your holiday, then you should be aware that ways of managing high BP differ from country to country. This has been discussed in more detail in the answer to the question about working abroad in the section on **Work** at the beginning of this chapter. I would also suggest that you read that answer if you are planning an extended foreign trip or if you are going to one of the more exotic holiday locations.

Like many other families, we want to get some medicines from the chemist here before we go away – we don't want our holiday to be spoiled by one of us being travel sick or having a tummy upset. Is it safe to take these medicines with my blood pressure drugs if I need to?

The drugs commonly used to prevent or suppress travel sickness or vomiting are hyoscine (sold under various brand names such as Joyrides, Kwells, Scopoderm) which can be bought from chemists without prescription in the UK, and metoclopramide (Maxolon) which is only available on prescription. These are safe to take with almost all BP-lowering drugs. If you are taking methyldopa (Aldomet) for your blood pressure then this can sometimes (although rarely) interact with metoclopramide to cause involuntary movements of your face and limbs. This side-effect is not serious and will not last, but it can be frightening if you are not prepared for it.

Drugs to stop diarrhoea probably do little if anything to shorten the course of this usually self-limiting disorder, but they are reassuring. Diarrhoea is caused by rapid movement in the gut, and this movement can be slowed by small doses of traditional remedies such kaolin and morphine mixture or tablets of codeine phosphate, or newer drugs such as diphenoxylate (Lomotil) or loperamide (Diareze, Imodium, Loperagen). Loperamide can be bought over the counter from a chemist's; for the other drugs you will need a doctor's prescription. They can all be safely used with your BP-lowering tablets. None of them can be given safely to young children.

Persistent diarrhoea acquired on holidays is usually caused by an infection by a protozoan called *Giardia lamblia*. It responds well to the antibiotic metronidazole, and neither the infection nor the treatment has any effect on blood pressure.

What should I do about taking my medication if I get diarrhoea or vomiting while I'm abroad?

Travellers' diarrhoea and/or vomiting is rarely severe. It usually gets better by itself after three or four days without needing antibiotics or any treatment other than increasing the amount of fluids you drink. You should continue with your usual medication except in the extremely unlikely case that you are so ill that you have to be admitted to hospital (in which case you should obviously inform the doctors about your high BP and the drugs you are taking for it).

The main risk of diarrhoea and vomiting is that you become dehydrated and lose the essential salts (sodium and potassium) that your body needs to function properly. Sensible treatment mainly depends on correcting these losses by drinking large quantities of water with glucose (which helps you absorb the extra water), sodium and potassium added in the correct proportions. You will need to drink about a pint (half a litre) of such a mixture after each bout of diarrhoea or vomiting. You can make up a suitable mixture yourself, based on either fruit

Living with high blood pressure

juice or ordinary (not diet) Coca-cola (both of these will provide glucose and potassium). If you are using fruit juice, then dilute it with with some water (add some extra sugar if you like) and add half a level teaspoon of ordinary table salt to each pint (half litre) of the mixture. If you are using Coca-cola then you obviously don't need to dilute it before adding the salt (the quantities are the same), but you may like to let it go flat first so that the fizz doesn't upset you further. If you are worried about making up your own mixture you can instead buy sachets of oral rehydration salts (sold under brand names such as Dioralyte or Rehidrat) from a chemist and dissolve these in water strictly according to the instructions.

The only people on BP-lowering medication who really have to worry about diarrhoea and vomiting are people who are taking ACE-inhibitors (there is more information about these drugs in Appendix 1). The normal kidney mechanisms for correcting sudden fluid and salt loss cannot operate in people taking these drugs, and they therefore have much higher risks of collapsing from dehydration and salt (sodium and potassium) depletion. People on ACE-inhibitors must take rehydration and salt replacement much more seriously than other people. If their illness does not begin to improve within a few hours, then intravenous fluids through a drip may be necessary, which means admission to hospital.

Sports

Are there any sports that are particularly good or bad for high blood pressure?

Aqualung (scuba) diving may be dangerous for anyone either with uncontrolled high blood pressure, or on BP-lowering drugs. They will have to be satisfied with snorkelling, diving to not more than two or three metres (6–10 ft).

Squash and other similar extremely active and exhausting competitive sports are unwise, and so are all kinds of static exercise such as weightlifting, press-ups, and body-building.

Boxing is out of the question. Otherwise there is virtually nothing that people with treated and controlled high blood pressure cannot do, providing they get themselves sensibly into training, and do not rush into very demanding activities for the first time in middle age.

People who exercise regularly tend to have lower blood pressures than couch potatoes. Swimming is probably the best form of exercise of all, as it remains possible even for elderly people with joint and back pain. Cycling is a good alternative for people without back pain. The section on *Exercise* in Chapter 5 will tell you more about these and other forms of exercise, the best way to approach them, and their beneficial affect on your blood pressure.

Are there any sports which I won't be allowed to do?

There may be some. Most BP-lowering drugs interfere with your body's normal responses to extreme changes in atmospheric pressure or acceleration. Because of this, it is reasonable for the governing bodies of sports which involve you in such conditions to be concerned about your high BP. They may perhaps suggest that you should not do them, or should have a medical before you take part. Examples which spring to mind are motor racing, parachuting and recreational flying, but I doubt this list is exhaustive. If you want to take part in a sport of this type, I suggest that you contact its governing body to see if they impose any restrictions and, if so, what they are. The Sports Council (address in Appendix 2) should be able to tell you the names and addresses of the appropriate governing bodies.

Sex

Does high blood pressure affect sexual appetite or performance?

The vast majority (90% or more) of people with high blood pressure, both male and female, are able to lead completely full and normal sex lives.

Living with high blood pressure

What about the other 10%? There is no evidence to suggest that high blood pressure itself causes problems of diminished desire and/or sexual performance, but in any large group of men with high blood pressure, about 10% will have such problems (the average figure for the general population is about 5%). The difference is caused by other health changes often associated with high blood pressure (eg circulation problems, diabetes), or by BP-lowering medication (discussed in the answer to the following question), or simply by the worry and loss of confidence which can be associated with the diagnosis of high BP. Although these figures refer to men (in whom the problem tends to be more obvious), there is no reason to doubt that the effects in women are dissimilar, simply less discussed and unresearched.

Sex starts in the mind. If the mind is disturbed or preoccupied with other worries (whatever they are), the sequence of first emotional and then physical changes which must occur before successful love-making can take place may not even begin; or, having begun, it may at any point be interrupted. Depending on where this interruption occurs, the consequences may be loss of desire, failure to obtain or maintain an erection (impotence), premature ejaculation, or failure of orgasm.

Men who usually have good erections when they wake in the morning can be sure that their machinery is in good order, and that whatever problems they have are probably connected in some way with their own mind, or the interaction between minds necessary for a successful partnership. Problems of this sort can often be solved simply by discussing them frankly with your partner, a simple step many find difficult to take. If you find it difficult to start talking, you could look for help from an experienced and sympathetic counsellor. Local family planning clinics and marriage guidance organisations such as Relate (address in Appendix 2) can usually organise this for you.

Do BP-lowering drugs cause impotence?

All BP-lowering drugs can occasionally cause partial or complete failure of erection (impotence) in men, but the fact that they can does not mean that they will. To put it in context, about

5% of men are affected by worries about their potency anyway – this figure doubles to about 10% for men on BP-lowering medication. Impotence caused by BP-lowering medication is always reversible: in other words, it is a side-effect that disappears soon after stopping the drug. If it doesn't, the drug is unlikely to be the cause.

The worst offenders are thiazide diuretics, mainly when prescribed in unnecessarily large doses (which still happens all too often). Runners-up are the drugs acting mainly on the brainstem and the beta-blockers. (There is more information about all these drugs in Appendix 1.) If you are taking one of these drugs and are having potency problems, then it would be worth going back to your doctor to see if a change of dosage or a change of drug would be helpful.

If I am impotent, what can I do about it? Can I get any sort of treatment or do I just have to grin and bear it?

I'm assuming that you have ruled out causes of temporary impotence such as your medication, any worries or emotional problems, tiredness and overwork, too much alcohol, and so on, and that you no longer have good waking erections. Men who rarely or never have good erections when they wake up in the morning nearly always have problems with their sexual machinery, usually because of impairments either to the blood supply or the nerve supply to the penis. Erectile failure from this cause (organic impotence) can be treated.

Depending on the actual cause of your impotence, there are various different and effective forms of treatment. One of the simplest is vacuum therapy, with a device which looks rather like a rigid condom – this is harmless (although it can be an expensive purchase) and has helped many people. Injections of papaverine into the penis, and penile implants (which require an operation) are more invasive treatments but also effective. The best treatment for you as an individual will require a lot of thought and discussion with your doctor. There are now clinics specialising in erection problems in most large hospitals, and you could ask your GP to refer you to one of these.

Meanwhile, you can use what you have (on the 'if you don't use it, you lose it' principle). Most men and women can both reach orgasm without an erect penis, or at least without an erection sustained throughout intercourse, but you must be prepared to talk to each other frankly about the difficulty, and discover your own personal ways round it.

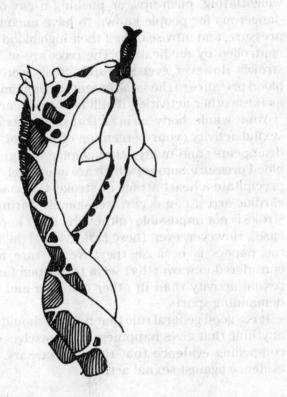

Does sex raise blood pressure?

Yes, but only briefly. As in any other vigorous physical activity, blood pressure rises moderately in anticipation, steeply during performance, and falls quickly afterwards. There is some evidence that regular sexual activity may reduce rather than increase average blood pressure at other times.

If we're warned off doing things that can suddenly raise our blood pressure, why doesn't this apply to sex? After all, you

read in the papers about people dying of heart attacks then. Can you really reassure me that sexual activity isn't dangerous for people with high blood pressure?

Activities that cause very high peaks in blood pressure, such as weightlifting, push-ups, or pushing a car out of a ditch, are dangerous for people known to have uncontrolled high blood pressure, and unwise even if their high blood pressure has been controlled by medication. The risks are of heart attacks and strokes. However, even if sexual activity were capable of raising blood pressure to the same extent and for similar lengths of time as these other activities, it still might not carry the same risks.

Your whole body is in a transiently exalted state during sexual activity (your perception of pain, for example, virtually disappears) and many other changes occur other than raised blood pressure, some of which are more likely to prevent than to precipitate a heart attack or stroke. Coronary thrombosis and cardiac arrest can occur occasionally during intercourse, and stroke is not impossible (although I don't know of any recorded case). However, even these rare events (the reason they are in the papers is because they are so rare and are therefore considered newsworthy) seem to happen far less often during sexual activity than in other common and equally physically demanding sports.

It is a good general rule that nobody should ever give up doing anything that gives happiness to themselves or others, without compelling evidence that this is necessary. There is no such evidence against sexual activity.

Contraception

Can I go on the pill if I have high blood pressure?

Although everyone use the term 'the pill' when they talk about oral contraceptives, here we need to be a bit more specific because more than one type of pill is available.

Combined oral contraceptives (COCs) are the most commonly used. They contain two hormones – oestrogen and progestogen. If your blood pressure has ever been high enough to cause concern, you should not use COCs. The reason for this is that they cause a small rise in blood pressure in most women (and you certainly don't want this if you already have high blood pressure) – in women in their 20s, COCs raise blood pressure by an average 8 mmHg after two years, and 12 mmHg after five years. In a few women they cause a rise that is huge, rapid and dangerous. This happened fairly often with the higher dose COCs used in the 1960s and 1970s, but is probably rare with the low-dose COCs in use today.

The other type of pill is the progestogen-only pill (POPs). As the name implies, this contains only one hormone – progestogen. You may be able to use this pill under proper supervision from your GP or family planning clinic. You will need to remember that POPs are slightly less effective than COCs, that they tend to cause irregular bleeding, and that they need to be taken at about the same time of day every day: if you are at all absent-minded, then this will not be the best form of contraception for you. They probably do not cause any significant rise in blood pressure.

What does 'proper supervision' mean?

You should have your blood pressure carefully checked before you start taking any sort of oral contraceptive, and the doctor should review your medical history (after all, there may be other reasons why you should avoid oral contraceptives, not just that you have high blood pressure).

You should then have regular blood pressure checks all the time that you are on the pill: perhaps once a month for the first few months, and then every 3–6 months after that. The easiest arrangement to remember is to have it checked every time you collect your repeat prescription (doctors, practice nurses and their office staff are busy people and may easily forget to do this, so don't be afraid to remind them). You will also need to be sensible about any worries you may have (if you start having unusual headaches, for example, or unexplained leg pain) and report them to your doctor.

I was on a combined pill but my blood pressure went up a lot so I had to stop taking it. My doctor did check my blood pressure before I went on the pill, so why did she put me on it in the first place? And will I always have high blood pressure even though I've stopped taking it?

It is difficult for me to comment in detail without knowing your exact figures for your blood pressure before you started on the pill. If your figures were about average (say about 125/70 mmHg) and there is no history of high BP in your family, then your doctor had no way of knowing that the pill would have the effect it did on you. Even if your BP was in the borderline region for taking the combined pill (at about 140/90 mmHg), she still had no way of knowing exactly what would happen to you. By keeping a regular check on your blood pressure she was able to do the sensible thing, which was to take you off the pill as soon as your BP went up too high.

Will you always have high BP? Even very high blood pressure brought on by taking the pill falls rapidly to normal once you stop taking it. The only exception would be someone who has not had regular BP checks while on the pill, in which case high blood pressure might have continued for long enough to cause kidney damage, which would mean that the high BP was irreversible. The fact that your BP was high while you were on the pill may indicate that you have inherited the tendency to develop high blood pressure (does anyone else in your family have high blood pressure?), so you should be aware of this. It means that you should be sensible about what you eat and drink and how much exercise you take, and that you should not smoke. Your GP will advise you on how often you will need to have your BP checked.

Last time I was pregnant I had high blood pressure, although I don't have it normally. Can I take the pill?

Your doctor will probably be quite happy for you to take a progestogen-only pill (POP). Depending on your exact medical history, you may also be able to take a combined oral contraceptive (COC) providing that you do not smoke and have careful supervision, with your blood pressure being checked at very frequent intervals.

There is more information about high blood pressure in pregnancy in Chapter 8.

As I have high blood pressure, if I can't go on the pill, then what other forms of contraception can I use?

The only contraceptives where your high blood pressure has to be considered are those which involve hormones. The pill is obviously the most important of these, but there are others.

One is Depo-Provera (depot medroxyprogesterone acetate or DMPA), a form of progestogen given as an injection every three months or so. If you are considered suitable for progestogen-only pills (POPs) then you may be able to have this instead. Its use in the UK has been quite controversial, with some people expressing concern about side-effects (you cannot reverse the injection once it has been given, so any side-effects are bound to last for several weeks until the effects of the hormone wear off) and others finding it an excellent method of contraception. Anyone who wants to take Depo-Provera is required to have proper counselling before having their first injection, regardless of their blood pressure levels. It probably has no effect on blood pressure.

Other forms of hormonal contraceptive are less commonly available - they may be only available through certain clinics, or still be in the testing stage. They include a ring impregnated with progestogen that you insert into your vagina, slow release hormone implants (Norplant) that are placed under your skin, and a hormone-impregnated form of intra-uterine device (IUD). If you are offered any of these, you should mention your high blood pressure and discuss with the doctor whether or not they will be suitable for you, but I cannot see any reason why they should not be.

Emergency or post-coital contraception (popularly called the 'morning-after pill') contains the hormone oestrogen. Although this will be a high dose, it is given for too short a time to have any significant effect on blood pressure.

Apart from these hormonal contraceptives, your choice is as wide as anyone else's – you can use any of the barrier methods (condoms, the female condom, the diaphragm or cap, spermicides), or have a standard IUD (sometimes called a loop or a coil) fitted. If you have completed your family, you may want to consider sterilisation for yourself or a vasectomy for your partner. None of these methods will have any effect on your own or your partner's blood pressure.

The menopause

I've now started the menopause, and my high blood pressure was discovered when I first went to see my doctor about it. Has the menopause caused my high blood pressure?

No, it's simply coincidence. Most women have their last menstrual period between 48 and 53 years old, with 52 as the average age. Blood pressure rises with age and as (like you) many women consult their doctors around this time, so discovery of their high blood pressure often coincides with the menopause.

I have high blood pressure. When I reach my menopause, will I be more likely to have problems with hot flushes, night sweats or palpitations?

The first thing to remember is that not all women going through the menopause have the symptoms you mention, whether or not they also have high blood pressure. Certainly high blood pressure does not cause either hot flushes or night sweats.

People are normally unconscious of their heart beating, unless they are taking strenuous exercise (such as running) or are frightened (say having to make a public speech for the first time). Whatever the cause, when you become aware of your heart beating, then these obvious heartbeats are called palpitations. During the menopause your circulation becomes less stable, with unpredictable shifts of blood from one place to another, and equally unpredictable changes in heart rate. This can cause palpitations. Even if your blood pressure happens to be high, this is not in itself the cause of palpitations.

Occasionally, very high blood pressure may cause a rapid irregular heart beat, whether or not you are going through the menopause (it can also happen in men). If you listen to your heart beat or feel your pulse carefully, and the beats seem not to be regular, then you should see your doctor. Most of these apparently irregular beats are completely harmless, but you do need an examination by an experienced doctor to be sure of this.

Does HRT have any effect on blood pressure? I have high blood pressure, so can I use HRT safely and will it be effective?

HRT (hormone replacement therapy) is given to women who are suffering unpleasant symptoms because of the menopause. Symptoms caused directly by hormone insufficiency and relieved by HRT may include hot flushes, night sweats, vaginal dryness, and thinning of bone (osteoporosis). They vary enormously from one woman to another, and decisions about your treatment therefore must be tailored to your personal needs. The fact that you have high blood pressure should not affect your decision about whether or not you take HRT as it has no effect, up or down, on blood pressure, despite the fact that it contains oestrogen.

HRT is very effective in suppressing flushes and sweats for as long as you take it. If you stop taking it and your body has not yet got used to the normal drop in oestrogen hormones which occurs when you stop having periods, then the flushes and sweats will recur. It is also effective in preventing vaginal dryness, but if this is your only really troublesome symptom, you can do this just as well by using small quantities of an oestrogen vaginal cream. Very little of this is absorbed into your body, so you don't have to worry about any wider effects. If vaginal dryness is not treated at all (not even by using a little lubricant such as saliva or a product such as KY Jelly or Replens), then this may lead to loss of confidence and a gradual slide into sexual inactivity.

HRT prevents osteoporosis by stopping loss of calcium from bone. This is important for women with a light, slender bone structure, or with a family history of osteoporosis (if your mother or grandmother became crumpled up like a question mark in her old age then she probably had osteoporosis). However, if you have high blood pressure, treatment with thiazide diuretics will not only bring down your BP, but also reduce the output of calcium through your kidneys, thus preventing osteoporosis just as efficiently as HRT.

Controlled trials have shown that HRT has no effect at all on menopausal depression, probably because most depression at this time depends not on hormones, but the big life changes symbolised by no more periods, no more children, and facing up to the meanings of marriage stripped down to its original two actors, without any supporting cast.

There is some evidence that HRT may reduce the risks of coronary heart disease (and if you have high blood pressure, your risks of this are increased). We are not sure about this, as the proper trials have yet to be started, let alone completed. However, even if HRT does turn out not do much good for your heart, on present evidence we can be reasonably sure that it won't do it any harm.

Miscellaneous

If I move to a new area, or for any other reason need to change my doctor, how do I go about choosing a new one to treat my high blood pressure? And how soon will the new practice get my medical records?

Your local Health Authority and the Community Health Council for your area (addresses in your phone book) can both give you information about local GPs – who they are, when they qualified, whether it is a fund-holding practice, and so on. It is then up to you to find out more about them: you can always ring up a practice and ask if they have a doctor who takes a keen interest in high blood pressure. Many practices now issue leaflets which tell you more about the doctors and other health professionals working there, surgery hours, and all the other things you may want to know. If you want to know what other people think about a particular GP, then you will have to ask around – neighbours, people in the Post Office, and nurses at local hospitals are all good sources of opinion about local practices, but it is seldom wise to rely on just one person's word.

It usually takes about three months, but may take much longer, for your new practice to get your records – it depends on the efficiency of your former GP and the Health Authorities involved. It is probably wise to ask your former doctor (or the practice manager if there is one) to let you have either a photocopy of the relevant parts of your medical record, or a computer print-out if their records are largely computer-held. You can then hand this directly to your new doctor as soon as you move.

If I'm going to be on BP-lowering drugs for a long time, then do I still have to pay prescription charges?

Needing BP-lowering drugs regularly does not qualify you as exempt from prescription charges. However, you may be exempt for other reasons – because of your age, because of some other medical condition (eg diabetes), because you are pregnant, or because you are on income support or have a low income. (If you are on a low income you will need to fill in an AG1 form from the Department of Social Security and they will then consider your application.)

If you are not exempt but still need a lot of prescriptions, then it may be worth considering pre-paying your prescription charges by buying a 'season ticket' for a four or 12 month period. This season ticket will cover all your prescription charges, not just those for your BP-lowering drugs. Before you go ahead and get one, you need to do a careful calculation, based on the current price of ordinary prescriptions, the price of season tickets, and your average number of prescriptions in a year, to see whether a season ticket will be worth it for you. If you decide to go ahead and buy one, you will need to fill in form FP95 which is available from most doctors' surgeries, from pharmacies, from

Post Offices or from your local Health Authority (address in your local phone book).

You may also be interested to know that at the current cost of NHS prescriptions, some BP-lowering drugs are actually cheaper bought direct from your chemist on a private prescription, so it may be worth asking about this.

Will my blood pressure be affected by how much sleep I get?

Waking blood pressure seems to be unaffected by sleep, but as blood pressure falls profoundly during sleep in most people with high blood pressure, wear and tear on their arteries may be reduced by spending more time asleep.

Can I carry heavy shopping?

In this case most of the hard work is done by your legs, and is good exercise – but very unpleasant. It should not affect your blood pressure. Why not use a wheeled shopping trolley and get your exercise is some other way?

Can I drive safely when I am on BP-lowering drugs?

Some drugs used to lower BP can make you drowsy, and this may cause problems for some drivers. The problem is most likely to arise with the drugs acting mainly on the brainstem and some of the beta-blockers, although all BP-lowering drugs can cause some drowsiness in some people. All the drugs which do make people drowsy will do so much more if they are combined with alcohol. The possibility of fainting may be another problem, particularly with adrenergic neurone blockers or alpha blockers. (There is more information about all these drugs in Appendix 1.)

The answer is (of course) to be sensible – if you know your drugs make you drowsy or faint, then don't drive. If they don't have this effect, then you can obviously continue driving.

It may be worth mentioning here that beta-blockers have been effectively prescribed for people nervous about taking their driving test, because of the calming effect that they have.

Are there any support groups or self-help organisations for people with high blood pressure?

Not specifically that I know of. However, some of the medical charities and similar organisations have a strong interest in high blood pressure, often because their main field of interest is in some way associated with it or its consequences (eg the British Heart Foundation, the Stroke Association, the British Diabetic Association). Their addresses, and those of other potentially useful organisations, are given in Appendix 2.

8
Pregnancy

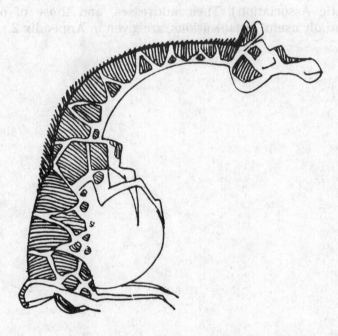

High blood pressure in pregnancy

Does blood pressure change in pregnancy?

Yes, it normally falls during pregnancy. If it rises, this is always important, because it may indicate that you have pre-eclampsia or eclampsia (the next section in this chapter deals with both these conditions). That's why nurses, doctors, and midwives keep measuring your blood pressure all through your pregnancy.

Pregnancy

Pregnancy normally lasts between 38 and 42 weeks. This is usually divided into three periods of development, called trimesters. The first 13 weeks (the first trimester) roughly corresponds to the time when the baby is being formed. The second trimester is from 14 to 27 weeks: it used to be the time when the baby was thought to be too immature to survive, but now some babies as young as 24 weeks do survive with intensive neonatal care. Babies were considered able to survive if they were born during the third trimester (which runs from 28 weeks of pregnancy until the birth), although before modern intensive care many failed to do so.

From whatever level it starts, your blood pressure normally falls during the second trimester (from 14 to 27 weeks). It then usually rises slowly until your baby is born (which is normally at 38 to 42 weeks) although it may still be a bit lower than before you became pregnant. After your baby is born your blood pressure rises slowly over the first five days to regain its usual level before your pregnancy.

Why does blood pressure usually fall in pregnancy?

When you are pregnant, not only do you need oxygen, but so does your developing baby. Your body therefore makes more blood to carry enough oxygen for both of you, so the total volume of your blood rises rapidly during the first 12 to 13 weeks of your pregnancy. All other things being equal, a rise in blood volume should cause a rise in blood pressure. To prevent this, your placenta (which nourishes your baby in your womb, links your blood supply with your baby's, and is expelled in the afterbirth following the birth of your baby) releases hormones (mainly progesterone) which relax the walls of your veins and small arteries so that they become larger to make room for this increased blood volume, without any rise in your blood pressure. Because of this your heart doesn't have to pump so hard and your blood pressure falls.

Because your blood vessels are relaxed, they do not respond as quickly to instructions from your brain, so blood may remain in your legs when you get up out of a chair. Your BP then falls, and you may feel dizzy or faint. All this usually happens in the first 12 weeks or so when your circulation is changing most rapidly, but even later in pregnancy you may find yourself feeling faint in a hot room or if you get up too quickly from lying down.

When I'm pregnant, how high must my blood pressure be to be called high blood pressure?

A blood pressure of 140/90 mmHg or more is conventionally considered to be high blood pressure in pregnancy. The significance of these figure will depend on whether you high blood pressure is new (ie developing for the first time in your pregnancy) or whether it was already high before you became pregnant.

Why is it important to know if my raised blood pressure developed before I became pregnant or whether it is something new?

The difference between pregnancy in women with high blood pressure (ie having raised BP before you became pregnant) and high blood pressure starting in pregnancy (ie developing a raised BP after you become pregnant) is simply the rate of change of your blood pressure. Ordinary high blood pressure starts very slowly, in childhood or adolescence, with plenty of time for every part of your body to get used to it. High blood pressure developing for the first time during pregnancy develops over a very short time, never more than a few weeks and occasionally even over a few hours. During this time you may get very serious damage to your small arteries, particularly in the kidneys and brain (this is eclampsia, which is discussed in more detail in the next section in this chapter). The same kinds of damage may occur in ordinary high blood pressure, but only at much higher levels of blood pressure, and usually over much longer periods of time.

If I get high blood pressure during my pregnancy, who should look after it, my GP or my obstetrician?

If your blood pressure rises for the first time during pregnancy, and you didn't have high blood pressure before you were pregnant, then your obstetrician will take the decisions about your treatment, although your GP also needs to know what medication (if any) you are taking. Because blood pressure can change very quickly in pregnancy, your GP (or someone else in the primary care team looking after you, perhaps your midwife) should check your blood pressure if at any time you feel ill, have pain in the upper part of your abdomen, or a prolonged headache. Your antenatal clinic should give you your maternity notes so that you can shown them to anyone you need to consult, although in some areas you may instead be given a card called a shared-care card on which all this information can be recorded. Don't forget to take your notes with you whenever you go to the clinic or to see your GP.

Not many women are both young enough to be pregnant and at the same time old enough to have blood pressure high enough to need BP-lowering medication. This means that not many obstetricians see women with long-standing high blood pressure, who have already had treatment for it for months or years. If you are one of these women then you need joint care, intelligently shared between your GP or your hospital physician (this choice probably depending on which of them has shown most interest in your BP), your obstetrician, and your midwife. Because your medication is likely to be changed during your pregnancy, you will need more frequent BP measurements than most women, and they will need to be very accurate.

I'm in my first pregnancy, and my blood pressure has gone up a bit. My doctor says she'll keep an eye on it but that I don't need any drugs for it yet. If I do need to take BP-lowering drugs, when will I start on them?

You don't say either what your blood pressure is, or how far on you are in your pregnancy, so we can't give you a specific answer. Speaking generally, if blood pressure rises for the first time after 36 weeks of pregnancy, then it is usually best to deliver the baby, so labour is induced (brought on) early. If BP starts rising between 24 and 28 weeks, doctors often try to control it with BP-lowering drugs so that the baby is more mature when born and has a better chance of surviving. Doctors vary in their opinions on how high your BP should be before you start treatment. There is good evidence that treatment benefits both mother and baby when BP measures 160/100 mmHg or more. However, these decisions also depend on whether or not there is any evidence of kidney damage: if there is, this will show up as protein in your urine (something which is checked for during your regular urine tests).

We hear a lot about how drugs taken in pregnancy can damage unborn babies – I'm especially thinking of thalidomide, but I know there are others. Can BP-lowering drugs be safely taken in pregnancy?

The time when we are most concerned about drugs affecting the foetus (the unborn baby) is in early pregnancy. Your pregnancy begins before you miss your period, but for the first week when the fertilized egg is moving down your fallopian tube it is probably not at risk from drugs in your bloodstream. Women who are planning a pregnancy are advised to take extra folic acid (a vitamin which plays an important part in the development of the foetus) for three months before stopping using contraceptives and for the first three months of pregnancy. If you are taking BP-lowering drugs, then it is during this time that you should discuss with your GP (or whoever else is looking after your blood pressure) whether or not you need to change your type of drug. After the first three months of pregnancy the baby is mostly just growing, and is much less vulnerable to any effects from drugs.

Ever since thalidomide (which, incidentally, was a sleeping tablet – it was NOT a BP-lowering drug), all drugs have been tested on animals (mostly rabbits or rats) to see if they may cause organ damage to the foetus during pregnancy. Because very large numbers of animals can be used, these tests are fairly sensitive, but because they are not on humans, we can never be entirely sure they exclude risks to a human foetus.

Thousands of women and babies have been checked for evidence of foetal damage from drugs taken in pregnancy and, on the whole, these studies have been reassuring. None of the BP-lowering drugs in common use have been shown to produce foetal damage, although many women have conceived while taking their regular BP-lowering medication. Foetal damage on the same scale as that caused by thalidomide is certainly not occurring now from any of the BP-lowering drugs.

However, we do know that for all drugs at all times (not just in pregnancy), any harmful events which happen to fewer than 1% of the people who take them are in practice virtually undetectable by even the best and largest-possible trials. Although damage on the scale of thalidomide is certainly not happening, serious damage to as few as one baby in every 1000 born is possible. As this is the same frequency as death from eclampsia (discussed in the next section in this chapter and the event which all treatment for high blood pressure in pregnancy aims to prevent) we have to take this risk seriously, while at the same time not being alarmist about it.

What does this mean in practice? In my opinion, for women of reproductive age, this means remembering three things. First, don't accept medication with BP-lowering drugs unless your raised BP is serious enough to justify this (bearing in mind that most of the risks of high blood pressure are much less in women than men); second, plan your pregnancies; and third, consider (with advice from an interested and well-informed doctor) the possibilty of temporarily interrupting your treatment with BP-lowering drugs during the weeks when you are attempting to conceive and during the first 13 weeks of your pregnancy.

I am 35 years old, and have just missed my first period in my third pregnancy. I have had rather a high BP for the last five years, and my GP thinks I ought to start treatment. How should this decision be influenced by my pregnancy?

A lot depends on how often your blood pressure has been measured, and exactly how high the readings are. Providing the average of your last three BP readings was not more than about 160/100 mmHg, and providing you have regular weekly measurements of your BP throughout your pregnancy, then you and your baby will probably do better if you put off starting any BP-lowering drugs until after the birth. If, however, your average BP has been much higher than this, or if your BP rises during your pregnancy, then balance of advantage will probably shift to your starting on BP-lowering treatment.

If you have to start treatment during your pregnancy, then the next thing to decide is which are the most suitable BP-lowering drugs for you to take. You will obviously want to avoid any drugs which could cause any risk to you or to your baby. This means that diuretics, often the first choice for medication for high BP, are ruled out because they may make pre-eclampsia worse (pre-eclampsia is discussed in the next section in this chapter), and they can also cross the placenta and reach the unborn baby. Beta-blockers are well tolerated and apparently without risk to the baby after the 24th week (before this, they may slow down the baby's growth, and should be avoided if possible). The drugs which really need to be avoided for your baby's sake belong to two groups which are anyway much less commonly prescribed for high BP: the ACE-inhibitors and the calcium-channel blockers. As you will see from Appendix 1 (where there is more information about all these drugs) that still leaves you and your doctor with plenty of choices.

Pre-eclampsia and eclampsia

I presume 'pre-eclampsia' just means 'before eclampsia', but what exactly is eclampsia?

The word eclampsia comes from the Latin, and literally means 'flashing lights'. In practice it means fits (seizures) caused by brain damage, caused in turn by very high blood pressure that develops very fast, usually in late pregnancy. Anyone suffering eclampsia sees flashing lights just before a fit begins: hence the name. Soon after this, the sufferer suddenly loses consciousness, her whole body shakes symmetrically and uncontrollably, with clenched teeth and severe spasm of all muscles, all for only a minute or two but seeming much longer.

Eclampsia is very dangerous both to the mother and to the unborn child. Before modern antenatal care, deaths from eclampsia in pregnancy were common. They still happen, although very rarely – only in 10 pregnancies in every million.

In nearly all cases eclampsia is preceded by pre-eclampsia – either by several weeks of slowly rising blood pressure, or by dramatic warning signs (mainly pain in the upper abdomen caused by congestion of the liver), or by severe persistent headache. The existence of these changes and warning signs mean that nearly all eclampsia can be prevented by good antenatal care. Because pregnancy is now normally well-supervised, eclampsia has become very rare, and when it occurs, it may indicate a serious breakdown in health care.

Eclampsia is treated by urgent admission to hospital, by giving drugs to control BP and seizures, and delivering the baby as quickly as possible, after which BP usually falls rapidly to normal without any other treatment.

In my last pregnancy one doctor said I had PIH, another said I had PRH, and the midwife said I had PET. What was going on?

Once upon a time eclampsia and pre-eclampsia were together called toxaemia of pregnancy. At that time there was no attempt to separate several different conditions affecting pregnant women, some of which were caused by problems unrelated to high blood pressure. In recent years doctors have tried to make things clearer (or at least more specific) by trying out different names for high blood pressure in pregnancy. Toxaemia is a term rarely heard today, but pre-eclamptic toxaemia (PET) is still used. Pregnancy-induced hypertension (PIH), pregnancy-related hypertension (PRH), pregnancy-associated hypertension (PAH), hypertension-oedema-proteinurea syndrome (HOP), hypertensive disease of pregnancy (HDP) and gestosis are names which all mean the same thing: blood pressure that is raised during the latter part of pregnancy and which gets better after the baby is born.

If we must use abbreviations, the most sensible would seem to be PE (for pre-eclampsia), because eclampsia is real, and is what we are trying to prevent. However, if there is no protein in the urine then you may well find the abbreviations PIH or PRH being used, and many doctors and midwives use PET (pre-eclamptic toxaemia) when there is protein in the urine (there are questions about protein in urine later in this section).

What is fulminating pre-eclampsia?

Fulminating is yet another word that comes from the Latin, and roughly means 'like lightning'. It can be applied to any illness or condition (not just pre-eclampsia) when it occurs suddenly and with great intensity (in other words, one which strikes like lightning).

Fulminating pre-eclampsia happens very rarely, but when it does, it is an emergency. The term is used to describe the extremely rapid development of pre-eclampsia, over hours or days rather than the more usual weeks. In this rare emergency, blood pressure rises rapidly, large and increasing amounts of protein are passed in urine, and the woman retains fluid so that her face swells up visibly over a few hours. When this happens, her brain also becomes swollen, and she is then in immediate danger of eclamptic fits. Drugs will be used to bring down her BP and to prevent fits, and her baby will be delivered as soon as possible either by inducing labour or by caesarean section. Recent research has shown that the best available treatment for women who develop an eclamptic fit is with magnesium given into a vein or into a muscle. This hospital treatment decreases the risk of further fits and reduces the danger to both mother and baby.

Does anyone know what causes pre-eclampsia and eclampsia?

We still do not know the fundamental cause of pre-eclampsia (and it is said that there will be a Nobel Prize for the person who discovers it). I think when we do understand the cause we will find that we should actually be talking about causes in the plural. We already know there are different patterns to pre-eclampsia, which may have different underlying causes.

However we do know that, as with 'ordinary' high blood pressure, there is an inherited tendency for pre-eclampsia to run in families, which is why midwives and doctors ask you about blood pressure in your relatives, particularly in your mother or sisters. Pre-eclampsia is also more common in first pregnancies, in women over 40, and in people who already have raised blood pressure before they get pregnant.

Pre-eclampsia is somehow related to the placenta. The placenta has its own arteries. In pre-eclampsia these arteries do not penetrate the wall of the uterus (womb) so well as in women without pre-eclampsia, and they seem to be narrowed by plaques of cholesterol and blood clots in much the same way as the coronary and leg arteries are in 'ordinary' high blood pressure. This reduces placental blood supply, which somehow induces raised blood pressure throughout the body, with reduced blood flow through the liver and kidneys (untreated, this can lead to kidney failure). The way the blood clots may also be affected and, again if untreated, may prevent blood clotting altogether, leading to severe bleeding before, during or immediately after the birth.

All these changes sound frightening, but they are rare in modern practice, with regular antenatal supervision and prompt action at the first signs of pre-eclampsia.

How likely is it that I will get pre-eclampsia in my first pregnancy?

In Western countries, where almost all women are well nourished, about 5% of women expecting their first babies will get pre-eclampsia. In most women it will be in a mild form, but about one woman in 250 may get more severe symptoms.

In some studies as many as a quarter of all women have been found to have some rise in blood pressure during their first pregnancy, instead of the expected fall. However, as we have seen in other parts of this book (especially Chapter 3 on *Measuring high blood pressure*) the accuracy and reliability of BP readings can be affected by many different things, so these rises may be because of anxiety or the number of different people taking the blood pressure measurements.

I had pre-eclampsia in my first pregnancy, am I likely to get it again?

About one woman in 50 (ie about 2%) with mild pre-eclampsia

in a first pregnancy and about 7.5% of those who had it severely go on to get severe pre-eclampsia in their second pregnancies. About one-third of all women who had PE in their first pregnancies (regardless of whether it was mild or severe) get mild PE in their second.

Or, looking at it the other way, two-thirds of those with severe PE and nearly three-quarters of those with mild PE have no problems with raised blood pressure in their second pregnancies.

I would like to start a family, but I'm worried that I may get pre-eclampsia when I get pregnant as I already have high blood pressure. Am I at greater risk than women of my age who don't already have high BP?

Yes, but we don't know by exactly how much. Depending on your age, weight and family history, your risk of pre-eclampsia can be anything from twice to 10 times that of a woman who did not have raised BP at the beginning of her pregnancy.

The truth is that because most obstetricians over the past 50 years or so have worked from hospitals, they often don't have much information about women's BPs before their pregnancies began. If women are not seen for antenatal care until they are well into their pregnancies at 15–20 weeks (which is still fairly common in women at the highest risk of pre-eclampsia), and if nobody looks at their previous medical records (or if these records contain no useful information about BP), then there is simply no way of knowing whether a rather high BP is recent and important, or is of long standing and therefore much less important. A lot of research on this subject has been weakened by this lack of information, so any conclusions have to remain rather uncertain.

The moral of this is that if any doctor or nurse has at any time been concerned about your blood pressure, you should make sure the details of this concern are available to whichever professionals become responsible for advising you during your pregnancy.

My mother and my sister both had pre-eclampsia in their

first pregnancies. I've head that it runs in families, so what are my chances of having it?

Most of the work on the inheritance of pre-eclampsia has been carried out by an American obstetrician called Chesley. In his research he found that of 248 women whose mothers had had an eclamptic fit, one in four got PE in their first pregnancy, and one in 50 of these women had an eclamptic fit, so their risk was increased 20-fold. When you look at these figures you do need to remember that these women were having babies in the 1930s and 1940s, and their daughters were having their babies in the 1960s and 1970s. Much has changed in the last 20 to 30 years, so we would expect the chances of developing PE or eclampsia to be less today, with our improved antenatal care and earlier inductions when PE does occur.

The chance of sisters getting either PE or eclampsia is much less. And as its inheritance is through the female line, any problems in a husband's or partner's mother's pregnancies are irrelevant.

It would be sensible for you to tell your obstetrician and the other people caring for you during your pregnancy about this family history of pre-eclampsia. The more they know about your medical history and background, the better they can look after you.

If I do develop pre-eclampsia, will it harm my baby?

The risk to your baby is from prematurity. Pre-eclampsia may cause premature birth, usually with a birthweight under 2.5 kg (5 lb 8 oz), or your baby may need to be induced early to protect you, the mother. Either way, depending on the degree of prematurity, this does slightly increase the risk of harm to your baby. Babies who are very immature may need special care in a neonatal intensive care unit.

I had eclampsia in my first pregnancy and was very ill. I would like to have another baby but I'm scared that it will happen again. What are the chances that I will get eclampsia next time?

Eclampsia is rare. Of the 10 women who had it in the largest research study so far reported, none had eclampsia in their second pregnancy, eight had normal blood pressure and two had mild pre-eclampsia. If you developed kidney failure because of your eclampsia then it would be worth asking your doctor to check your kidney function – this will involve doing a 24 hour urine collection test and having an ultrasound scan to check the size of your kidneys. If these tests are normal your risk of getting eclampsia or severe PE are very small. Some studies suggest that a good diet may reduce the risk of PE and eclampsia, so you might also like to arrange to see a dietitian to discuss this.

Diagnosing and treating PE

If I already had high blood pressure before my pregnancy, how can they recognise if I develop pre-eclampsia?

Blood pressure normally falls during pregnancy (see the answers to the first two questions in this chapter for more about this) even in a woman who already had high blood pressure before she became pregnant (like you). Whatever your starting point, a rise above your pre-pregnancy BP level would be a cause for concern, and would alert your doctor or midwife to the possibility of pre-eclampsia.

For those women for whom good pre-pregnancy BP measurements are not available, then BP measurements taken later in pregnancy can be compared with the readings taken early in pregnancy. Research suggests that a diastolic pressure rising by more than 15 mmHg or a systolic pressure rising by more than 30 mmHg indicate a cause for concern.

Does a doctor deciding that you have pre-eclampsia depend only on high blood pressure measurements, or do they rely on other evidence as well?

Your BP readings are important but yes, they do take other evidence into account. Pre-eclampsia will be suspected if your BP is 140/90 mmHg or more and is known to have been less than this before your pregnancy began, and/or if there is protein in your urine, and/or if you have some swelling of your whole body from increased fluid (oedema). Although most pregnant women will have some mild oedema (usually affecting their ankles and legs), protein in your urine and more severe oedema indicate that raised blood pressure has caused some kidney damage. These are the earliest changes in the sequence of events which may, untreated, end with eclampsia.

You are considered to have mild PE if your diastolic pressure is between 90 and 99 mmHg, moderate PE if it is in the range 100-109 mmHg, and severe PE if it is 110 mmHg or more. If you have significant amounts of protein in your urine then PE is considered to be severe whatever the level of your blood pressure.

Does protein in the urine always mean that a woman has pre-eclampsia?

No. A bladder or kidney infection may also cause protein to appear in your urine, so the urine sample you provide should also be checked for infection. The urine tested needs to be a 'clean catch' or 'midstream' specimen, otherwise the germs which normally live in the vagina may be washed into the collecting tube and cause the sensitive urine testing strips (dipsticks) to give a false positive result. You provide a midstream (MSU) specimen by passing a little urine first before you collect your sample in the container provided.

Sometimes you may be asked to collect all the urine you pass in 24 hours, to measure the total protein lost in your urine throughout the day. This should be less than 300 mg in 24 hours. Some people lose protein from their kidneys from time to time, without this signifying any damage.

Why is there protein in the urine in pre-eclampsia?

Urine normally contains only water with a large variety of rather simple waste products (mainly urea and salt) dissolved in it. Proteins (which are large and complex chemical molecules) are normally filtered out and retained by your kidneys, and so do not appear in your urine.

When blood pressure rises for the first time in pregnancy, it rises much faster than 'ordinary' high blood pressure in people who are not pregnant. Even though the actual level of raised blood pressure may not be very high, because it has happened quickly, your kidneys have had less time to adapt to the new higher level and so are more easily damaged. The effect of even minor damage is that your kidneys begin to leak protein into your urine. The amount of protein in your urine is roughly proportional to the severity of the damage to your kidneys.

My legs got very swollen the last time I was pregnant, so my GP was a bit concerned about pre-eclampsia, but stopped worrying when my BP and urine tests turned out to be OK. Please can you explain what was happening?

In severe pre-eclampsia, so much protein may be lost in the urine that the level of protein in blood falls. The blood cannot then retain all the water it contains; some leaks through the walls of the capillaries (the smallest blood vessels) to other parts of your body, making them swell (oedema or, as it used to be called, dropsy). Because water tends to fall to the lowest point, this swelling first becomes obvious in your legs.

However, swollen legs are extremely common in pregnancy, and usually have nothing to do with pre-eclampsia. Anything which obstructs the flow of blood up your leg veins can cause raised blood pressure in your veins (not your arteries, and arterial blood pressure is what we are concerned with in pre-eclampsia). Fluid can then leak out of the veins into the skin, causing the same signs of oedema. The most obvious cause of such obstruction is the pregnant uterus (womb), and in late pregnancy some degree of oedema is almost inevitable in almost every pregnant woman. It can happen earlier in pregnancy in women who are overweight, or wear tight clothing, or stand for hours on end.

All these common causes of swollen legs can be distinguished from pre-eclampsia because they are not accompanied by protein in the urine.

Finally, don't forget that if only one leg swells, or one leg swells more than the other, the cause may be a deep vein blocked by a clot, a common and important complication of late pregnancy which may need urgent treatment. See your doctor or midwife if you think this is happening.

Can I do anything to lessen my chance of getting pre-eclampsia?

Perhaps, as there is some evidence that a healthy diet may help. Research work carried out in Canada during and in Australia after World War II suggested that careful attention to diet reduced the risk of PE. In Scotland one obstetrician advised women to eat a high protein, low carbohydrate diet, and induced their babies. PE and eclampsia were reduced, and so was the average birthweight and caesarean section rate. An American doctor, Dr Brewer, also believes that a high protein diet protects against the development of pre-eclampsia. Results of all this research are not completely clear because most of these studies were not randomised controlled trials (see Chapter 10 for an explanation of these types of trials). Opinions on just what constitutes a healthy diet have also changed in recent years, and the recommendations now are that for our general health we should all eat more of the high carbohydrate, high fibre foods (wholemeal breads and cereal, pasta, pulses, fruit and vegetables and so on – see Chapter 5 for more information) rather than cutting down on them.

So the best we can say is that eating a well balanced diet and having a normal weight before you try to get pregnant may help – it certainly won't do you any harm. (If you need any help with this, you could ask your doctor to refer you to a dietitian for individual advice.) We also know that stress can affect blood pressure in some people, and that pregnant women usually need more rest than they did before they were pregnant, so consider how to modify your working life if these are problems for you.

Would cutting down on salt help?

Women are still sometimes told to reduce their salt intake if their blood pressure rises in pregnancy. As with other nutrients, salt is needed in larger quantities during pregnancy and a controlled study in 1958 showed that restricting salt intake was ineffective. You can use salt as usual in cooking and add it to your food to your own taste. However, you may wish to remember that in this country we all eat far more salt than we need, so there is certainly no need for you to increase the amount you eat. You will find more information about salt in the section on **Sodium and salt** in Chapter 5.

If I do develop pre-eclampsia, is there a way for my doctors to treat it or even cure it?

Pre-eclampsia stops when the baby is born. In late pregnancy it can therefore be treated by starting labour early (induction) or by a planned or emergency caesarean section (an operation to deliver the baby through the abdomen) before labour starts.

Although severe, rapidly progressing pre-eclampsia can occasionally begin at 24-26 weeks into the pregnancy, this is very uncommon. Most women who get it develop a mild form of the disease at 34-36 weeks with small amounts of protein in the urine, and diastolic BP (the second of the two BP figures) in the 90-100 mmHg range. They usually do well if labour is induced a little early and deliver good sized babies, who can stay with their mothers on the ward. Babies who are very immature may need special care in a neonatal intensive care unit. Depending on how far you are on in your pregnancy, or whether this is your first or a later pregnancy, labour may be induced either by breaking your waters (called artificial rupture of membranes, or ARM) or by using prostaglandin (PG) pessaries or gel inserted into the vagina. Synthetic oxytocin (Syntocinon) may be used to make the uterus contract if labour does not start after the ARM or PG pessary. Sometimes this may be given immediately the ARM has been done.

If your obstetrician decides that your PE needs drug treatment, then the BP-lowering drugs they are most likely to use are either methyldopa or beta-blockers. Methyldopa is an old drug which, although it does have some side-effects, has a good track record for safety and effectiveness at all stages of pregnancy. Beta-blockers are well tolerated and apparently without risk to the baby after 24 weeks (before this they may slow down the baby's growth and so should be avoided, but as PE rarely starts before 24 weeks this is not usually a problem). If these drugs are ineffective then most obstetricians would admit women with pre-eclampsia to hospital for treatment with hydralazine (a vasodilator drug), either by tablets or, in an emergency, by an injection into a vein. You will find more information about all these drugs in Appendix 1.

I've heard that taking aspirin can prevent pre-eclampsia. I had pre-eclampsia in my first pregnancy, so should I start taking aspirin now that I'm pregnant again?

No, for two reasons. The first (and most obvious) is that self-medication can be dangerous. The second is that a number of clinical trials have shown that aspirin is unlikely to be effective in preventing pre-eclampsia. The theory behind the trials was that aspirin would help prevent blood clots in the placenta, but we now know from the results that taking it has no beneficial effects. The only possible exception to this might be in those very few women with very severe pre-eclampsia which had started early in a previous pregnancy: if this is what happened to you, then you may want to discuss it further with your obstetrician.

We used to be told that rest in bed was the most important treatment for pre-eclampsia, but obstetricians and midwives today don't seem so concerned about this. Can you explain this?

Research studies have compared pregnant women with PE treated by traditional bed rest in hospital with similar women who simply took things easy at home – and have shown no difference at all in how well they (and their babies) got on. Physical and mental rest are important, but many women get more rest if they are allowed up and about in their own homes than if they are compelled to lie in a hospital bed. However, women with pre-eclampsia who are being treated at home do need careful supervision, and should have their BP measured and their urine tested for protein at least once a day, and should be admitted to hospital immediately if they get abdominal pains or headaches.

9
Long-term consequences and complications

What can go wrong

Why do we need to know about all these dreadful complications? I think it just frightens people to know about what can go wrong.

The only reason anyone needs treatment for high blood pressure is to prevent the possible complications discussed in this chapter. Today many people like to be fully informed about their health and to be able to discuss all aspects of their condition

Long-term consequences and complications

with the professionals involved in their care. They find it less frightening to know what might happen, how to prevent it and how to recognise when something is going wrong than to treat possible complications as a taboo subject which can never be mentioned. That is why this chapter describes all the awful things that can happen to people with uncontrolled high blood pressure. Please remember that even if you have no treatment at all, it is most unlikely that any of them will happen to you in the next few days, weeks, or even years, and few of them will ever happen at all. Still, one day we all have to die of something, and most people with fairly severe high blood pressure do eventually die from one or other of the conditions discussed here. If you get good advice and follow it conscientiously, you can greatly reduce your risks and postpone them for many years (that after all is the whole point of having treatment, and of reading this book), but you will also be in the happy or unhappy position (depending how you look at it) of knowing what is most likely to happen eventually.

How does high blood pressure cause damage?

Imagine a fluid flowing through a tube which tapers at the end (after all, blood is a fluid, and arteries are basically tubes which get smaller as they go further from the heart). If the fluid flows through at a higher pressure than the tube walls can cope with, then you can expect one of two consequences: the walls of the tube may be damaged with pieces breaking off which block the tube or its tapered outlet, or the whole tube may burst. These correspond to the two ways in which high blood pressure may harm arteries and the organs to which the arteries supply blood: we can call them 'blocking effects' and 'bursting effects'. This is obviously a considerable simplification of the actual processes involved, but a great help in understanding them.

Although arteries do behave in some ways like the plastic or copper tubes used for plumbing, they are different in that they are made of living material which is able, within limits, to adapt to higher pressure – providing it is not impossibly high and rises relatively slowly (over months or years rather than hours, days or weeks). Arteries are usually elastic enough to cope with very high pressures indeed, if these are sustained only for an hour or two of exertion.

The blocking effects of high blood pressure therefore develop slowly, over many years. Waxy plaques made of a mixture of clotted blood and cholesterol thicken the artery walls and make the artery linings more irregular, with the plaque piling up at points where the lining has been damaged. A large clot may form at such a point, become detached and spin off into the bloodstream (when it is called an embolus) and may then travel into – and block completely – a small artery (a process called embolism). Blocking effects therefore include the gradual narrowing or eventual complete blockage of arteries by clots, or their sudden obstruction by an embolism, both of which reduce or stop the flow of blood to all or part of the organs the affected arteries supply. Blocking effects depend not only on high blood pressure, but also on high blood cholesterol (there is a section on **High blood cholesterol** in Chapter 6) and tobacco smoking.

Bursting effects occur mainly in the arterioles (the smallest arteries) with the weakest walls, usually just where they divide into the network of capillaries (the smallest type of blood vessel) supplying blood to various body organs. They generally result from very high blood pressure, usually sustained for many years, and often with a very rapid recent rise in pressure over a few days or weeks so that the arteries either have insufficient time to adapt to high pressures, or the pressure is too extreme for even an adapted artery to contain it.

Where do these blocking and bursting effects happen? Do they affect different parts of the body in different ways?

The simplest way to answer your question is with a couple of lists, which don't make very pleasant reading. However, as you read them, remember that after a few years of treatment your chances of developing any of them will be reduced: the risk will become roughly proportional to the lower blood pressure level you will have reached with your treatment, not to the higher level you had before your treatment started. And to repeat what I have already said earlier in this chapter – even if you have no treatment at all, it is most unlikely that any of them will happen

Long-term consequences and complications

to you in the next few days, weeks, or even years, and few of them will ever happen at all.

Blocking effects

- **Heart**
  Partial blocking of the coronary arteries (the blood vessels supplying the heart) causes pain in the front of the chest when walking up hills or stairs (angina).

  Complete blockage of a coronary artery destroys part of the heart muscle (a 'heart attack', coronary thrombosis or myocardial infarction – these terms are usually used interchangeably).

- **Aorta**
  The aorta is the largest of all the arteries in the body, and normally the most elastic. After years of high blood pressure and high blood cholesterol it becomes less elastic, with its lining roughened by plaque, and stretches to produce a swelling (aneurysm) rather like a sausage-shaped balloon, usually in the upper abdomen. Blood clots may form on this roughened aortic lining, gradually building up to an inch or more in depth. Such a clot may break loose as an embolus, which may lodge further down in an artery supplying a kidney, or in a thigh artery, interrupting the blood supply to one kidney or leg.

- **Legs and feet**
  Partial blocking by plaque of the arteries in the lower trunk or thigh causes pains in the calf on walking uphill (claudication).

  Complete blockage of the leg arteries (either from an embolus originating in the aorta or from clots forming in the thigh arteries) causes gangrene in the toes or foot.

- **Brain**
  Roughening of the carotid arteries (on both sides of the front of the neck) may cause a build-up of blood clots, which may break up intermittently into very small fragments (called micro-emboli). These travel up to the brain, causing a

temporary loss of vision as they pass through the retina (the back of the eye), and giddiness, faintness or confusion lasting a few seconds (transient ischaemic attacks, or TIAs). They then break up into such small particles that they cause no further trouble.

If a blood clot in a carotid artery fails to break up into micro-emboli, but instead travels intact as a large embolus up into the brain, it may completely block the supply of blood to part of the brain, causing an embolic stroke.

Kinking of partially blocked arteries in the back of the neck, provoked by looking upwards and tilting the head backwards on the neck (as when hanging out washing or looking up at an aeroplane) may cause temporary blackouts or giddiness lasting a few seconds (vertebrobasilar insufficiency).

- Eyes

For reasons not fully understood, but presumably connected with changes in blood circulation, people with high blood pressure are more likely than others to develop obstructed arterial circulation in the eye (central retinal artery occlusion), obstructed veins in the eye (central retinal venous thrombosis) or retinal detachment. All these are less likely to occur when high blood pressure is well controlled by treatment.

- Other organs

Virtually any other organ in the body can have its blood supply impaired or stopped by all these blocking effects of high blood pressure, but serious effects are rare except in exceptional circumstances.

Bursting effects

- Heart

High blood pressure means extremely hard work for the heart, which has to pump against the increased resistance of a generally narrowed and tightened-up artery system. Eventually the heart doesn't actually burst, but fails to pump blood out of the left ventricle (the left side of the heart) as fast as it comes into the lungs from the right ventricle. If this happens suddenly, it causes acute heart failure, with extreme breathlessness and a sensation of drowning (an apt description, as the lungs are drowning in dammed-up blood). If it happens slowly, you gradually feel more and more short of breath, first on exercise, eventually even at rest, often with a dry cough and swollen ankles.

Strictly speaking, heart failure of this kind is not really a bursting effect, but as it behaves like one (it is almost entirely preventable by good control of high blood pressure), I have included it here.

- Aorta
As mentioned in the section on blocking effects, aneurysms (swellings) can occur in the aorta. Such an aortic aneurysm can burst at very high levels of blood pressure, or at lower pressures if it has become very large and its wall has become weaker. This usually happens in two stages: first, a split in the aortic lining so that blood spurts into and between the layers of the aortic wall (this usually takes place over several hours, causing chest pain easily mistaken for a coronary heart attack); and second a split into the outer aortic wall, fatal within seconds or minutes.

- Brain
Aneurysms in brain arteries are small bubble-like distensions of the artery wall. They may occur because you have had a local weakness in the artery wall since you were born, or because a normal artery wall has been stretched by high blood pressure. They may occur on the surface of the brain (when they are usually of the inborn type) or in its interior (when they are usually of the type caused by high blood pressure).

If a surface aneurysm bursts it releases blood into the cerebrospinal fluid which bathes the brain (subarachnoid haemorrhage), causing very severe headache, so suddenly that people often think someone has struck them from behind, but with no immediate loss of consciousness or paralysis. If an interior aneurysm bursts (intracerebral haemorrhage), this usually destroys part of the brain, sometimes with loss of consciousness and usually with paralysis, usually of one side (hemiplegia), developing either immediately or within an hour or two.

- Eyes

  The retina of the eye is the only part of the body where the smallest arteries (arterioles) are directly visible – they can be examined easily using an instrument called an ophthalmoscope. At very high pressures (diastolic always more than 120 mmHg, sometimes as much as 180 mmHg or even more) fluid begins to leak from these arterioles into the retina, causing blurred vision, and visible evidence of imminent serious risk of brain haemorrhage, kidney failure, or permanent blindness from destruction of the retina. It is therefore important for anyone with a diastolic pressure above 120 mmHg to have the retina of both eyes examined with an ophthalmoscope, either in a dark room or after the pupils of their eyes have been dilated with suitable eye drops. If BP is not reduced from this extremely high level within a few hours, there may be substantial bleeding from these arterioles, with permanent damage to vision.

  Similar changes may occur in people with diabetes at lower pressures – one reason why it is important for them to keep good control of both their diabetes and their blood pressure, and to have their eyes checked at least once a year.

- Kidneys

  At very high pressures (and as with eye damage, sometimes sooner and at lower BP in people with diabetes), the smallest arteries (arterioles) in the kidneys begin to burst in the same way as those in the retina, resulting in rapid but still reversible loss of kidney function and eventually (but usually only after weeks or months without treatment) irreversible kidney failure. The first easily detected sign of this is the appearance of protein in the urine (easily and quickly detected by a simple test on a urine sample), as it causes no symptoms until kidney failure is advanced.

Can my treatment really make a difference to whether or not I get any of these effects later in life?

Yes. However, you do need to remember that high blood pressure is not the only cause of these complications, so in no way can your treatment completely eliminate the possibility that one of them may occur in the future, although it will greatly reduce it.

As you might expect, because the blocking effects result from many years of sustained high blood pressure, usually combined with high blood cholesterol and often with smoking, they are only partly and slowly reversible by reducing blood pressure once they have occurred. Treatment for high blood pressure (and reduction of blood cholesterol and stopping smoking) then makes all of them roughly 20% less likely than in people with similar BP who have had no treatment, but the reduction in risk is gradual and incomplete. Hence the emphasis throughout this book on controlling your blood pressure before any of these complications occur: prevention really is the best medicine.

All the bursting effects are either largely or completely preventable by well controlled treatment for high blood pressure. Kidney and eye damage can be virtually eliminated, and so can heart failure as a direct result of uncontrolled high blood pressure. Because coronary heart attacks can be reduced only by 20–30%, and some of these destroy enough heart muscle to cause heart failure, this cannot be entirely eliminated as an eventual consequence, but it can be made extremely unlikely for many years. Strokes from all causes are reduced by about 45% by well-maintained treatment but some strokes still occur because there are many other contributory causes apart from high blood pressure. High blood cholesterol and smoking both make stroke more likely, but are much less powerful causes of stroke than of coronary heart disease.

Heart attacks

I have been treated for high blood pressure for more than 20

years. I realise I am still more likely than other people to have a heart attack. If I do get one, how can I recognise it?

At least 80% of coronary heart attacks start with pain in the middle of the front of your chest. The pain often goes up into your jaws and/or into your arms. If you have already experienced angina pain, the pain of a coronary heart attack is likely to be more or less the same, perhaps more severe, but always much more persistent. Angina pain rarely lasts longer than 5 minutes, providing you stop whatever you are doing and rest. If 'angina' lasts for 15 minutes or more, you should send for skilled help – an ambulance, your own doctor, or both.

The pain of a coronary heart attack may be very severe, but usually it is more like a rather bad attack of 'indigestion' or heartburn caused by an upward leak of stomach acid into the gullet (oesophageal reflux). In fact experimentally, if you put strong acid into the gullet through a tube, most people who have previously experienced either a coronary heart attack or oesophageal reflux are unable to tell them apart. None of us wants to have a heart attack, so naturally we hope for the best, and most people who actually have a heart attack start off by insisting that it must be 'indigestion'.

In about 20% of heart attacks there is either no pain at all, or the pain may be so slight that people forget it. Severity of the pain is no indication of the seriousness of the attack: a heart attack bad enough to cause acute heart failure, with severe shortness of breath and congestion in the lungs, can occur with absolutely no pain at all.

Are there any warning symptoms before a definite heart attack?

Usually there are (about 60% of sufferers have symptoms for 1-2 weeks before a heart attack) but sometimes an attack can occur as the first symptom of coronary disease. People with long standing angina have a greater risk of developing a heart attack. Angina (discussed in more detail in the next section in this chapter) is often not recognised as such and may be dismissed as 'indigestion'. Any pain over the front of the chest (not necessarily at all severe) which comes on with exertion and is quickly relieved by rest is likely to be anginal pain. If angina attacks become more frequent, more severe and brought on by less exertion over a period of a week or two, this may indicate an imminent heart attack.

If I think I have a heart attack, what should I do?

Send for skilled help as soon as possible. Never wait longer than 15 minutes for the pain to go away by itself: make sure of this by noting the time when any chest pain begins. No good doctor, paramedic or ambulance driver will ever reproach you for calling them for a chest pain which eventually turns out to be a false alarm: we have all had too much experience of being sent for too late. Aspirin has been shown to reduce the death rate from heart attacks by about 20%, but it is best to wait for the paramedic's advice before slowly chewing an aspirin tablet if you suspect a heart attack.

If you are not on your own, then tell whoever is with you what is happening, because he or she is much more likely than you are to take a sensible decision, and give you the benefit of any doubt. If you have angina and have taken a dose of nitroglycerin (glyceryl trinitrate), then don't take any more – if the first dose didn't work, nor will others, and in overdose it can make you ill.

The results of early treatment for coronary heart attacks, using injected drugs which dissolve the clot obstructing one of your coronary arteries, are now very good indeed, but they absolutely depend on giving treatment as early as possible after a recognised onset.

If I think I'm having a heart attack, should I send for my doctor, for an ambulance, or both?

Both. Almost anywhere in the United Kingdom, your most sensible plan is to send for the ambulance first (by dialling 999) and then telephone for your doctor, saying that you have already asked for an ambulance. If, having read this book, you have a strong suspicion that you are having a heart attack, this suspicion will be shared by any experienced doctor who sees you, and he or she will then send you to the nearest hospital Coronary Care Unit (CCU). There will be less delay if you start this process yourself.

An experienced doctor today will send you to a CCU regardless of any immediate results from examining your heart with a stethoscope, checking your blood pressure, or checking your heart using an electrocardiogram (ECG). If the doctor arrives before the ambulance, all of these may be useful in assessing the severity of the attack, and may indicate a need for emergency measures outside hospital, but none of them (including the ECG) can exclude a heart attack at this stage. Even very small attacks, causing no fall in BP and no significant change in the ECG in the first few hours, may suddenly and without warning lead to an unstable heart rhythm, which can be most effectively treated in a specialised CCU at a hospital.

Roughly 50% of all deaths after a heart attack occur within the first two hours after onset of pain. In the UK today, the average delay before someone reaches a CCU is about three hours after the onset of chest pain, of which about two hours is the delay before people even start to seek any skilled help, and about one hour is the delay waiting for an ambulance, getting the person into the ambulance, transporting them to hospital and then getting them into the CCU. So more than half the deaths that are going to occur now occur outside hospital, with little or no application of the life-saving knowledge we now possess. This will not change until people stop letting themselves die of optimism, and their mortal fear of bothering busy doctors, paramedics, ambulance drivers and hospital staff. You're what we're there for.

Can I do anything to avert a heart attack?

Yes, plenty. First, if you have not already done so, you need to minimise all the three major risk factors for coronary disease: no smoking (including pipes and cigars), a greatly reduced fat intake, and well-controlled blood pressure. Attention to these reduces coronary risk even at a very late stage, although obviously it is better to attend to them earlier.

Second, if you have angina and the attacks are becoming more frequent, then current evidence (and medical opinion) endorse the value of regular low dose aspirin, which probably reduces the risk of a fatal attack by about 20%.

Aspirin works by making your blood less likely to form a clot inside a narrowed coronary artery, the final step which precipitates a coronary heart attack. A much more drastic although more effective step is to take a more powerful anticoagulant drug such as warfarin. Because blood coagulability varies from day to day and week to week, anticoagulant treatment is safe only under close medical supervision, with regular blood tests to check whether the dose needs to be changed. The possible benefits from this treatment have to be balanced in each individual case against risks of bleeding from the stomach or gut, and on present evidence it is not justified except in a few people at exceptional risk, usually people with increasingly frequent and severe angina.

Third, bearing in mind the greatly increased effectiveness of 'clot-busting' (thrombolytic) treatment today (providing it is given early) you should agree with a friend, a colleague at work or your partner on a sensible course to follow if you develop any pain in the front of the chest lasting 15 minutes or more. If you have already foreseen this event, you are more likely to take a sensible decision to get help early, rather than pretend it's not happening.

Angina

What's the connection between high blood pressure and angina?

High blood pressure over many years is one of the main causes of hardening and narrowing of the coronary arteries, the underlying reasons for angina. High blood pressure is also an immediate and reversible cause of angina, because high BP increases the work the heart has to do, and therefore its demands on an inadequate blood supply. So if your blood pressure is reduced, you will be less likely to have angina, even if your arteries are already hardened and narrowed. Better control of high blood pressure, usually by adjusting medication, is often all many people need to abolish their angina altogether, at least for many years.

Is angina a serious disease, something I really need to worry about?

Angina is a stern reminder of mortality, a sign that you are unlikely to live forever. On average, people live another 12 years following their first attack of angina – some much more, some less. How much this worries you will partly depend on how you regard your own life, and whether you have already learned to accept that death is eventually a price that has to be paid for the benefits of having been born.

In his preface to his play *The Doctor's Dilemma*, George Bernard Shaw set out 10 good rules for a healthy life. Two of the best were firstly not to try to live forever, and secondly to use your life as energetically as you can, so that when you eventually die, you have used it all up and none has been wasted.

The great majority of people with angina can live with it comfortably, by reasonable adjustments to how they live. Roughly half of all people with angina never consult a doctor about it, and may not recognise what it is. They find that the pain they get in the front of the chest is quickly relieved by slowing up or stopping whatever activity provoked it in the first place, and may be avoided by doing everything a bit more carefully.

Angina is caused by excessive demands on the blood supply to your heart muscle. Anything which reduces this supply or increases the demand is likely to cause pain. So cold weather, which requires more work from your body just to keep warm, reduces the exercise threshold for angina, and so does a big meal, requiring a big shift of blood to the gut in order to digest it. Wrap up warmly in cold weather, and if it's really freezing, stay indoors. Eat smaller meals more often. You soon learn from experience how fast you can walk up hills or stairs, how often to stop for a breather, and where you can do this without looking silly (a stick can be a great help, both to lean on and to look busy with).

I get chest pains which several doctors thought were angina, but the tests were all normal and didn't show anything. Can you get angina with normal tests?

Yes. Many people with recurrent pain in the front of the chest but negative tests do ultimately turn out to have coronary disease, but this may be many years later.

You don't say what sort of tests you had, but I expect that they included an ECG (electrocardiogram), performed either when you were at rest, or during or after a standard exercise test (an 'exercise' ECG). Although angina usually causes some changes to show up on these ECGs, they can appear perfectly normal in people with significant coronary artery disease.

Angina is nearly always caused by partial obstruction of one or more coronary arteries by cholesterol plaque, although there are other possible causes such as severe anaemia. This obstruction can be shown by injecting a dye which is opaque to X-rays into your bloodstream, and then filming its passage through your coronary arteries (coronary angiography). Most, but not all, authorities accept a normal coronary angiogram as proof that there is no coronary disease, but as this test always involves a small but not negligible risk, it is probably not justified simply to prove a still doubtful negative.

If I go to my doctor, can I get treatment for my angina? If so, what's available?

The 50% of people with angina who do consult a doctor find plenty of help available from drugs. By using some or all of them, and with sensible changes in how they live, the large majority of people with angina can get along with very little chest pain.

The oldest and one of the best of these drugs is nitroglycerin (glyceryl trinitrate or GTN), the stuff that sank the *Bismarck*. GTN should be used as and when you need it. As angina is always relieved within 30 seconds by rest, and GTN takes at least as long as this to be absorbed even if you chew up the tablets or use the more fashionable (but no more effective) sprays under your tongue, it is more sensible to use it to prevent attacks than to treat them. Angina is usually completely predictable: at constant temperature, constant speed, wearing the same weight of clothing, and at the same time of day in relation to meals (which divert blood to the gut and thus reduce your angina threshold), the pain comes on at exactly the same distance from the bottom of the hill, the stairs, or the beginning of whatever else you are doing. If you chew up a GTN tablet when you start, you'll find you can go further and do more.

GTN works by dilating your veins so that your heart has less work to do. The same action can often cause a headache, which is rarely severe. If you find you have to take bigger and more frequent doses, you should see your doctor, not go on taking more and more. Chest pain that is not relieved within 15 minutes is likely to be caused by a coronary heart attack, not angina, and so you should send for an ambulance, not take more GTN (see the previous section on **Heart attacks** for more information on exactly what to do if this happens).

A wide range of other drugs are available which can be taken regularly once or twice a day, either to prevent angina completely (if you don't try to do too much), or to reduce the frequency and severity of attacks. These drugs include variations on GTN which have a longer-lasting action (and the same side-effects), for example isosorbate (Isordil), and drugs in the beta-blocker and calcium-channel blocker groups which are also used to treat high blood pressure (there is more information about these BP-lowering drugs in Appendix 1).

I know my tablets for angina are effective in relieving the pain, but do they help to prevent heart attacks?

There is no evidence that they prevent heart attacks as such, but there is some evidence that some drugs in the beta-blocker group may reduce the chance of a heart attack proving fatal, probably by stabilising heart rhythm. There is better evidence that in people who have already survived one heart attack, treatment with certain beta-blockers (propranolol, timolol or metoprolol) makes further attacks less likely.

Calcium-channel blockers have no effect either way on the risk of a coronary heart attack, as long as they are taken only in slow-release (SR) form. Taken as unmodified rapid-action tablets they can increase the risk of a heart attack, as well as often causing minor side-effects.

There is more information about both these groups of drugs in Appendix 1.

Some doctors tell you to avoid angina by doing less, while others tell you to protect your heart by doing more. How can they both be right?

This is how it works. Regular additional exercise, just a bit more than you are already doing, always has some training effect on the heart. One of the great myths of coronary disease prevention is that exercise must be violent and exhausting to do any good. Doing the most you can, within the limits set by anginal pain, claudication, breathlessness, or whatever your particular limiting factor happens to be, is always worthwhile. Even people in heart failure find that if they walk or shuffle as far as they can before becoming too breathless to carry on, then within a week or two this limiting distance gets longer, and they feel a bit better. Use it or lose it.

However, while you should do the most you can, you should stop at your own personal threshold for angina or leg pain (claudication). If you keep doing this regularly, you (like most people) will find that the distance you can cope with slowly improves, and so does your morale and general well-being.

We seem to hear a lot these days about coronary artery bypass graft operations for angina. Are they really the cure-all they sometimes sound?

Coronary artery bypass grafts (CABGs) are generally very effective in relieving the symptoms of angina but, contrary to most public opinion, they seldom extend life and, for most cases, are not an effective way of preventing heart attacks. Although the operation itself is usually very successful, like any other operation it can be a very painful and frightening experience, and it is certainly not an easy alternative to treatment by medication. Most experts on the subject think that CABGs should only be considered for people with angina whose chest pains really cannot be controlled by drugs alone. These people are a minority of those who have angina, and a much smaller minority of those with coronary disease.

Before you can be considered for a CABG, you will need to have a coronary angiogram. This involves injecting a dye which is opaque to X-rays into your bloodstream and then filming its passage through your coronary arteries, and this procedure itself involves a small risk. The angiogram shows up any obstructions in your coronary arteries. Controlled trials have shown that only the minority of people with significant obstructions in two or more of the three coronary arteries, or with obstructions in the left anterior descending branch, are likely to live longer with the operation than without it, but most in all groups will get relief (complete or almost complete) from anginal pain.

Coronary angioplasty, in which you have a sort of rebore of the lining of the coronary artery, is an alternative operation, less invasive than a CABG and usually involving only a day or two in hospital. However, it is a less permanent alternative to a CABG and often has to be repeated in two or three years.

My doctors feel that I would benefit from a CABG, but tell me that I can't have one until I stop smoking. Do you really think this is right - both medically and morally?

Unless you have really tried your utmost to give up smoking and have still failed then, in my opinion, your doctors are right. I feel that everyone involved in our free NHS, whether as health care professionals, managers, or patients, have a moral duty to do the best they can. This means that the people being treated should (and generally do) work just as hard at getting themselves better as their carers do to help them.

That being said, nicotine dependence is real and, for some people, stopping smoking seems to be as difficult as getting off heroin. People who have never been nicotine-dependent have little right to judge the efforts of those who still need tobacco despite serious attempts to get off the stuff. We also have to remember that within the group of people with artery problems who would benefit from surgery, because smokers are at the highest risk, they also stand to gain most.

Long-term consequences and complications

In my experience, the prospect of heart surgery can be a turning point. When referring them for evaluation for CABG, I told my patients who still smoked that I thought they owed it to those who would be giving them their medical and nursing skills to make a final effort, surpassing whatever they had previously done to stop smoking. All of them succeeded. Perhaps you should do the same; and if you fail, well, so do doctors and nurses, and you certainly have a right to be helped like anyone else. If you have tried and failed, your doctors are wrong. If you haven't really tried, they are right.

Heart failure

I have been treated for high blood pressure for 15 years, starting when I was 55. It was never very well controlled. For the past year my BP has been much lower than it used to be when I go for a check-up, but I feel much worse, very tired and short of breath. What's happening?

The most likely cause of what you describe (falling blood pressure combined with increasing breathlessness and failing health in someone who has had many years of treatment for originally high blood pressure) is heart failure. Your heart muscle has become too weak to maintain your normal blood pressure, so your BP falls. One of the commonest causes of heart failure is uncontrolled (or very poorly controlled) high blood pressure over many years.

Heart failure does not mean, as some people imagine, that your heart suddenly stops beating, but that it fails to pump blood out of the left side of the heart as fast as it comes in from the right side of the heart. This causes congestion in your lungs, increased breathlessness and/or wheezing when lying flat, sometimes a dry cough (mainly at night), and eventually swollen ankles. As the volume of blood expelled by each heartbeat falls, a failing heart speeds up, with a pulse rate usually over 80 beats a minute, often much more. The heartbeat may also become irregular, but there are other common and generally harmless causes of irregular heartbeats, and nobody should think their heart is failing just because of irregular or 'missed' beats.

Treatment of heart failure has become much more effective in the past few years, as we now have ACE-inhibitor drugs available as well as the more traditional treatment with digitalis (digoxin) and diuretics (water tablets). ACE-inhibitors greatly improve heart function in heart failure, whether or not this has been caused by high blood pressure, and as they can also be used to treat high blood pressure, they can be very useful for people in your situation. Most people can be made very much better, and survive several years more than they would without treatment.

Stroke

They say the main cause of strokes is high blood pressure, but my father had a stroke only a week after his doctor told him his blood pressure was entirely normal. Why?

As with coronary heart attacks, there are several different causes of stroke, all of which interact. High blood pressure is only one of these causes, but taking all strokes as a group, it is the most important cause, and also the easiest target for stroke prevention. Other causes, in descending order of importance, are high blood viscosity (usually from too many red blood cells, the opposite of anaemia), diabetes, high blood cholesterol, and smoking. A skinful of alcohol may precipitate stroke, probably by raising blood pressure too much and too fast. On the other hand, there is fairly good evidence that people who eat a lot of fresh fruit and vegetables are much less likely to get strokes.

Are there any warning symptoms before a stroke?

Usually, but not always. Most people who have a major stroke have had warning symptoms months or years earlier but these are often not recognised and never brought to medical attention.

These warning symptoms are most commonly caused by small fragments of clot detached from cholesterol plaque in the lining of neck arteries. These fragments (called micro-emboli) can travel up into the brain and the retina (the back of the eye), causing temporary symptoms which may include disturbed vision or blindness, weakness of one side of the face or one hand or one leg, loss of speech, or partial or complete loss of consciousness. These brief losses of function are called transient ischaemic attacks or TIAs. None of these symptoms lasts for more than a few seconds or perhaps minutes, as the micro-emboli then disintegrate, leaving no permanent damage.

Less common warning symptoms are minor strokes. They may affect areas of the brain too small to cause symptoms (eg loss of movement in the right or left limbs, thought disturbance or speech impairment) that last long enough to be recognisable if and when you consult your doctor. Multiple very small strokes of this kind generally get almost completely better within 24 hours. They can cause lasting memory loss, thought disturbance and emotional distress, usually with big ups and downs in ability (and quite different from the steadily advancing impairment of Alzheimer's disease). The disturbance and distress may be obvious to members of the same household or close friends, but not at all apparent to people (such as doctors and nurses) who don't live with the person affected.

Can anything be done to prevent strokes?

Yes. If you are not already having treatment for high blood pressure then it is important to have your BP checked and get it well controlled if it turns out to be high – your aim is a diastolic pressure below 90 mmHg if at all possible. If you still smoke, stop now: the reduction in risk is small, but at this point everything is worth having. You should also start taking aspirin regularly, usually one tablet a day, which will reduce your tendency to form blood clots. This is certainly very effective in reducing transient ischaemic attacks (TIAs), and probably effective in preventing strokes.

People who are at very high risk of strokes should consider full anticoagulant treatment with warfarin or some similar drug.

They usually have known carotid artery disease (ie affecting one or other of the arteries along the sides of the neck) and will probably be under supervision from a neurologist. What decision to take on this type of treatment depends on balancing probable gains against possible penalties, and will differ from person to person.

Surgical removal of clots and plaque from the carotid artery has been popular in North America as a way of preventing strokes, but most evidence suggests that it is seldom an effective treatment.

I woke up one morning with one side of my face paralysed. I thought it was a stroke, but my doctor says it isn't, it's a Bell's palsy. What's the difference? Does it have any connection with my high blood pressure? And will I be more likely to have a stroke later?

To allay your worries first: there is no connection between a Bell's palsy and your high blood pressure, and having had a Bell's palsy does not make it more likely that you will have a stroke in the future.

A Bell's palsy is paralysis of the 7th cranial nerve (also called the facial nerve), a nerve which starts in the brain and then branches out to reach most parts of the face. This nerve controls the muscles in the face, so if it becomes paralysed, then so do the facial muscles. The paralysis usually affects either the left or the right side of the face (including the eyelids and the forehead); occasionally it may recur later on on the other side; and rarely it can affect both sides at the same time. (Buster Keaton, the silent movie comedian, made a fortune from his deadpan face caused by a permanent Bell's palsy on both sides, but this was exceptional.) It can occur at any age, but is most common in people who are between 20 and 50 years old. There may be a little pain just in front of the ear on the affected side for the first day or two, and there is loss of taste on the same side of the tongue, but otherwise there are no sensory changes.

The paralysis usually extends rapidly for the first two days and then stays the same. After about six weeks, 85% of cases begin to get better without any treatment, and eventually recover completely. The other 15% have some permanent weakness, occasionally complete paralysis. Steroid injections within 24 hours of the paralysis starting may reduce swelling and nerve damage, but are ineffective later.

The cause of a Bell's palsy is still unknown, but is probably a virus infection causing swelling of the 7th cranial nerve where it lies encased in bone close to the ear. It has nothing to do with high blood pressure.

Virtually everyone who first notices a facial paralysis is afraid they are having a stroke, but in fact there is absolutely no connection between a Bell's palsy and a stroke. Strokes certainly can begin with facial weakness on one side or the other, but usually hand movements will be affected on the same side, and often the foot on that side will drag. Although a Bell's palsy can cause some difficulty in speaking clearly if the paralysis is complete, there is no difficulty in choosing the right word or understanding the words of other people. When speech is affected by stroke there is usually at least some difficulty in remembering the right meanings of words.

I'm not afraid of a big stroke that just finishes me off, but I've always dreaded being left as a vegetable with double incontinence, a burden to everyone. What can I do to avoid that contingency?

Apart from taking all the steps you can to prevent your having a stroke, you should make it clear to your closest family members and to your doctors that if you do have the misfortune to reach such a helpless state of dependence you do not wish to have your terminal illness unnaturally prolonged by excessive treatment. After very severe strokes swallowing becomes difficult, and small bits of food or drink tend to be inhaled into the lungs, causing pneumonia. This is the natural and painless mode of death after major irreversible brain injury, and most doctors will not interfere with it by prescribing antibiotics, if they and your closest family know this was your wish. It may help to put this in writing and lodge it with your doctor. Such documents have no legal force in this country, but they can affect commonsense decisions.

10
Research and the future

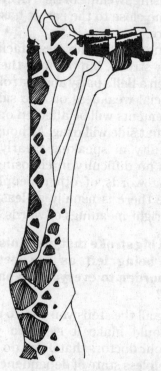

Drug testing and clinical trials

Do any other animals get high blood pressure, and can they be used in research on human high blood pressure?

While I recognise that some people have strongly held views both for and against the use of animals in medical research, I do not think that a book of this type is the place to discuss these controversies. So what follows is a description of what is happening; your opinion of whether it is a good or a bad thing is your own.

In practice, rats are the only laboratory animal extensively used for studies on high blood pressure. All breeds of rat fed a normal diet have a distribution of blood pressure, some higher and some lower, but some breeds have a much higher average pressure, some very high indeed, and they get strokes, damaged retinas, heart failure and kidney failure, more or less like humans. These special breeds have been extensively used for research. A few studies have been done on pigs and rhesus monkeys, but they are too expensive for routine studies.

Studies of possible harmful side-effects of BP-lowering drugs mainly use rats, mice, and rabbits.

Only the broad outlines of either treatment for high blood pressure or its causes and effects can be studied in laboratory animals, even those whose diets and digestive systems resemble those of humans, as with rats and pigs. Human responses to drugs are often substantially different from those of other animals, and humans do not lead their lives in standard laboratory conditions. Drugs developed to control human high blood pressure are never used even experimentally on people until they have been thoroughly tested on a variety of animals, but unexpected effects, both harmful and beneficial, have always been found years after even the most successful drugs have been in use.

What are clinical trials? Are they different from controlled trials?

Clinical trials (or clinical studies) are closely-supervised scientific studies into treatments for diseases. If the treatment is a drug, then the expression 'drug trials' may sometimes be used. A clinical trial may investigate a completely new treatment, or a new way of giving an existing treatment, or compare a new treatment with the best treatment currently available. Trials usually involve close observation of a series of patients, with measurement of the various indicators of the disorder in question before, during and after days or weeks of treatment. Such a trial is said to be 'controlled' if the treated group of patients is compared with an another group whose members are untreated or treated differently – the 'controls'.

Uncontrolled trials – reports of alleged benefits from treatment based simply on comparing measurements before and after treatment – are generally agreed by medical scientists to be meaningless because of the great variabilty of illness, the tendency of most disorders to get better without treatment, and above all because of the placebo effect (discussed in the answer to the next question). Unfortunately many enthusiastic people continue to rely on personal experience of this kind. (In my experience, this may be particularly true of the complementary therapies.) Reports of uncontrolled trials are not normally published by reputable medical journals, but (again unfortunately) poor quality journals abound.

Whenever I have referred to trials or research studies in this book, I have meant the results of properly-conducted controlled clinical trials.

What are placebos, and what is the placebo effect?

The word 'placebo' comes from the Latin, and means 'I will please'. A placebo drug is an inert or 'dummy' version of a drug – it looks like a drug, you take it like a drug, but in fact it has no active ingredients at all.

Placebo drugs were originally used to reassure people that their illness was really being treated, although in fact their doctors were giving them a completely inactive substance, usually tricked out with colours, tastes and odours to convey an impression of potency. Although this entailed some deception, it was generally less dishonest, and certainly less dangerous, than most of the biologically active drugs that were available up to about 1935. Until then, the number of drugs that were both active and useful (if used accurately and cautiously) could certainly be counted on the fingers of both hands. Of the vast number of useless remedies then in common use, many contained lead, arsenic, mercury, strychnine and other poisons, which undoubtedly caused a great deal of illness.

It was true then, and remains true today, that if people cannot accept (or if doctors assume that they cannot accept) that many problems are still best left alone, either until recovery takes place or until accurate diagnosis is possible, then they are likely to be harmed less by innocently taking a placebo than by the prescription of active but innapropriate drugs. Whatever doctors may say, prescription of a placebo is a common delaying tactic when what the prescriber really wants to do is to wait and see. This may be a better course than rushing into treatment with only a snap diagnosis. Inappropriate treatment can be worse than placebo treatment, not only because the wrong treatment might do more harm than good, but also because it may halt the search for the real sources of problems.

You might think that taking an inert dummy drug would make no difference to you and have no effect on your symptoms – but it can, and this is the placebo effect. People can actually benefit from taking a placebo simply because they believe it will have a positive effect as, of course, they are not aware that it is inactive. Anyone prescribed a placebo will have also consulted a professional carer (a doctor, nurse or some other therapist), and all the evidence shows that just having such a consultation and starting on some sort of treatment often makes someone with an illness or problem feel better.

The placebo effect is real, not imaginary. Nearly all trials of treatments show a substantial although often only temporary placebo effect (usually benefiting about one-third of patients in any trial for at least two or three weeks), even for serious illnesses such as coronary heart disease or cancer, and for surgery as well as medication.

Placebos can even reduce your blood pressure, although not by enough or for long enough to make them a useful form of treatment. They work because anything that calms and relaxes people will reduce blood pressure to some extent compared with their BP in some more anxious state (such as knowing you have high BP and worrying that it is not being treated). All this is important evidence that caring, kindness and willingness to listen are important to the outcome of medical care, all too easily overlooked with the current pressures for higher health service 'productivity'.

If placebos are only imitation drugs, why do doctors use them in clinical trials?

Placebos are now used on a huge scale in controlled trials of treatments in order to separate the usually substantial effects of the whole package of being looked after by caring professionals (not just the medication but all that goes with the consultation process) from the specific effects of the drug under trial. We could say that everyone in the trial gets the same placebo effect, but that some of them get that plus the active drug being tested.

Trials using placebo-treated controls have two other advantages compared with trials which compare treated patients with untreated controls. The first is that all the participants in the trial with the untreated controls (including the doctors and any other health professionals involved) know exactly who is receiving treatment and who is not. This can, and usually does, strongly affect the apparent outcome: both doctors and patients tend to find what they want to find. With placebo-treated controls, it is usually possible to design a type of trial called a 'double-blind trial' in which neither doctors nor patients know which group is which while they are measuring and recording the apparent effects of both drug and placebo. This gives more impartial results, as no-one's expectations can affect the outcome.

The second advantage is that, by comparing the side-effects reported by the placebo-treated controls with those reported by the actively-treated patients, the true side-effects of a new drug can be separated from the apparent side-effects of the placebo, which can often be substantial.

If so many things can affect the impartiality of a clinical trial, what can doctors do to make sure that their research really is impartial?

Yes, it is often difficult to ensure that controls do not differ from treated patients in ways that make comparisons between the results of treatment versus no treatment (or of treatment versus placebo or some other established treatment) either meaningless or at least very difficult to interpret. For example, if you ask for volunteers to test a new drug, they may be younger and healthier than the people who agree to be controls, or they may be more sick and more desperate. If doctors are asked to select suitable subjects for a trial, they may choose the patients they think are most likely to benefit from it, or those who have fewer other complicating disorders.

The only way to ensure that test subjects and controls are as nearly as possible the same in all other respects is to allocate them randomly to test or control status – this type of trial is called a 'randomised controlled trial'. Obviously this should be done only after all the people asked to take part have understood what the trial is for, why it needs to have a randomised controlled design, and have agreed to take part under these conditions.

Even with randomised controls, if numbers are small, there may still be substantial differences between the test subjects and the controls, due entirely to chance. It is very difficult to get good results from any trials that involve fewer than 30 participants. The most powerful trials, giving the most useful results, are large double-blind randomised controlled trials, usually conducted in several different places in order to get sufficient numbers. These are the 'gold standard' for research, and future advances in medical science depend mainly on trials of this kind.

I can see that taking part in a clinical trial will help medicine as a whole, but – if it doesn't sound too selfish – what good will it do me personally?

Participation in well-organised and reputable controlled clinical trials is not only of enormous value for medical science, it is also of great benefit to the participants, even if they are controls being treated with either established drugs or placebos. All trials consistently show better health outcomes for people who participate (both the study group and the controls) than for those who refuse. Some of this difference may arise from generally less thoughtful behaviour among refusers than among participants (for example, they may smoke or drink more, or be more careless about remembering their pills) but some of it certainly arises from the fact that everyone taking part in a research trial (both the participants and the health professionals involved) tends to work more conscientiously and self-critically. Participation in research is a powerful motive for better quality care.

Reputable research is designed to answer questions which do not yet have a reliable answer. No reputable researcher will ask you to accept a treatment that is already known to be inferior, or deny you a treatment already known to be better. The temptation with all new treatments is to believe that they are substantially better than the older treatments they are intended to replace and that their advantages will not be outweighed by new and sometimes unforseen risks. The whole point of trials is to find out whether this is actually so, as quickly as possible, using the smallest possible number of subjects needed to give a reliable answer. Once we have that answer, all can benefit, and those who took part in the less successful arm of the trial usually benefit first.

In 1956 I was responsible for treating children with leukaemia at Hammersmith Hospital, using the new chemotherapy then becoming available for the first time. Though most of these children returned to good health for 6 to 9 months, within a year they all died. Twenty years later most such children lived to become normal adults, and now nearly all of them do. This huge advance depended entirely on the results of double-blind randomised controlled trials, first comparing the new treatments with nursing support alone, then comparing established treatments with new treatments. Step by step, by systematically building a body of evidence rather than letting the different specialists pursue their own prejudices, we solved an apparently insoluble problem.

All this applies to reputable trials, run or supported by the Medical Research Council, the research units of the various Royal Colleges, by university medical school departments, or other independent groups such as the British Heart Foundation. Many excellent trials also have some support from the pharmaceutical industry, but this must be clearly subordinated to independent institutions with enough weight to ensure that their independence is real. Unfortunately there are other types of trials around, some of which are thinly-disguised marketing strategies, and some of which are intended rather more for the benefit of the sponsor or the researcher rather than for the benefit of medical science or the individual participants. With this in mind, if you are asked to take part in a trial, I would suggest that you ask for a full written account of its nature, its aims, its sponsorship, and of any benefits accruing to the hospital or the practice from your participation. Nobody with a serious commitment to research will take offence. Otherwise, thanks, but no thanks.

My doctor has asked me to take part in a clinical trial. How should I decide whether or not to accept this offer – are there any particular questions I should ask?

I suggest that you first find out who is running the trial and why (as discussed at the end of the answer to the previous question). Once you have satisfied yourself that it is an independent, reputable and properly-conducted trial, then you need a proper explanation of the reasons for it and exactly what is involved, and you should receive this both in a face-to-face discussion with your doctor or the researcher and also in writing. During the discussion you can raise any questions about the drug (or other treatment) being tested and how taking part in the trial will actually affect you. You might, for example, want to ask any or all of the following questions.

- Has the drug been tested on people before and, if so, on how many people and with what results?
- What, if any, side-effects can you expect?
- What tests and measurements are they going to take? For example, do they just want to measure your blood pressure at set intervals, or will they want to perform blood or urine tests, or have they anything else in mind?
- How often will they want to perform these tests?
- How long will each set of tests take?
- Where will the tests take place – at your doctor's surgery, or do you have to travel to a hospital?
- If the tests will take a long time or if they expect you to travel,

will they pay your expenses or compensate you for any loss of earnings?
- Will taking part in the trial inconvenience you in any way?

Once you have answers to all the questions that you want to ask, then you can think about whether you want to take part – you do not have to give an answer immediately, and you can always go back and ask more questions should you wish to do so. Deciding to take part is not a commitment to stay in the trial until it is completed, as you have the right to withdraw at any time and without having to give any reasons.

If you decide to go ahead, then you will be asked to sign a consent form stating that you understand what is involved in the trial and that you agree to take part. If there is anything on the form that you do not understand or which has not been mentioned to you before, than ask about it, and do not sign until you are quite happy with the answers. You will have realised from my previous comments in this chapter that I feel that properly conducted research is extremely important – but it is also important that everyone taking part does so willingly and with properly informed consent and that they do not feel pressurised in any way.

The future

These days there seem to be more and more local GP clinics for things – diabetes and asthma, for example – which always used to be dealt with in hospital clinics. Will we see these sorts of clinics for high blood pressure and, if so, what will the hospital specialists be doing?

I certainly think that in the next 10 years we will see more and more treatment for 'straightforward' high blood pressure being carried out by teams based in GPs' surgeries, although not necessarily in separate clinics. This implies very big changes in GP teams, with huge improvements in the quality and comprehensiveness of care they provide, requiring big investments in more staff, and time for the team members (who could include doctors, nurses, dietitians, clerical staff and so on) to develop their approach to the work involved. These teams must also be prepared to involve you, the people being treated for high blood pressure, in the decisions that are made about your treatment.

Then, as 'simple' high blood pressure becomes more completely detected and better followed-up by these GP teams, malignant hypertension will become increasingly rare, and eventually (I hope) a potential cause for serious concern about the quality of preceding care, just as eclampsia is for management of pregnancy and childbirth. Not all these cases are the result of neglect, but most of them are. This will reduce the function of hospital specialists almost entirely to the sophisticated search for classical causes of secondary high blood pressure (this was explained in Chapter 1), mostly in the kidney, requiring the extremely specialised resources of perhaps five or six centres in the whole of the UK.

How is treatment for high blood pressure likely to change over the next 10 years or so?

The most likely – and perhaps the most important – change will come as primary high blood pressure (also known as 'essential hypertension' and explained in Chapter 1) is recognised as being not a single category (including all people with high blood pressure of unknown cause and all treated in more or less the same way) but to consist of separate subgroups for which different causes are known, and therefore different treatments (and not necessarily drug treatment) are most appropriate. To some extent this has already happened, though neither traditional teaching nor textbooks seem to recognise this. Many young men with both high blood pressure and either weight or alcohol problems can attain normal pressures if they lose weight, stop drinking and start a vigorous exercise programme.

As matters now stand, it seems unlikely that it makes any difference to people with primary high blood pressure how (ie with which drugs) their BP is lowered. What matters is how much it is lowered – in general, the more the better. We simply use whichever drug seems to work and is well tolerated when first used. Sooner or later this position will probably change. As we find more distinct causes, we shall use more distinct solutions. Treatment and management will thus become more complex, but because the intelligence of you, the people with high blood pressure, will at last be recognised and used, the job will become much easier for us all.

Glossary

acupuncture A traditional form of treatment in China, acupuncture involves inserting special very fine needles into the skin at particular sites on the body in order to balance the 'life energy' or 'vital force' which the Chinese call 'ch'i' or 'qi'.
aneurysm A swelling or bubble-like stretching of the wall of an *artery*.
angina Pain over the front of the chest on exertion (eg when walking up hills or stairs), caused by reduced oxygen supply to heart muscle.
anticoagulants Drugs which reduce the tendency of the blood to clot.
aorta The largest *artery* in the body, leading directly from the heart.
aromatherapy A *complementary therapy* involving treatment with essential oils, which are aromatic (scented) oils extracted from the roots, flowers or leaves of plants by distillation. Aromatherapy often involves massage, but the oils can also be inhaled or added to baths.
arterial blood pressure The blood pressure in your *arteries*. Raised arterial blood pressure is what we mean by 'high blood pressure' throughout this book.
arteries Blood vessels carrying oxygenated blood away from the heart to the *capillary network* supplying blood to all parts of the body. They have firm muscular walls and contain blood under relatively high pressure.
arterioles The smallest *arteries*, which end in the *capillary network*.
atrial fibrillation Rapid *fibrillation* affecting the atria (auricles), which are the upper chambers of the heart. It may be treated with drugs to restore a normal heart rhythm and to reduce the heart rate or, in some circumstances, by an operation to insert a pacemaker.
bile A substance produced by the liver which has two main functions. It helps to break down fats in the gut so that they can be digested, and

it also carries away waste products produced by the liver.
blood volume The total amount of blood in your body.
body mass index or **BMI** A way of ranking any group of people with various heights according to how fat they are. It is calculated by dividing your weight in kilograms by the square of your height in metres. A 'normal' BMI value is between 20 and 25.
brachial artery The main *artery* in the upper arm, used when measuring blood pressure.
brainstem The area lying between the brain and spinal cord which controls many unconscious bodily functions, including heart output, urine output (which affects *blood volume*), and the diameter of small *arteries* in different parts of the body (the main determinent of blood pressure).
brand name or **trade name** Most drugs have at least two names: the brand or trade name is the name given to a drug by its manufacturer, and is usually written with a capital first letter. The other name is the *generic name*.
caesarean section An operation to deliver a baby through the wall of the abdomen.
calories Units in which energy or heat are measured. The energy value of food is measured in calories. If we are to be strictly correct, we should really be talking about the energy value of food being measured in kilocalories (often abbreviated to kcal or written as Calories with a capital first letter). But most people simply use the shorthand term 'calorie' when they mean kilocalories, and that is what has been used in this book.
capillaries The smallest blood vessels in the body, through which body cells receive oxygen and dispose of their waste products.
capillary network The network of capillaries carries blood from the *arterioles* (the end of the arterial system) to the *venules* (the beginning of the vein or venous system).
cholesterol A fat-like substance which is an essential component of all body cells. Excess cholesterol in the blood may be deposited as *plaque* on the walls of *arteries*.
claudication Leg pain from obstruction or hardening of the leg *arteries*, caused by a shortage of oxygen in leg muscles.
clinical trials or **clinical studies** Scientific research studies into treatments for diseases. They may investigate a completely new treatment, or a new way of giving an existing treatment, or compare a new treatment with older treatments.

Glossary

clotting factors Substances in the blood which take part in the chemical processes which lead to the formation of blood clots.

coarctation of the aorta A rare condition in which the aorta (the huge artery carrying blood out of the heart) is tightly narrowed a few inches beyond its origin, and then expands to its normal diameter.

complementary therapies Non-medical treatments which may be used in addition to conventional medical treatments. Popular complementary therapies include *acupuncture*, *aromatherapy* and *homeopathy*.

controlled trial A *clinical trial* in which the group of patients receiving treatment are compared with an untreated or differently treated group, called the 'controls'.

coronary arteries The *arteries* which supply the muscles of the heart with blood.

coronary heart disease or **coronary artery disease** or **coronary disease** Narrowing or blockage of the *coronary arteries* by *plaque*. It can lead to *angina* or a *heart attack*.

coronary thrombosis Obstruction of a *coronary artery* by a blood clot. Also called a *heart attack*.

corticosteroids A group of drugs derived from *hormones* naturally present in the body which affect the immune system and distribution of sodium and potassium salts. They are used for treating asthma, rheumatoid arthritis and other problems involving the immune system. Although often referred to simply as 'steroids', they should not be confused with the anabolic steroids which we often hear about being abused by athletes.

cuff A piece of fabric containing an inflatable rubber bladder which is wrapped around your upper arm when your blood pressure is measured with a *sphygmomanometer*. Cuffs are available in different sizes to suit everyone from children up to adults with very large upper arms.

depression Feeling sad, hopeless, pessimistic, withdrawn and generally lacking interest in life. Most people feel depressed at some point in their lives, usually in reaction to a specific event such as a bereavement. The most severe forms of depression are often cyclical, occurring at intervals of months or years. These forms of depression seem to arise spontaneously, perhaps because of changes in brain chemistry, and are strongly inherited.

diabetes or **diabetes mellitus** Too high a level of glucose (sugar) in the blood, caused by the body's inability to produce enough of a *hormone* called insulin or by the resistance of body cells to the effect of insulin.

diastolic pressure The pressure of the blood in the arteries between heart beats. It is the bottom of the two figures in the blood pressure 'fraction' (eg someone with a BP of 150/85 mmHg has a diastolic pressure of 85 mmHg).

dietitian A health professional trained in nutrition who can provide advice and information on all aspects of diet and eating behaviour.

double-blind trial A *controlled trial* in which neither doctors nor patients know which group of patients is receiving the test treatment and which are the controls. This gives more impartial results, as no-one's expectations can affect the outcome of the trial.

drug trial A *clinical trial* where the treatment being investigated is a drug.

eclampsia A rare dangerous condition that occurs in late pregnancy. A woman with eclampsia has fits (seizures) caused by brain damage, caused in turn by very high blood pressure that has developed very fast. Nearly all eclampsia can be prevented by good antenatal care.

embolus (plural emboli) A fragment of material (usually a blood clot) that travels in the bloodstream. Emboli can form in arteries (most commonly the carotid arteries in the neck) and in veins (most commonly deep veins in the legs).

essential hypertension An alternative term for *primary high blood pressure*.

fibrillation Independent, irregular and unco-ordinated movement of the fibres of the heart muscle, so that instead of acting effectively together to squeeze blood through the heart, they tremble or flutter ineffectively, producing irregular, rapid heartbeats.

fibrinogen A substance found in blood which is involved in the chemical processes that lead to the formation of blood clots.

foetus The baby in the womb.

fulminating An adjective describing any illness or condition which starts suddenly and accelerates rapidly.

generic drugs or **generic names** Most drugs have at least two names: the generic name is the scientific name (usually written with a small first letter) and applies to all the versions of that drug, regardless of the manufacturer. The other name is the *brand name*.

genes The 'units' of heredity that determine our inherited characteristics, such as eye colour.

gestosis Another name for *pre-eclampsia*.

Glossary

gout A type of arthritis usually affecting the small joints, most commonly but not always in the big toe. It occurs when your body fails to get rid of one of its waste products, a substance called uric acid.

HDL cholesterol or **high density lipoprotein cholesterol** One of the *cholesterol*-containing substances found in the bloodstream. HDL cholesterol is considered to be 'good' cholesterol because high blood levels predict lower death rates from *coronary heart disease*. Cholesterol is carried away in this form from the walls of the *arteries* to be stored in the liver or excreted in *bile*.

heart attack Death of an area of heart muscle because its blood supply is interrupted, usually because one of the *coronary arteries* is blocked. The severity of a heart attack (and whether or not it is fatal) depends on the amount of heart muscle affected and whether heart rhythm is disturbed.

heart failure Inability of the heart to keep up with its work of pumping blood around the body – it fails to pump blood out of the left side of the heart as fast as it comes in from the right side. It does NOT mean that the heart is not beating or is about to stop.

holistic treatment Treatment which aims at treating the whole person (body, mind, feelings, lifestyle etc) rather than simply responding to and treating individual symptoms.

homeopathy A *complementary therapy* based on the principle that 'like can be cured with like' (the word homeopathy comes from two Greek words that mean 'similar' and 'suffering'). The remedies used (which are completely safe) contain very dilute amounts of a substance which in larger quantities would produce similar symptoms to the illness being treated. Although there is as yet no scientific explanation for why homeopathy works, and almost no evidence that it has more than a *placebo effect*, it is available through the NHS although the provision is limited.

hormones Chemical messengers that circulate in the bloodstream and help control the body's functions.

hypertension An alternative term for high blood pressure.

hypertension-oedema-proteinurea syndrome or **HOP** Another name for *pre-eclampsia*.

hypertensive disease of pregnancy or **HDP** Another name for *pre-eclampsia*.

hypokalaemia Low blood potassium.

impotence Failure of erection of the penis.

induction or **induction of labour** Starting labour and childbirth early by artificial means, for example by breaking your waters or by using drugs to make your womb contract.

joules Units of work or energy in the metric system – the metric equivalent of *calories* (one calorie equals about 4.2 joules).

LDL cholesterol or **low density lipoprotein cholesterol** One of the *cholesterol*-containing substances found in the bloodstream. LDL cholesterol is considered to be 'bad' cholesterol because it is one of the sources of *plaque*, and because high blood levels predict high death rates from *coronary heart disease*.

lipids Fatty substances. Lipids found in the bloodstream include *cholesterol* and *triglyceride*.

malignant hypertension Blood pressure so high that it destroys *arterioles* in the *retina*, brain and kidneys. It is the most serious form of high blood pressure, a rare medical emergency which occurs either when very high blood pressure has persisted untreated for many years, or when blood pressure has risen very fast indeed.

mmHg Abbreviation for millimetres of mercury, the units in which blood pressure is recorded.

myocardial infarction Another name for a *heart attack*.

NSAIDs or **non-steroidal anti-inflammatory drugs** A class of drugs commonly used for arthritis, other rheumatic conditions, and generally for pain relief.

oedema Swelling of the body from water accumulating in the tissues. Because water tends to fall to the lowest point, this swelling first becomes obvious in the legs.

ophthalmoscope An instrument, consisting of a special lens on an electric torch, which is used for examining the *retina*.

osteoporosis Loss of density (thinning) of bone due to aging. The bones become more brittle and fracture more easily. Women are more vulnerable to osteoporosis after the menopause, because their ovaries stop producing the *hormone* oestrogen, which helps maintain healthy bones. A calcium-rich diet, plenty of exercise and (where necessary) hormone replacement therapy (HRT) can all help prevent osteoporosis.

palpitations Feeling or hearing your own heart beating fast.

placebo An inert or 'dummy' version of a drug which looks, tastes and smells like the 'real' drug but which contains no active ingredients at all.

placebo effect Anyone with an illness or problem tends to feel better after they have consulted a doctor (or another health professional or

Glossary

professional carer of any sort) and started some plan of treatment (with or without medication). This 'feeling better' is the placebo effect.

placenta The placenta provides the interface between the mother's circulating blood and her unborn baby's circulating blood.

plaque Fatty deposits (consisting mainly of *cholesterol* and clotted blood) on the walls of *arteries* that may ultimately weaken or block these vessels.

pre-eclampsia You have pre-eclampsia if in pregnancy your BP is 140/90 mmHg or more and is known to have been less than this before your pregnancy began, if there is protein in your urine and if you have some swelling of your body from increased fluid (*oedema*). If left untreated, pre-eclampsia can lead to *eclampsia*. Pre-eclampsia stops when the baby is born.

pre-eclamptic toxaemia or **PET** Another name for *pre-eclampsia*.

pregnancy-associated hypertension or **PAH** Another name for *pre-eclampsia*.

pregnancy-induced hypertension or **PIH** Another name for *pre-eclampsia*.

pregnancy-related hypertension or **PRH** Another name for *pre-eclampsia*.

primary high blood pressure High blood pressure which is not caused by some other medical condition. It is the most common type of high blood pressure.

pulmonary circulation Blood circulation through your lungs, where it takes up oxygen.

randomised controlled trial A *controlled trial* in which participants are allocated to receive the active treatment or to be a 'control' on a completely random basis, so that the choice of subjects for treatment cannot be affected by the researchers running the trial.

retina Usually described as 'the back of the eye', this is the inner surface of the eyeball which is sensitive to light and colour. All the signals to do with your vision originate in your retina, from where they go to your brain to be organised into a picture of what you are seeing. It has a rich blood supply of very fine *arterioles*, *venules* and *capillaries*. The retina is the only place in the body where the circulation can be seen directly without cutting anything open. This is done by looking through the pupil of the eye with an *ophthalmoscope*, usually in a dark room or after dilating the pupils with special eyedrops.

secondary high blood pressure High blood pressure for which the cause is known, that is high blood pressure which is secondary to some other medical condition. Fewer than 1% of people with high blood pressure have secondary high blood pressure.

side-effects Almost all drugs affect the body in ways beyond their intended actions. These unwanted 'extra' effects are called side-effects. Side-effects vary in their severity from person to person, and often disappear when the body becomes used to a particular drug.

slow-release or **sustained-release** or **SR** Tablets or capsules designed to delay absorption of a drug in the gut and so help to supply the drug more evenly through the day.

sphygmomanometer The instrument used for measuring blood pressure.

steroids In this book, an abbreviation for *corticosteroids*.

stroke Damage caused to part of the brain because its blood supply has been interrupted. A stroke may be caused by a *thrombosis* in a brain artery, or the artery may have been blocked by an *embolus*. Some strokes are caused by haemorrhages (bleeding) within the brain. Strokes may affect movement, sensations, speech, thought and other functions of the brain. Which part or function is affected depends on which part of the brain has been damaged.

subconjunctival haemorrhage A small amount of bleeding in the white of the eye. This may appear after coughing, sneezing or straining when emptying the bowels, and shows up as a bright red area on the white of the eye which then disappears slowly over six weeks or so. It is completely harmless.

systemic circulation Blood circulation through the whole of your body other than your lungs.

systolic pressure The pressure at which blood is pushed out of the heart into the arteries when the heart muscle is squeezing. It is the top figure in the blood pressure 'fraction' (eg someone with a BP of 150/85 mmHg has a systolic pressure of 150 mmHg).

thrombosis Formation of a blood clot inside a blood vessel.

total blood cholesterol A measure of all forms of *cholesterol* in your blood, including *HDL*, *LDL* and *VLDL cholesterol*. A rough indication of the amount of 'bad' cholesterol in the blood.

toxaemia or **toxaemia of pregnancy** An old name for *eclampsia* and *pre-eclampsia*.

trade name Another name for *brand name*.

transient ischaemic attacks or **TIAs** Temporary disturbance of vision, giddiness, faintness and confusion lasting for a few seconds and

Glossary

caused by micro-emboli (very small fragments of blood clots) travelling up to the brain, where they break up into minute particles that cause no further problems. They often precede a major *stroke* and require treatment with aspirin or *anticoagulants*.

triglyceride The form in which fat is first absorbed from the gut.

uterus The womb.

veins Blood vessels which carry blood back from your body tissues to your heart. Unlike *arteries*, they have thin flabby walls.

venous blood pressure The blood pressure in your *veins*. Although exertion raises your venous blood pressure, this is NOT the type of high blood pressure we are considering in this book, which is high *arterial blood pressure*.

venules The smallest *veins*, beginning at the ends of the *capillary network*.

VLDL cholesterol or very low density lipoprotein cholesterol One of the *cholesterol*-containing substances found in the bloodstream. VLDL cholesterol is considered to be 'bad' cholesterol because it is one of the sources of *plaque*, and because high blood levels predict high death rates from *coronary heart disease*.

white coat hypertension This refers to the effect that doctors have on some people – simply entering a doctor's surgery can make them so nervous that their blood pressure shoots up. The nickname comes from the fact that so many doctors (especially those in hospitals) wear white coats when they are working.

Appendix 1

Drugs used in treating high blood pressure

As you can see from the lengths of the lists in the tables in this appendix, a very large number of drugs is used in treating high blood pressure. I have tried to make the lists as complete as possible, and they were correct at the time this book went to press. But you should be aware that drugs come and go very rapidly – manufacturers introduce new drugs and withdraw older ones all the time. If you cannot find your particular drug or drugs on this list, then ask your doctor for more information about it. If it is a new drug, your doctor should be able to tell you to which drug group it belongs, and you can then look that up here. Alternatively, if your drug is not in this list, it may be because it is being given to you for some other reason: it may not be for your high blood pressure.

Prices also change: the speed with which current prices go out of date, and so the task of updating them in future editions of this book, means that we have omitted them. This has been a reluctant decision. Drug prices are hugely variable and in some cases very high, and these variations in price are important. At the current cost of NHS prescriptions, some drugs are actually cheaper bought direct from your chemist on a private prescription, and it may be worth you asking about this. If you need to buy more of your tablets or capsules when you are travelling abroad, you may have to meet the full cost (another reason for knowing what it is). You should either make sure you have enough to cover all your needs before you go, or check with your chemist to find out what the likely costs will be.

No doctor, not even the greatest specialists, can possibly have personal experience of all these different drugs. Good doctors make themselves familiar with one or two from each group, and stick to them. So please remember the lists are inclusive – they are not lists of recommendations.

Drug names

All drugs have two names – the generic (or scientific) name given to each drug when it is first developed, and the brand (or trade) name, which is the name given to a drug when it is manufactured by a particular drug company.

Drug companies patent the drugs they develop, and these drug patents last for eight years. Because of this, many drugs (especially those introduced within the past eight years) are available only under one brand name. For drugs introduced more than eight years ago (and therefore outside patent protection) each generic name may have several equivalent brand names. Brand names abroad are not necessarily the same as in the UK. Generic names are internationally standardised and recognised by pharmacists. They must, by law, be printed somewhere on the original container (although this is often in very small print).

About the groups

Available BP-lowering drugs can be divided into 10 groups according to how they work. If you use the tables to find out to which group (or groups, if you are on a mixed or combined preparation) your medication belongs, you can then find out more about it by looking up that group in the section on *Drug groups* later in this appendix. The numbers I have given to the drug groups are simply to make the information easier to find – they are not in any sense 'official' numbers.

There are usually so many different drugs and brands in each group, with so few significant differences between them, that you may safely assume that whatever is said about the group applies equally to all drugs included within it. The few exceptions to this are mentioned individually. The explanations of how the drugs work are necessarily somewhat simplified, but although a little knowledge may be a dangerous thing, it is less dangerous than no knowledge at all.

We have included the year in which the first-available drug in each group came into common use because, very generally speaking, although the more recently introduced drugs may be less likely to cause obvious unwanted side-effects, we know a lot more about the older drugs than the newer ones, particularly about their long-term side-effects. All BP-lowering drugs have some side-effects, although few of these may be noticed by the person taking them. Reading lists of side-effects can be alarming, so it is worth remembering two things. First, that the fact that side-effects are possible does not mean that they are either inevitable or severe; and second that it is possible to have beneficial side-effects as well as unpleasant ones.

The groups are presented in the order of preference currently recommended by the British Hypertension Society, starting with those most likely to be prescribed and ending with those least likely. A few are described out of sequence because, although they may rarely be used, explanations of the way they work resemble those of more commonly used drugs. In reality, after the first two or three choices, no such simple sequence exists. As all the drug groups work in different ways, and as everyone responds individually to treatment, the fact that yours happens to be one of the less commonly prescribed drugs is not something to worry about.

British Hypertension Society order of preference

First-line drugs
Group 1   Diuretics
   1A   Thiazide and thiazide-like diuretics
   1B   Potassium sparing diuretics
   1C   Diuretics with potassium supplements
   1D   Loop diuretics

Second-line drugs
Group 2   Beta-blockers

Third-line drugs
Group 3   Angiotensin Converting Enzyme (ACE) inhibitors
Group 4   Angiotensin inhibitors
Group 5   Vasodilators
Group 6   Alpha-blockers
Group 7   Calcium-channel blockers

Fourth-line drugs
Group 8 Drugs acting mainly on the brainstem

Last resorts
Group 9 Adrenergic neurone blockers
Group 10 Ganglion blockers

About the tables

Table 1 lists the drugs alphabetically by brand name, with the manufacturer's name given in brackets underneath. Against each brand name you will find the generic name(s) of the drug(s) it contains, the range of dose sizes available, and the drug group(s) to which it belongs.

Table 2 lists the same drugs but in alphabetical order of their generic names. Against each generic name you will find a list of all the brand names that contain that particular drug (remember, some of these brand names may contain that particular drug in combination with other drugs) and also the drug group to which it belongs.

In both tables, all drugs are tablets or capsules unless otherwise stated. Long-acting (slow-release or sustained-release) tablets are indicated by an asterisk (*).

Table 1: Drugs in alphabetical brand name order

Brand name & manufacturer	Generic name	Unit dose	Group number
Accupro (Parke-Davis)	quinapril	5, 10, 20, 40 mg	3
Accuretic (Parke-Davis)	quinapril + hydrochlorothiazide	10 + 12.5 mg	3 + 1A
Acepril (Squibb)	captopril	12.5, 25, 50 mg	3
Acezide (Squibb)	captopril + hydrochlorothiazide	50 + 25 mg	3 + 1A
Adalat LA* (Bayer)	nifedipine	30, 60 mg	7

Brand name & manufacturer	Generic name	Unit dose	Group number
Adalat LA* (Bayer)	nifedipine	10, 20 mg	7
Adipine MR* (Trinity)	nifedipine	10, 20 mg	7
Adizem-60 (Napp)	diltiazem	60 mg	7
Adizem-SR* (Napp)	diltiazem	90, 120, 180 mg	7
Adizem-XL* (Napp)	diltiazem	120, 180, 240, 300 mg	7
Adizem XL Plus (Napp)	diltiazem + hydrochlorothiazide	12.5 + 150 mg	7 + 1A
Aldomet (MSD)	methyldopa	125, 250, 500 mg suspension 250 mg/5 ml	8
Amias (Astra/Takeda)	candesartan	2, 4, 8, 16 mg	4
Amil-Co (Baker Norton)	amiloride + hydrochlorothiazide	5 + 50 mg	1B + 1A
Angiopine MR* (Ashbourne)	nifedipine	20 mg	7
Angitil SR* (Trinity)	diltiazem	90, 120, 180 mg	7
Apresoline (Ciba)	hydralazine	25, 50 mg	5
Aprinox (Knoll Pharma)	bendrofluazide	2.5, 5 mg	1A
Aprovel (BMS/Sanofi)	irbesartan	75, 150, 300 mg	4
Arelix* (Hoechst)	piretanide	6 mg	1D

Appendix 1

Brand name & manufacturer	Generic name	Unit dose	Group number
Arfonad (Cambridge)	trimetaphan	5 ml ampoule	10
Baratol (Monmouth)	indoramin	25, 50 mg	6
Baycaron (Bayer)	mefruside	25 mg	1A
Bendogen (Lagap)	bethanidine	10 mg	9
Beta-Adalat (Bayer)	atenolol + nifedipine	50 + 20 mg	2 + 7
Beta-Cardone (Evans)	sotalol	40, 80, 200 mg	2
Beta-Prograne* (Tillomed)	propranolol	160 mg	2
Betaloc (Astra)	metoprolol	50, 100 mg	2
Betaloc-SA* (Astra)	metoprolol	200 mg	2
Betim (Leo)	timolol	10 mg	2
Blocadren (MSD)	timolol	10 mg	2
Burinex (Leo)	bumetanide	1, 5 mg	1D
Burinex A (Leo)	bumetanide + amiloride	1 + 5 mg	1D + 1B
Burinex K (Leo)	bumetanide + potassium chloride	0.5 + 573 mg	1C
Calanif (Berk)	nifedipine	20 mg	7

Brand name & manufacturer	Generic name	Unit dose	Group number
Capoten (Squibb)	captopril	12.5, 25, 50 mg	3
Capozide (Squibb)	captopril + hydrochlorothiazide	50 + 25 mg	3 + 1A
Capozide LS (Squibb)	captopril + hydrochlorothiazide	25 + 12.5 mg	3 + 1A
Carace (DuPont)	lisinopril	2.5, 5, 10, 20 mg	3
Carace 10 Plus (DuPont)	lisinopril + hydrochlorothiazide	10 + 12.5 mg	3 + 1A
Carace 20 Plus (DuPont)	lisinopril + hydrochlorothiazide	20 + 12.5 mg	3 + 1A
Cardene (Roche)	nicardipine	20, 30 mg	7
Cardene-SR* (Syntex)	nicardipine	30, 45 mg	7
Cardilate MR* (Norton)	nifedipine	20 mg	7
Cardura (Invicta)	doxazosin	1, 2, 4 mg	6
Catapres (Boehringer Ingelheim)	clonidine	0.1, 0.3 mg	8
Catapres Perlongets* (Boehringer Ingelheim)	clonidine	0.25 mg	8
Celectol (Rhone-Poulenc Rorer)	celiprolol	200, 400 mg	2

Appendix 1

Brand name & manufacturer	Generic name	Unit dose	Group number
Co-Betaloc (Astra)	metoprolol + hydrochlorothiazide	100 + 12.5 mg	5 + 1A
Co-Betaloc SA* (Astra)	metoprolol + hydrochlorothiazide	200 + 25 mg	5 + 1A
Coracten* (Evans)	nifedipine	10, 20 mg	7
Cordilox (Baker Norton)	verapamil	40, 80, 120, 160 mg	7
Corgard (Sanofi Winthrop)	nadolol	40, 80 mg	2
Corgaretic 40 (Sanofi Winthrop)	nadolol + bendrofluazide	40 + 5 mg	2 + 1A
Corgaretic 80 (Sanofi Winthrop)	nadolol + bendrofluazide	80 + 5 mg	2 + 1A
Coversyl (Servier)	perindopril	2, 4 mg	3
Cozaar (MSD)	losartan	25, 50 mg	4
Cozaar-Comp (MSD)	losartan + hydrochlorothiazide	50 + 12.5 mg	4 + 1A
Cozaar Half-strength (MSD)	losartan	25 mg	4
[no brands]	debrisoquine	10 mg	9
Dilzem-SR* (Elan)	diltiazem	60, 90, 120 mg	7
Diovan (Ciba)	valsartan	40, 80, 160 mg	4

Brand name & manufacturer	Generic name	Unit dose	Group number
Diurexan (Asta Medica)	xipamide	20 mg	1A
Doralese (Bencard)	indoramin	20 mg	6
Dyazide (SmithKline Beecham)	triamterene + hydrochlorothiazide	50 + 25 mg	1B + 1A
Emcor (Merck)	bisoprolol	10 mg	2
Emcor-LS (Merck)	bisoprolol	5 mg	2
Eucardic (Boehringer Mannheim)	carvedilol	12.5, 25 mg	2
Gopten (Knoll Pharma)	trandolapril	0.5, 1, 2 mg	3
Half-Inderal LA* (Zeneca)	propranolol	80 mg	2
Half Securon-SR* (Knoll Pharma)	verapamil	120 mg	7
Hydrosaluric (MSD)	hydrochlorothiazide	25, 50 mg	1A
Hygroton (Geigy)	chlorthalidone	50 mg	1A
Hypovase (Invicta)	prazosin	0.5, 1, 2 mg	6
Hytrin (Abbott)	terazosin	1, 2, 5, 10 mg	6
Inderal (Zeneca)	propranolol	10, 40, 80 mg	2

Appendix 1

Brand name & manufacturer	Generic name	Unit dose	Group number
Inderal LA* (Zeneca)	propranolol	160 mg	2
Inderetic (Zeneca)	propranolol + bendrofluazide	80 + 2.5 mg	2 + 1A
Inderex* (Zeneca)	propranolol + bendrofluazide	160 + 5 mg	2 + 1A
Innovace (MSD)	enalapril	2.5, 5, 10, 20 mg	3
Innozide (MSD)	enalapril + hydrochlorothiazide	20 + 12.5 mg	3 + 1A
Ismelin (Ciba)	guanethidine	10, 25 mg	9
Istin (Pfizer)	amlodipine	5, 10 mg	7
Kalspare (Cusi)	chlorthalidone + triamterene	50 + 50 mg	1A + 1B
Kalten (Zeneca)	atenolol + hydrochlorothiazide + amiloride	50 + 25 + 2.5 mg	2 + 1A +1B
Kerlone (Lorex)	betaxolol	20 mg	2
Loniten (Upjohn)	minoxidil	2.5, 5, 10 mg	5
Lopresor (Geigy)	metoprolol	50, 100 mg	2
Lopresor SR* (Geigy)	metoprolol	200 mg	2
Metanix 5 (Borg)	metolazone	5 mg	1A

Brand name & manufacturer	Generic name	Unit dose	Group number
Mudocren (Morson)	timolol + hydrochlorothiazide + amiloride	10 + 25 + 2.5 mg	2 + 1A + 1B
Moduret 25 (DuPont)	amiloride + hydrochlorothiazide	2.5 + 25 mg	1B + 1A
Moduretic (DuPont)	amiloride + hydrochlorothiazide	5 + 50 mg	1B + 1A
Monocor (Lederle)	bisoprolol	5, 10 mg	2
Monozide 10 (Lederle)	bisoprolol + hydrochlorothiazide	10 + 6.25 mg	2 + 1A
Motens (Boehringer Ingelheim)	lacidipine	2, 4 mg	7
Natramid (Trinity)	indapamide	2.5 mg	1A
Natrilix (Servier)	indapamide	2.5 mg	1A
Natrilix SR (Servier)	indapamide	1.5 mg	1A
Navidrex (Ciba)	cyclopenthiazide	0.5 mg	1A
Navispare (Ciba)	cyclopenthiazide + amiloride	0.25 + 2.5 mg	1A + 1B
Neo-Naclex (Goldshield)	bendrofluazide	5 mg	1A
Neo-Naclex K* (Goldshield)	bendrofluazide + potassium chloride	2.5 + 630 mg	1C
Nephril (Pfizer)	polythiazide	1 mg	1A

Appendix 1

Brand name & manufacturer	Generic name	Unit dose	Group number
Nifensar XL* (Theraplix)	nifedipine	20 mg	7
Odrik (Roussel)	trandolapril	0.5, 1, 2 mg	3
Perdix (Schwartz)	moexipril	7.5, 15 mg	3
Physiotens (Solvay)	moxonidine	0.2, 0.4 mg	8
Plendil* (Schwartz)	felodipine	5, 10 mg	7
Prescal (Ciba)	isradipine	2.5 mg	7
Prestim (Leo)	timolol + bendrofluazide	10 + 2.5 mg	2 + 1A
Prestim Forte (Leo)	timolol + bendrofluazide	20 + 5 mg	2 + 1A
Probeta LA* (Trinity)	propranolol	160 mg	2
Saluric (MSD)	chlorothiazide	500 mg	1A
Secadrex (RPR)	acebutolol + hydrochlorothiazide	200 + 12.5 mg	1 + 1A
Sectral (RPR)	acebutolol	400 mg	2
Securon-SR* (Knoll Pharma)	verapamil	240 mg	7
Slow-Trasicor* (Ciba)	oxprenolol	160 mg	2
Slozem (Lipha)	diltiazem	120, 180, 240 mg	7

Brand name & manufacturer	Generic name	Unit dose	Group number
Staril (Squibb)	fosinopril	10, 20 mg	3
Syscor MR* (Bayer)	nisoldipine	10, 20, 30 mg	7
Tenif (Zeneca)	atenolol + nifedipine	50 + 20 mg	2 + 7
Tenoret 50 (Zeneca)	atenolol + chlorthalidone	50 + 12.5 mg	2 + 1A
Tenoretic (Zeneca)	atenolol + chlorthalidone	100 + 25 mg	2 + 1A
Tenormin (Zeneca)	atenolol	25, 100 mg	2
Tenormin-LS* (Zeneca)	atenolol	50 mg	2
Tensipine MR* (ethical generic)	nifedipine	10, 20 mg	7
Tildiem-LA* (Lorex)	diltiazem	300 mg	7
Tildiem Retard* (Lorex)	diltiazem	90, 120 mg	7
Torem (Boehringer Mannheim)	torasemide	2.5, 5, 10 mg	1D
Totamol (CP Pharmaceuticals)	atenolol	25, 50, 100 mg	2
Trandate (Duncan Flockhart)	labetalol	50, 100, 200, 400 mg	2
Trasicor (Ciba)	oxprenolol	20, 40, 80, 160 mg	2

Brand name & manufacturer	Generic name	Unit dose	Group number
Trasicrex* (Ciba)	oxprenolol + cyclopenthiazide	160 + 0.25 mg	2 + 1A
Triam-Co (Baker Norton)	triamterene + hydrochlorothiazide	50 + 25 mg	1B + 1A
Tritace (Hoechst)	ramipril	1.25, 2.5, 5 mg	3
Unipine XL* (ethical generic)	nifedipine	30 mg	7
Univer* (RPR)	verapamil	120, 180, 240 mg	7
Vasace (Roche)	cilazapril	0.25, 0.5, 1, 2.5, 5 mg	3
Viskaldix (Sandoz)	pindolol + clopamide	10 + 5 mg	2 + 1A
Visken (Sandoz)	pindolol	5, 15 mg	2
Zanidip (Napp)	lercanipidine	10 mg	7
Zestoretic 10 (Zeneca)	lisinopril + hydrochlorothiazide	10 + 12.5 mg	3 + 1A
Zestoretic 20 (Zeneca)	lisinopril + hydrochlorothiazide	20 + 12.5 mg	3 + 1A
Zestril (Zeneca)	lisinopril	2.5, 5, 10, 20 mg	3

Table 2: Drugs in alphabetical generic name order

Generic name	Brand name	Group number
acebutolol	Secadrex, Sectral	2
amiloride	Amil-Co, Burinex A, Frumil, Kalten, Moducren, Moduret 25, Moduretic, Navispare	1B
amlodipine	Istin	7
atenolol	Beta-Adalat, Kalten, Tenif, Tenoret 50, Tenoretic, Tenormin, Tenormin-LS*, Totamol	2
bendrofluazide	Aprinox, Corgaretic 40, Corgaretic 80, Inderetic, Inderex*, Neo-Naclex, Neo-Naclex K, Prestim, Prestim Forte	1A
benzthiazide	Dytide	1A
betaxolol	Kerlone	2
bethanidine	Bendogen	9
bisoprolol	Emcor, Emcor-LS, Monocor, Monozide 10	2
bumetanide	Burinex, Burinex A, Burinex K	1D
candesartan	Amias	4
captopril	Acepril, Acezide, Capoten, Capozide, Capozide LS	3
carvedilol	Eucardic	2
celiprolol	Celectol	2
chlorthalidone	Hygroton, Kalspare, Tenoret 50, Tenoretic	1A
chlorothiazide	Saluric	1A
cilazapril	Vascace	3

Appendix 1

Generic name	Brand name	Group number
clonidine	Catapres, Catapres Perlongets*	8
clopamide	Viskaldix	1A
cyclopenthiazide	Navidrex, Navispare, Trasidrex	1A
debrisoquine	[no brand names]	9
diltiazem	Adizem-60, Adizem-SR*, Adizem-XL*, Angitil SR*, Dilzem-SR*, Slozem, Tildiem-LA*, Tildiem Retard*	7
doxazosin	Cardura	6
enalapril	Innovace, Innozide	3
ethacrynic acid	Edecrin	1D
felodipine	Plendil	7
fosinopril	Staril	3
guanethidine	Ismelin	9
hydralazine	Apresoline	5
hydrochorothiazide	Accuretic, Acezide, Amil-Co, Capozide, Capozide LS, Carace 10 Plus, Carace 20 Plus, Co-Betaloc, Co-Betaloc SA*, Cozaar-Comp, Dyazide, Hydrosaluric, Innozide, Kalten, Moducren, Moduret 25, Moduretic, Monozide 10, Secadrex, Triam-Co, Zestoretic 10, Zestoretic 20	1A
hydroflumethiazide	Aldactide 25, Aldactide 50	1A
indapamide	Natramid, Natrilix, Natrilix SR	1A
indoramin	Baratol, Doralese	6
irbesartan	Aprovel	4
isradipine	Prescal	7

Generic name	Brand name	Group number
labetalol	Trandate	2
lacidipine	Motens	7
lercanipidine	Zanidip	7
lisinopril	Carace, Carace 10 Plus, Carace 20 Plus, Zestoretic 10, Zestoretic 20, Zestril	3
losartan	Cozaar, Cozaar-Comp, Cozaar Half-strength	4
mefruside	Baycaron	1A
methyldopa	Aldomet	8
metolazone	Metenix 5	1A
metoprolol	Betaloc, Betaloc-SA*, Co-Betaloc, Co-Betaloc SA*, Lopresor, Lopresor SR*	2
minoxidil	Loniten	5
moexipril	Perdix	3
moxonidine	Physiotens	8
nadolol	Corgard, Corgaretic 40, Corgaretic 80	2
nicardipine	Cardene, Cardene-SR*	7
nifedipine	Adalat LA*, Adalat Retard*, Angiopine MR*, Beta-Adalat, Calanif, Cardilate MR*, Coracten*, Nifensar XL*, Tenif, Tensipine, Unipine	7
nisoldipine	Syscor MR*	7
oxprenolol	Slow-Trasicor*, Trasicor, Trasidrex*	2
perindopril	Coversyl	3

Generic name	Brand name	Group number
pindolol	Viskaldix, Visken	2
polythiazide	Nephril	1A
potassium chloride	Burinex K, Diumide-K Continus, Lasikal, Lasix+K, Neo-Naclex K	1C
prazosin	Hypovase	6
propranolol	Beta-Prograne, Half-Inderal LA*, Inderal, Inderal LA*, Inderetic, Inderex*, Probeta LA*	2
quinapril	Accupro, Accuretic	3
ramipril	Tritace	3
sotalol	Beta-Cardone	2
terazosin	Hytrin	6
timolol	Betim, Blocadren, Moducren, Prestim, Prestim Forte	2
torasemide	Torem	1D
trandolapril	Gopten, Odrik	3
triamterene	Dyazide, Frusene, Kalspare, Triam-Co	1B
valsartan	Diovan	4
verapamil	Cordilox, Half-Securon-SR*, Securon, Securon-SR*, Univer	7
xipamide	Diurexan	1A

Drug groups

Group 1: Diuretics

1A Thiazide and thiazide-like diuretics
1B Potassium sparing diuretics
1C Diuretics with potassium supplements
1D Loop diuretics

FIRST INTRODUCED 1957

As you can see, diuretics are available in four subgroups. Of these, only those in the first subgroup – thiazide diuretics – are generally useful for treating high BP, and they are the drugs most commonly used today. Use of the others for this purpose is occasionally justified by special circumstances, but in general they should be avoided, and if there are special reasons why you need them, you should ask what these are.

- Diuretics in general

Although they are very effective BP-lowering drugs, the main purpose of diuretics (and the origin of their name) is to increase urine output. For this reason they are often loosely referred to as 'water tablets'. This can lead to misunderstandings, because although the volume of your urine output will rise when you take them, the frequency with which you need to empty your bladder may or may not rise – so there is a chance that you may think they're not working when they are actually working well. More importantly, if you are already bothered by the need to make frequent trips to empty your bladder, you may wonder why on earth your doctor wants to make you go even more often.

The main way diuretics reduce BP is probably by increasing output of sodium through the kidney, although they also widen small arteries and reduce blood volume. They are a little more effective if you also reduce your salt intake.

- 1A Thiazide diuretics

When these were first introduced they were mainly intended for treatment of heart failure. They were soon found to be useful for reducing high BP, and have been the mainstay of treatment ever since. They have a few side-effects, but because they have been in use for so long and have been so intensively studied, their faults are relatively well understood, and can mostly be avoided by keeping the dose down (they rarely cause side-effects unless they are used in unnecessarily high doses). The British Hypertension Society advises them as the usual first choice for treatment, and this is endorsed by a large majority of experienced doctors.

The only important differences between the vast number of competing varieties available are the speed with which they work and how long their effects last. If your doctor wants you to have a thiazide diuretic with a slow, steady effect for a once-daily dosage, then you will probably be prescribed chlorthalidone, chlorothiazide or hydrochlorothiazide. Otherwise there is nothing to choose between bendrofluazide and all the rest: all of them will give good control through the day after a morning dose, but if you take them twice daily, you may need to take the second dose in the late afternoon rather than last thing at night, to avoid getting up during the night.

Thiazides have their full BP-lowering effect at very low doses: if you take more than this, you greatly increase the risk of side-effects, without any advantage in reducing your BP. Many doctors, nurses and chemists have still not taken this on board, partly because pharmaceutical companies continue to produce and promote high-dosage tablets. There is ample evidence that it is pointless to take more than 2.5 mg a day of bendrofluazide, 25 mg a day of chlorthalidone (which means half a 50 mg tablet as no 25 mg tablet is currently available), 25 mg a day of hydrochlorothiazide, or 0.25 mg of cyclopenthiazide.

Beneficial side-effects
Thiazide diuretics reduce excretion of calcium through the kidney, resulting in two important beneficial side-effects. People with a tendency to form stones in the kidney, and women with a tendency to develop osteoporosis (brittle bones) after the menopause, are both much less likely to do so if they take thiazides regularly. Multiple fractures from osteoporosis are the main cause of severe curvature of the spine in elderly women, a condition easily prevented but very difficult to treat. The risk is highest in women with a family history of osteoporosis, and who are slightly built with a slender bone structure.

Other side-effects
Thiazide diuretics can cause impotence, mainly when prescribed in

unnecessarily large doses. Reducing the dose to the minimum may help, as side-effects are rare at low doses. There is more information about impotence in the section on *Sex* in Chapter 7.

They should not be used in pregnancy, because they cross the placenta and therefore reach the unborn baby, and because they can bring on eclampsia (there is a section on *Pre-eclampsia and eclampsia* in Chapter 8).

There are many possible harmful side-effects from thiazide diuretics, but only two of real importance at the low doses recommended. The first is gout; the second is diabetes and glucose intolerance. You will find more information about both of these in Chapter 6.

Their reputation for causing dangerous falls in blood potassium (hypokalaemia) is undeserved, although admittedly at one time this was thought to be a common side-effect of thiazide diuretics. You will find more information about the effect of drug treatment on blood potassium in the section on *BP-lowering drugs* in Chapter 4.

- Thiazide diuretics in combination with other drugs

At least half of all people with high blood pressure treated with BP-lowering drugs can only get good BP control by combining two drugs from different groups, usually a thiazide diuretic plus something else. Almost all the other BP-lowering drugs are available as combined preparations, containing a fixed dose of diuretic with a drug from one of the other groups. With the current cost of prescription charges, and with doctors under pressure only to prescribe about one month's supply of drugs at a time, it can obviously be much less expensive for people who have to pay prescription charges to use these combined preparations. However, because nearly all these fixed combinations contain unnecessarily high doses of thiazides, those who use them are more likely to have side-effects than those who instead take the lowest effective dose of thiazide as a separate tablet. (The *Miscellaneous* section in Chapter 7 includes information about prescription charges, exemption from them and pre-paid 'season tickets'.)

- 1B Potassium sparing diuretics
- 1C Diuretics with potassium supplements

As was mentioned in the section on thiazide diuretics (Group 1A), low blood potassium was first thought to be a common side-effect of taking diuretics for high blood pressure. This concern led to the development and promotion of these two groups of drugs. As their names imply, the potassium sparing diuretics (group 1B) were intended to prevent excessive potassium loss, while the addition of potassium supplements to diuretics (group 1C) was intended to replace any potassium that had been lost.

We now know that thiazide diuretics rarely lead to low blood potassium in people leading a normal life. For the vast majority of people treated for high BP with thiazide diuretics, low blood potassium is not a significant risk, and none of these drugs should be used routinely for treatment of high BP. One reason for this is that they could cause the level of potassium in the body to become too high (hyperkalaemia) – this is discussed further in the section on *BP-lowering drugs* in Chapter 4. For the large majority of people with high blood pressure who are apparently fairly well and lead a normal life, this danger of high blood potassium now seems much greater than its opposite, low blood potassium. There is therefore a professional consensus that potassium supplements are normally unnecessary, and potassium sparing diuretics are inappropriate. Unfortunately they are still promoted for routine treatment of high blood pressure by some companies.

- 1D Loop diuretics

Loop diuretics (of which the most commonly prescribed is probably frusemide) push sodium and water out of the kidneys more powerfully than thiazide diuretics. Unlike thiazide diuretics, they cause a noticeable and often inconvenient increase in the frequency with which you need to empty your bladder, but they are much less effective in lowering BP. They are rightly used for heart failure and in kidney failure, both common complications of long-standing high BP, so many people with high BP are treated with diuretics in this group, but they should not be used routinely to control high BP in otherwise healthy people. Few pharmaceutical companies now promote them for this purpose.

Group 2: Beta-blockers

FIRST INTRODUCED 1966

After the thiazide diuretics, these have been the next most commonly prescribed group of BP-lowering drugs during the past 15 years or so, although the ACE-inhibitors are now catching them up. They work mainly by blocking transmission of nerve messages from the brainstem to the spiral muscle sheath around the small arteries, and by reducing heart output. They reduce BP by slightly less than thiazide diuretics, but by about the same amount as most other BP-lowering drugs. For reasons not yet understood, and unlike other BP-lowering drugs, they seem to have no preventive effect at all against coronary heart disease in people who continue to smoke. There is also some evidence that they work less effectively in people of African descent than in people in other ethnic groups.

Beneficial side-effects
A possible beneficial side-effect of beta-blockers is a calming effect on nervous people. Beta-blockers have been used successfully to control nervousness in people speaking in public for the first time, in people taking their driving tests, and in people undergoing other similar stressful events. They have also been prescribed by psychiatrists to control minor anxiety. In spite of these effects, they are not addictive.

Beta-blockers are also very effective in preventing attacks of angina. This is a common complication of high blood pressure, and there is a section on **Angina** in Chapter 9. For people who have already had a heart attack (coronary thrombosis), some beta-blockers (metoprolol, propranolol and timolol) have been shown to reduce the risk of a fatal disturbance of heart rhythm during the next two or three years.

Other side-effects
Unpleasant side-effects in some people are tiredness and a generally reduced level of energy, and athletes or people doing heavy manual work may notice that they become fatigued more quickly. Cold hands and feet are common with beta-blocker drugs. This is seldom severe and you may be able to avoid it by dressing warmly, and wearing gloves and extra tights or long johns in the winter. The effect may be avoided by combining beta-blockers with another BP-lowering drug that increases blood flow through the limbs, perhaps one of the calcium-channel blockers.

Beta-blockers may cause erection problems and impotence in some men, but the effect soon disappears if the drug is stopped (there is more information about impotence and its treatment in the section on **Sex** in Chapter 7).

Having bad dreams is common in people who take fat-soluble beta-blockers (such as propranolol) which reach the brain. If you have this problem, ask your doctor if you can switch to a water-soluble beta-blocker (such as atenolol) which does not reach the brain.

All beta-blockers slow the heartbeat, but this is usually of no consequence. However, people who already have a very slow heartbeat (around 60 a minute or less) may get fainting attacks, and so should not use them.

In pregnancy, beta-blockers are well tolerated and apparently without risk to the baby after the 24th week (for some obstetricians they have replaced methyldopa as the first choice for treating high blood pressure in late pregnancy). Used earlier in pregnancy they may slow down the baby's growth, and so should be avoided.

There are two serious side-effects associated with beta-blockers. The first is narrowed lung airways in people with asthma. Because of this effect, even a single dose of a beta-blocker can be dangerous for people with asthma, so your doctor should check if you have it before prescribing them (there is more information about how this is done in the section on *Asthma and other breathing problems* in Chapter 6). The second and much rarer side-effect is further reduction in heart output in people who have heart failure (or who are on the verge of heart failure). However, high blood pressure itself is more likely to be a cause of heart failure (discussed in more detail in Chapter 9) than taking beta-blockers – in fact, for the large majority of people treated for high BP before it has caused heart failure, beta-blockers seem to be as effective as other BP-lowering drugs in preventing this complication.

Group 3: Angiotensin Converting Enzyme (ACE) inhibitors

FIRST INTRODUCED 1981

These are the most recently introduced major group of BP-lowering drugs currently in common use. They have not yet been evaluated in any large-scale long-term randomised controlled trials, so although they seem generally effective and they have some theoretical advantages, we cannot yet be sure that they will perform as well on a mass scale as the older, better-known drugs. However, they are already the first choice of many doctors for routine treatment and for people with diabetes. There is now a bewildering choice of different ACE-inhibitors available but, as usual, there is little significant difference between them. As we know more about them, the older ones are probably preferable to their more recent competitors.

These drugs are generally well tolerated, and may be particularly useful for treating the minority of people with high BP who need to start drug treatment under 40. They greatly improve heart function in heart failure (whether or not this has been caused by high blood pressure) and are therefore particularly useful in elderly people. There are big individual differences in response to these drugs, and they are ineffective in over one-third of people, unless they either greatly reduce their normal salt intake (discussed in the section on *Sodium and salt* in Chapter 5), or take thiazide diuretics as well. There is some evidence that people of African descent get a smaller fall in BP from all ACE-inhibitors than other ethnic groups.

ACE-inhibitors reduce blood pressure by interfering with the normal mechanism which increases salt excretion by the kidneys when there is too much of it in the body, and conserves salt when there is not enough. This means that the normal mechanisms for correcting sudden fluid and salt loss cannot operate in people taking these drugs, which can cause serious problems if an attack of severe diarrhoea and/or vomiting leads to dehydration. You need to be aware of this if you are on ACE-inhibitors, otherwise there could be a risk of you collapsing, with a very low BP and impaired kidney function if you have an attack of diarrhoea and vomiting. You will need to drink large quantities of extra water with one level teaspoonful of salt and one tablespoon of sugar added to each litre (2 pints) of water. You can also make up rehydration solutions based on fruit juice or Coca-cola, or buy sachets of oral rehydration salts from your chemist, and you will find more information about all these in the section on **Travel and holidays** in Chapter 7.

Side-effects

The commonest side-effect of the ACE-inhibitors is a chronic dry cough, which affects about a quarter of the people who take them, women more often than men. In spite of this there is no evidence that they have any worsening effect on asthma.

Captopril (which was the first of these drugs to be introduced) causes a bitter or salty taste in the mouth in about 20% of the people who take it. The taste disappears about 14 days after stopping the drug. Other drugs in this group seem to be free from this side-effect.

Otherwise minor side-effects are uncommon, but they do present two major risks. Firstly, if ACE-inhibitors are started in people who are already taking thiazide diuretics, then their blood pressure may fall so quickly and so far that there is a risk that they may collapse in kidney failure. People already taking thiazides should stop taking them, and leave at least seven days to go by before starting on ACE-inhibitors. Thiazide diuretics can then be added later (if and when necessary) when response to a low dose of ACE-inhibitor is known. Secondly, ACE-inhibitors can tip people with impaired kidney function into kidney failure. They can – and sometimes must – be used in people with impaired kidney function, but this is not safe without skilled supervision by a specialist. As the early stages of impaired kidney function cause no symptoms, you should always have a blood test first to check your kidney function before you start taking ACE-inhibitors.

ACE-inhibitors should be avoided in pregnancy because they affect the baby's blood pressure control, may impair the development of the baby's skull, and may reduce the volume of amniotic fluid (the fluid which surrounds the baby in the womb).

Group 4: Angiotensin II receptor antagonists

FIRST INTRODUCED 1994

These descendants of ACE-inhibitors are often called ACE II agents, with the first generation called ACE I. Only four have so far reached the market, but there will be more. They will probably come into routine use over the next few years. These are losartan (brand name Cozaar), valsartan (Diovan), candesartan (Amias) and irbesartan (Aprovel). They are useful for people who get a persistent dry cough with first-generation ACE-inhibitors.

Group 5: Vasodilators

FIRST INTRODUCED 1951

A very wide range of these drugs is available, some old and well-tested, others newer (introduced in the late 1970s) and still not finally evaluated in long-term, large-scale randomised controlled trials. The simplest and oldest of these drugs reduce blood pressure by relaxing the arteries and increasing their diameter. They therefore tend to increase heart rate and heart output unless they are combined with a beta-blocker.

Side-effects

Hydralazine (Apresoline) was once used very widely in N. America, but was never popular in the UK. Some people already established on it will continue if it seems to suit them. It is seldom effective on its own, but combines well with beta-blockers. The main problem with hydralazine is that at doses above about 200 mg daily it may induce an autoimmune disease called lupus erythematosus (LE) in about one-third of the people who take it, and in 1–3% of people even below this dose. This happens more commonly in women than men, and may start months or even years after beginning treatment. LE usually starts as widespread joint pains and swelling, closely resembling rheumatoid arthritis. Unless the possibility of LE is kept in mind, it is easy to imagine that someone has simply had the bad luck to develop another disorder, and to start treating the consequences instead of the cause. Hydralazine-induced LE disappears completely after the drug is stopped, although it may take a long time to go. Hydralazine is also a fairly common cause of impotence, reversible when the drug is stopped.

Minoxidil (Loniten) is a last-resort drug for severe high blood pressure, which should only be prescribed by hospital-based specialists. It causes marked hair growth, giving women beards but causing some regrowth in bald men: it is marketed for this purpose as an ointment (which has no effect on BP). Unless combined with a diuretic, it also causes marked water retention and sodium retention, with swollen ankles.

Group 6: Alpha-blockers

FIRST INTRODUCED 1976

Alpha-blockers are not widely used in the UK, mainly because they are tricky to start at all ages. Individual response to these drugs varies a lot, so you have to start with a very small dose, and slowly build this up according to response, with weekly blood pressure measurements. Once the right dose has been found, alpha-blockers are generally trouble free for most people until they reach their late 70s. They are effective drugs, and seem to be safe in pregnancy. They reduce blood pressure by dilating (widening) the small arteries.

Beneficial side-effects

Unlike any other BP-lowering drugs, alpha-blockers reduce blood cholesterol significantly. As everyone with high BP is at increased risk of coronary heart disease, and as high blood cholesterol adds another risk factor, this cholesterol-lowering effect is an important advantage, particularly for people with unusually high blood cholesterol (say 7 mmol or more).

Another advantage is that they improve the flow of urine in men with moderate obstruction from benign enlargement of the prostate. This is extremely common from late middle age onwards, and alpha-blockers can make it possible either to postpone surgery (they improve urine flow by about one-third as much as an operation), or sometimes avoid it completely.

Other side-effects
The great disadvantage of alpha-blockers is that the first dose often causes fainting unless it is given last thing at night before going to bed. If treatment is interrupted for some reason, this procedure must be repeated. Fainting is rarely a problem after the first dose, except in elderly people (say in their late 70s or older) in whom there is a risk of fainting attacks even after the use of these drugs is well established. Alpha-blockers should not therefore be used for people of this age.

Group 7: Calcium-channel blockers

FIRST INTRODUCED 1979
These drugs impede the transfer of calcium ions across cell membranes, mainly in the heart and arteries (hence the name – they block the calcium channel). However, they have no effect on calcium in bone, and no effect one way or the other on osteoporosis. Like alpha-blockers, they reduce blood pressure mainly by dilating small arteries. Like beta-blockers, they are also effective in controlling angina, and are often prescribed for this regardless of their effect on blood pressure.

Calcium-channel blockers are a diverse group, and cannot be used interchangeably. Verapamil (Cordilox, Securon) has a large direct effect on the heart, and was originally recommended only for control of arrhythmias (abnormal heart rhythms). For many years it was used only by hospital specialists, but for the past five years or so it has also been promoted for use by GPs as a routine treatment for high blood pressure. It is a difficult drug to use, and can be dangerous if combined with beta-blockers, because this combination may precipitate heart failure or dangerous disturbances in heart rhythm. As it offers no special advantages to outweigh these risks, it is not a good routine treatment for high blood pressure, and we find it difficult to understand why approval was ever given for its promotion for this purpose.

Diltiazem (Adizem, Tildiem) is particularly effective for some people with angina but, like verapamil, must be used cautiously if combined with beta-blockers.

The others, nifedipine (Adalat), amlodipine, felodipine, isradipine, lercanidipine and nicardipine are all safe, effective, and well tolerated even in combination with beta-blockers. (This combination is often useful because calcium-channel blockers tend to improve circulation in hands and feet, thus counterbalancing the effects of beta-blockers.) There is little difference between any of them. They are all effective, all help to control angina, and all combine well with thiazide diuretics.

Side-effects

Minor unpleasant side-effects are mainly caused by increased blood flow. Flushing and headaches are common with standard short-acting preparations (particularly at high doses), but tend to wear off after a few days in most people. These side-effects are much less common with slow release (SR) preparations, and this is one of the few cases where we feel that routine prescription of SR drugs is justified. Ankle swelling is common, and resistant to diuretics. Calcium-channel blockers should be avoided in pregnancy, as they may delay the start of labour, and some drugs in this group have caused foetal deformities in animals. Many recent studies suggest that some of the drugs in this group may increase the risks of heart attacks in people who take them. There is now little doubt of this effect, or that it is increased by short-acting preparations. If at all, they should be used in long-acting, slow-release (SR) forms, or types with a sustained effect in once-daily dosage.

Group 8: Drugs acting mainly on the brainstem

FIRST INTRODUCED 1949

These drugs – methyldopa, clonidine and moxonidine – act on the brainstem, which lies between the brain and the spinal cord. The brainstem controls many automatic bodily functions, including heart output, urine output (which affects blood volume), and the diameter of small arteries in different parts of the body. Methyldopa (Aldomet) was once the most widely prescribed of all BP-lowering drugs. It remains very popular for treatment of high blood pressure in pregnancy, and is still used by many elderly people who started on it years ago, have well-controlled blood pressures, and therefore have had no reason to change. Clonidine (Catapres) was never widely used in the UK, but is still very popular in Germany and some other parts of continental Europe.

Moxonidine was introduced in 1996. It may occasionally be useful when drugs from all other groups have been tried and failed, but side-effects are common and often unpleasant.

Side-effects
These drugs are effective, but they tend to cause side-effects which although usually only a nuisance, can be intolerable. These side-effects occur mainly at high doses and include bad dreams, drowsiness, tiredness, depression, dry mouth, and stuffy nose. They can also cause impotence, reversible when the drug is stopped. None should be used for people already prone to severe depression.

Methyldopa's most obvious disadvantage is that it causes drowsiness, especially in doses over 1000 mg per day. As it is fully effective in once-daily doses, this effect can be minimised by taking the whole dose at bedtime. (Not all doctors approve of once-daily doses, arguing that spacing the drug out is actually more effective, but trial evidence is against them.) Less obviously but more importantly, it can cause liver damage, particularly in elderly people, and sometimes severe enough to cause jaundice. Blood tests in this condition resemble the test results typical of gallstones, infectious jaundice, or the toxic effects of phenothiazine drugs such as chlorpromazine (Largactil) which are mainly used for schizophrenia and other psychotic illness. It also has complex effects on the surfaces of red blood cells, which although rarely important to health, may cause very confusing results in a wide variety of laboratory tests, including cross-matching of blood for transfusion. You can see that if you are taking methyldopa and have to have blood tests for any reason, then the laboratory needs to be warned.

Clonidine can cause dangerously high blood pressure (rebound blood pressure) if it is stopped suddenly or if doses are spaced too widely apart, so it can only be used safely in a slow-release (SR) form. It often causes minor depression.

Group 9: Adrenergic neurone blockers

FIRST INTRODUCED 1959
These drugs are now very rarely used (they may be needed for people with very severe and intractable high blood pressure which can be controlled in no other way) and then usually only under the supervision of specialists in hospitals.

Side-effects
Fainting is common with adrenergic neurone blockers, but for people who really need these drugs, I'm afraid there is no alternative to putting up with it. Such people need to avoid rapid head movements, go up and

down stairs slowly, use a stick or umbrella for support when walking, and avoid heights. All of these drugs also tend to cause troublesome diarrhoea, and delayed or impaired ejaculation (but they do not impair orgasm).

Group 10: Ganglion-blockers

FIRST INTRODUCED 1959

Like the adrenergic neurone blockers, this is another group of drugs that is now used only rarely, and then usually by hospital specialist clinics rather than by GPs. Ganglion-blockers work by blocking the nerves that control the spiral muscles around the small arteries, so increasing their diameter.

Side-effects

As well as greatly reducing BP, these drugs tend to increase heart rate and may cause flushing. Because the nerve block is applied at the junction (ganglion) between the nerves coming from the brain and the nerves going to the whole circulatory system, their effects are widespread rather than concentrated on target arteries, and because the fall in pressure is usually large, they may cause fainting.

Appendix 2

Useful addresses

*These numbers will change on 22nd April 2000

Action on Pre-Eclamptic
  Condition
31–33 College Road
Harrow HA1 1EJ
Tel: 0181 863 3271*
Helpline: 0181 427 4217*
Fax: 0181 424 0653*
Email: apec@dial.pipex.com

Aromatherapy Organisations
  Council
PO Box 355
Croydon CR9 2CP
Tel: 0181 251 7912*

Arthritis Care
18 Stephenson Way
London NW1 2HD
Tel: 0171 916 1500*
Fax: 0171 916 1500*

Arthritis Research Campaign
Copeman House
St Mary's Court
St Mary's Gate
Chesterfield
Derbyshire S41 7TD
Tel: 01246 558033
Fax: 01246 558007
Email: info@arc.org.uk

ASH (Action on Smoking and
  Health)
16 Fitzhardinge Street
London W1H 9PL
Tel: 0171 224 0734*
Fax: 0171 224 0471*
Email: action.smoking.health@
  dial.pipex.com
Website: www.ash.org.uk

Association of Qualified Curative
  Hypnotherapists
10 Balaclava Road
King's Heath
Birmingham B14 7SG
Tel: 0121 441 1775

British Acupuncture Council
Park House
206–208 Latimer Road
London W10 6RE
Tel: 0181 964 0222*
Fax: 0181 964 0333*
Email: info@acupuncture.org.uk
Website: www.acupuncture.org.uk

British Diabetic Association
10 Queen Anne Street
London W1M 0BD
Tel: 0171 323 1531*
Fax: 0171 637 3644*
Email: bda@diabetes.org.uk
Website: www.diabetes.org.uk

British Dietetic Association
7th Floor
Elizabeth House
22 Suffolk Street
Queensway
Birmingham B1 1LS
Tel: 0121 643 5483
Fax: 0121 633 4399
Email: bda@dial.pipex.com
Website: www.bda.uk.com

British Heart Foundation
14 Fitzhardinge Street
London W1H 4DH
Tel: 0171 935 0185*
Fax: 0171 486 582*
Website: www.bhf.org.uk

British Herbal Medicine
  Association
Sun House
Church Street
Stroud
Gloucestershire GL5 1JL
Tel: 0145 375 1389
Fax: 0145 375 1402

British Holistic Medical
  Association
59 Lansdowne Place
Hove
East Sussex BN3 1FL
Tel/Fax: 01273 725951

British Homeopathic Association
27a Devonshire Street
London W1N 1RJ
Tel: 0171 935 2163*
(1.30–5 pm)

Appendix 2

British Medical Acupuncture
  Society
Newton House
Newton Lane
Lower Whitley
Warrington
Cheshire WA4 4JA
Tel: 01925 730727
Fax: 01925 730492
Email: bmasadmin@aol.com
Website: www.medical_
  acupuncture.co.uk

British Society of Medical and
  Dental Hypnosis
National Office
17 Keppelview Road
Kimberworth
Rotherham S61 2AR
Tel: 01709 554558

British Wheel of Yoga
1 Hamilton Place
Boston Road
Sleaford
Lincolnshire NG34 7ES
Tel: 01529 306851
Email: wheelyoga@aol.com
Website: www.aol.com/wheelyoga

Chest, Heart and Stroke
  Association (Northern Ireland)
21 Dublin Road
Belfast BT2 7HB
Tel: 01232 320184*
Fax: 01232 334 487*
Email: nichsa@compuserve.com

Chest, Heart and Stroke
  Association (Scotland)
65 North Castle Street
Edinburgh EH2 3LT
Tel: 0131 225 6963
Fax: 0131 220 6313
Email: chss@dial.pipex.com

Community Health Council
  The address and telephone
  number of your local CHC will
  be in the phone book.

Complementary Medicine
  Association
The Meridan
142A Greenwich High Road
London SE10 8NN
Tel: 0181 305 9571*

Consumer's Association
2 Marylebone Road
London NW1 4DF
Tel: 0171 486 5544*
Fax: 0171 830 7600*
Email: which@which.net
Website: www.which@which.net

Coronary Prevention Group
2 Taviton Street
London WC1H 0BT
Tel: 0171 927 2125*
Fax: 0171 927 2127*
Email: cpg@lshtm.ac.uk
Website: www.healthnet.org.uk

Council for Complementary and Alternative Medicine
CCAM Park House
206–208 Latimer Road
London W10 6RE
Tel: 0181 968 3862

Department of Health
Richmond House
79 Whitehall
London SW1A 2NS
Tel: 0171 210 3000*
Health Literature Line Tel: 0800 555777

English Sports Council
16 Upper Woburn Place
London WC1H 0QP
Tel: 0171 273 1500*
Fax: 0171 383 5740*
Website: www.english.sports.gov.uk

Family Heart Association (specialises in familial hypercholesterolaemia)
7 North Road
Maidenhead
Berkshire SL6 1PL
Tel: 01628 628638
Fax: 01628 628698

Health Education Authority
Trevelyan House
30 Great Peter Street
London SW1P 2HW
Tel: 0171 222 5300*

Health Education Board for Scotland
Woodburn House
Canaan Lane
Edinburgh EH10 4SG
Tel: 0131 536 5500
Fax: 0131 536 5501
Website: www.hebs.scot.nhs.uk

Health Information First
Corey's Mill Lane
Stevenage
Herts SG1 4AB
Tel: 0800 665544
Fax: 01438 781247
Website: www.nthames-healthpride.acuk/hifirst/index.htm

HOPE (High Blood Pressure Open Public Education) (Aims to provide the public with currently available information on the prevention, diagnosis and treatment of high blood pressure)
c/o 1 Fairbourne
Cobham
Surrey KT11 2BT

Institute for Complementary Medicine
PO Box 194
London SE16 1QZ
Tel: 0171 237 5165*
Fax: 0171 237 5175*
Email: icmedicine@aol.com
Website: www.icmedicine.co.uk

Appendix 2

International Federation of
  Aromatherapists
Stamford House
2–4 Chiswick High Road
London W4 1TH
Tel: 0181 742 2605*
Fax: 0181 742 2606*

International Society of
  Professional Aromatherapists
ISPA House
82 Ashby Road
Hinckley
Leicestershire LE10 1SN
Tel: 0145 563 7987
Fax: 0145 589 0956

Irish Heart Foundation
4 Clyde Road
Ballsbridge
Dublin 4
Ireland
Tel: 00 353 1668 5001 (from UK)
Fax: 00 353 1668 5896 (from UK)
Email:
  info@irishheartfoundation.ie

MIND (National Association for
  Mental Health)
Granta House
15–19 Broadway
Stratford
London E15 4BQ
Tel: 0181 522 2122*
Fax: 0181 522 1725*
Email: contact@mind.org.uk
Website: www.mind.org.uk

National Association of Citizens
  Advice Bureaux
Middleton House
115–123 Pentonville Road
London N1 9LZ
Tel: 0171 833 2181*
Fax: 0171 833 4371*
Website: www.nacab.org.uk

Scotland:
26 George Square
Edinburgh EH8 9LD
Tel: 0131 667 0156
Fax: 0131 668 4359
Website: www.cas.org.uk

North Wales:
Unit 7
St Afaph Business Park
Glascoed Road
St Afaph
Denbighshire LL17 0LJ
Tel: 0174 558 6400
Fax: 0174 558 5554

National Asthma Campaign
Providence House
Providence Place
London N1 0NT
Tel: 0171 226 2260*
Fax: 0171 704 0740*
Website: www.asthma.org.uk

National Back Pain Association
16 Elm Tree Road
Teddington
Middlesex TW11 8ST
Tel: 0181 977 5474*
Fax: 0181 943 5318*
Website: www.backpain.org

National Institute of Medical
  Herbalists
56 Longbrook Street
Exeter
Devon EX4 6AH
Tel: 0139 242 6022
Fax: 0139 249 8963
Email:
  nimh@ukexeter.freeserve.co.uk

Patients' Association
8 Guilford Street
London WC1N 1DT
Tel: 0181 423 8999*
Fax: 0181 423 9119*
Website: www.pat-assoc.org.uk

Quit (National Society for Non-
  smokers)
Victory House
170 Tottenham Court Road
London W1P 0HA
Tel: 0171 388 5775*
Fax: 0171 388 5995*
Quitline: 0800 002200

Rare Unspecified Disorders
  Support Group
160 Locket Road
Harrow Weald
Middlesex HA3 7NZ
Tel/Fax: 0181 863 3557*
Email: rarechromo@aol.com
  (The RUDSG puts families
  affected by rare genetic
  abnormalities, such as
  polycystic kidneys and
  coarctation of the aorta, in
  touch, and helps to set up
  support groups.)

Relate (National Marriage
  Guidance)
Herbert Gray College
Little Church Street
Rugby
Warwickshire CV21 3AP
Tel: 01788 573241
Fax: 01788 535007
Website: www.relate.org.uk

Royal National Institute for the
  Blind
224 Great Portland Street
London W1N 6AA
Tel: 0171 388 1266*
Fax: 0171 388 2034*
Helpline: 0345 669999
Website: www.rnib.org.uk

Appendix 2

Society of Homeopaths
2 Artizan Road
Northampton NN1 4HU
Tel: 01604 621400
Fax: 01604 622622
Email: societyofhomeopaths@
  btinternet.com

The Stress Management Training
  Institute
Foxhills
30 Victoria Avenue
Shanklin
Isle of Wight
Tel: 01983 868166
Fax: 01983 866666

Stroke Association
Stroke House
Whitecross Street
London EC1Y 8JJ
Tel: 0171 490 7999*
Fax: 0171 490 2686*
Email: stroke@stroke.org.uk
Website: www.stroke.org.uk

Trade Union Congress Health
  Committee
Congress House
Great Russell Street
London WC1B 3LS
Tel: 0171 636 4030*
Fax: 0171 636 0632*
Website: www.tuc.org.uk

Vegetarian Society
Parkdale
Dunham Road
Altrincham
Cheshire WA14 4QG
Tel: 0161 928 0793
Fax: 0161 926 9182
Email: info@vegsoc.org
Website: www.vegsoc.org

Women's Health
52 Featherstone Street
London EC1Y 8RT
Tel: 0171 251 6580*
Fax: 0171 608 0928*
Email: womenshealth@pop3.
  poptel.org.uk

Women's Health Concern
93–99 Upper Richmond Road
London SW15 2TG
Tel: 0181 780 3916*
Fax: 0181 780 3905*
Helpline: 0181 780 3007*

Yoga for Health Foundation
Ickwell Bury
Biggleswade
Bedfordshire SG18 0DN
Tel: 01767 627271
Fax: 01767 627266

Appendix 3

Useful publications

At the time of writing, all the publications listed here were available. For current prices, please check with your local bookshop or with the publishers. Your local library may have copies of some of the books mentioned, and you may well find some of the leaflets available in your doctor's surgery or your local health centre.

Food and cooking

Books
The Light-Hearted Cookbook: Recipes for a Healthy Heart, by Anne Lindsay, published by Grub Street/British Heart Foundation (1993)

The Everyday Light-Hearted Cookbook, by Anne Lindsay, published by Grub Street/British Heart Foundation (1994)

Which? Way to a Healthier Diet, by Judy Byrne, published by the Consumers' Association/Hodder Headline (1993)

Healthy Eating on a Plate, by Janette Marshall, published by Vermilion (1995)

Booklets and leaflets
Eight Guidelines for a Healthy Diet: Advice for Healthy Eating, from H.M.Government, produced by the Ministry of Agriculture, Fisheries and Food, the Department of Health and the Health Education Authority (1993). Obtainable from Food Sense, London SE99 7TT (Tel: 0208 694 8862).

The **British Heart Foundation** publishes a number of free booklets and leaflets on healthy eating – titles include *Trim the Fat from Your Diet*; *Food and Your Heart*; *So You Want to Lose Weight* and *Food Should Be Fun*. Contact the BHF at the address in Appendix 2 for further details.

The **Health Education Authority** publishes booklets and leaflets on healthy eating – titles include *Enjoy Fruit & Veg* and *Enjoy Healthy Eating*. There is a small charge for these publications: contact the HEA at the address in Appendix 2 for further details.

The **Vegetarian Society** publishes a number of information sheets and leaflets about being a vegetarian and vegetarian cooking, and can also supply a list of recommended vegetarian cookbooks. Contact the Society at the address in Appendix 2 for further details.

As the advice on a healthy diet for people with diabetes is now exactly what has been recommended for the population as a whole, you may find cookery books and leaflets intended for people with diabetes useful in extending your range of recipes – contact the **British Diabetic Association** at the address in Appendix 2 for a list of available titles.

Stopping smoking

Books

How to Stop Smoking and Stay Stopped for Good, by Gillian Riley, published by Vermilion (1992)

Kick it! Stop Smoking in Five Days, by Judy Perlmutter, published by Thorsons (1986)

Allen Carr's Easy Way to Stop Smoking, by Allen Carr, published by Penguin (2nd edition 1991)

Stop Smoking for Good with the National Health Association Stop Smoking Programme, by Robert Brynin, published by Coronet (1995)

Booklets and leaflets

The **British Heart Foundation** (address in Appendix 2) publishes a free leaflet called *Smoking and Your Heart* which includes advice on how to give up.

The **Health Education Authority** publishes booklets and leaflets on stopping smoking – titles include *Stopping Smoking Made Easier* and *Thinking About Stopping*. There is a small charge for these publications: contact the HEA at the address in Appendix 2 for further details. The HEA also produces videos on the subject.

ASH and **QUIT** (addresses of both organisations are in Appendix 2) produce a wide variety of information sheets and leaflets on smoking, passive smoking, and how to give up the habit – contact them for a current list.

Exercise

Books and videos
A wide range of exercise books and videos are currently available, far too many to list here. We suggest that you choose from the selection in your local bookshop and/or library, bearing in mind the advice given in Chapter 5 on the most suitable types of exercise for people with high blood pressure.

Booklets and leaflets
The **British Heart Foundation** (address in Appendix 2) publishes free leaflets on suitable types of exercise – titles include *Put Your Heart into Walking* and *Exercise For Life!*

The **Health Education Authority** publishes booklets and leaflets on exercise – titles include *Getting Active, Feeling Good* and *Exercise: Why Bother?* There is a small charge for these publications: contact the HEA at the address in Appendix 2 for further details. The HEA also produces videos on the subject.

Other relevant topics

Books
Heart Health at Your Fingertips, by Dr Graham Jackson, published by Class Publishing (1998)

Stop That Heart Attack! by Dr Derrick Cutting, published by Class Publishing (1998)

Diabetes at your Fingertips, by Professor Peter Sönkson, Dr Charles Fox and Sister Sue Judd, published by Class Publishing (4th edition 1998)

The Pill and Other Hormones for Contraception, by John Guillebaud, published by Oxford University Press (4th edition 1991)

The HEA Guide to Complementary Medicine and Therapies, by Anne Woodham, published by the Health Education Authority (1994)

Understanding Stress, by Professor Greg Wilkinson, published by Family Doctor Publications (1993)

Other publications
The **Coronary Prevention Group** publishes a booklet called *Stress and Your Heart* – contact them at the address in Appendix 2 for further details.

The **Health Education Authority** publishes booklets and leaflets about alcohol and sensible drinking – titles include *Cutting Down Your Drinking*; *That's The Limit* and *Women and Drinking*. There is a small charge for these publications: contact the HEA at the address in Appendix 2 for further details.

The **Department of Health** publishes a free booklet called *Traveller's Guide to Health* which is available through the Department's free Health Literature Line (phone number in Appendix 2). Your GP may have copies of this booklet available.

Which? magazine has published reports on a number of relevant topics such as *Bathroom Scales*; *Cooking Fats and Oils* and *Home-use Blood Pressure Monitors*. Your local library should have reference copies.

High blood pressure – further reading

Hypertension: Community Control of High Blood Pressure, by Julian Tudor Hart, published by Radcliffe Medical Press (3rd edition 1993)

Management guidelines in essential hypertension: report of the second working party of the British Hypertension Society.
Sever P, Beevers G, Bulpitt C *et al. British Medical Journal* 1993;**306**:983–7

Index

accuracy
  blood cholesterol measurements 168–9
  BP measurements 59–64, 65–6, 75
  sphygmomanometers 55–6, 60, 77–8
ACE-inhibitors 311–13
  BP level reduction obtained 87, 312
  causing dry cough 104, 312
  combined with lithium 199
  combined with thiazide diuretics 87, 103, 108, 116, 312–13
  compared to other BP-lowering drugs 85
  and dehydration 213, 312
  and diabetes 193
  for elderly people 104, 312
  ethnic variations in response 95, 312
  first introduced 93, 311
  for heart failure 181, 264, 312
  and kidney failure 198, 313
  not recommended in pregnancy 234, 313
  side-effects 104, 312–13

ACE-inhibitors *(continued)*
  sodium restriction necessary 103, 109, 116, 312
  for younger adults 103
acupuncture 161, 279
addresses, useful 319–24
adrenergic neurone blockers 317–18
aging, effect on arteries & BP 20, 44–5, 81, 142–3, 222
air travel 209–10
alcohol
  combined with BP-lowering drugs 108–9, 116
  effect on blood cholesterol 132, 170
  effect on gout 186–7
  effect on liver 201
  and heart disease 132
  high intake as cause of high BP 4, 22, 36, 47, 62, 102, 131–2, 200–1, 277
  precipitating stroke 132, 264
  recommended daily limits 4, 47, 108–9, 131, 170
alpha-blockers 85, 86–7, 93, 104, 314–15
alternative therapies 155

Index

altitude, effect on blood pressure 210
aneroid sphygmomanometers 53–4, 55–6
aneurysms 249, 251–2, 279
angina 279
   beta-blockers 113, 177–8, 260, 310
   calcium-channel blockers 113, 178, 260–1, 315
   causes 249, 257–8, 259
   coronary artery bypass grafts 261–3
   diagnosis 259
   distinguishing from a heart attack 254–5, 260
   and exercise 261
   how to live with it 258
   indicates that BP-lowering drugs may be needed 93
   nitroglycerin 178, 255, 259–60
   occurrence 114–15
angiograms, coronary 259, 262
angiotensin converting enzyme inhibitors *see* ACE-inhibitors
angiotensin inhibitors 93, 313
animals, use in research 232, 268–9
ankylosing spondylitis 186–7
antacids 196
antenatal care 230–1, 238
antibiotics 111, 196, 212
anticoagulants 181, 257, 265–6, 279
antidepressants 108, 198–200
anti-oxidants 176
anti-ulcer drugs 195–6
anxiety 33–4, 47, 67, 75, 215, 310
aorta 279
   aortic aneurysm 249, 251
   coarctation of the 21, 35–6, 281
   effect of plaque 164, 166, 249

arm girth, and cuff size 60–1, 77–8, 121
arm position, effect on BP measurements 70
aromatherapy 159, 279
arrhythmias 34, 315
arterial blood pressure 11–12, 16, 279
arteries 279
   artery damage assessment 49
   blocking effects of uncontrolled high BP 101, 247–50, 253
   brachial 12, 13–14, 55, 68–9, 73–4, 280
   bursting effects of uncontrolled high BP 251–2, 253
   carotid 249–50, 265, 266
   coronary 101, 164, 166, 257, 281
   diameter variability 3, 12
   effect of aging 20, 81
   effect of BP-lowering drugs 85, 313, 314, 315, 316, 318
   effect of diabetes 192
   effect of malignant hypertension 25
   effect of plaque 12–13, 81, 101, 164, 166, 237, 248
   effect of pregnancy 229
   in placenta 237
arterioles 16, 248, 252, 279
arthritis 182–7
artificial sweeteners 129–30, 142
aspirin
   combined with other drugs 111, 177, 184
   first introduced 85
   heart attack prevention & first aid 184, 255, 256–7
   ineffective for pre-eclampsia 245
   pain control 184

aspirin *(continued)*
  side-effects 184
  stroke prevention 184, 265
asthma 8, 76, 188–92, 311
atrial fibrillation 66, 181, 279

babies 229, 231, 239, 244
'bad' cholesterol *see* LDL
  cholesterol; VLDL cholesterol
barrier contraceptives 222
bathroom scales 126–7
bed rest, for pre-eclampsia 245
Bell's palsy 266–7
benign enlargement of the prostate
  63, 75, 198, 314–5
beta-blockers 309–11
  for angina 113, 177–8, 260, 310
  BP level reduction obtained 86,
    310
  combined with anti-ulcer drugs
    196
  combined with other BP-
    lowering drugs 179, 310, 313,
    315, 316
  compared to other BP-lowering
    drugs 85
  dangerous for people with
    asthma 188–9, 192, 311
  and depression 199, 200
  effect on hypo warning signs 193
  for elderly people 104, 179
  ethnic variations in response 95,
    310
  first introduced 93, 309
  and heart failure 179–80, 311
  less effective in smokers 153
  and rebound high BP 99, 113
  side-effects 201, 216, 310–11,
    316
  use in pregnancy 234, 244, 311
bicarbonate of soda 135, 142, 147

bile 166, 279–80
bile-acid binding resins 175
bladder, full, effect on BP 47, 63,
  75, 207
bleeding 32–3
  see also haemorrhages
blocking effects 247–50, 253
blood, circulation & functions
  10–11
blood cholesterol
  cholesterol-lowering diets
    171–3
  cholesterol-lowering drugs 170,
    173–7
  effect of alcohol 132, 170
  effect of alpha-blockers 314
  effect of eggs & dairy foods 133,
    165
  effect of exercise 148, 170
  effect of fat intake 138, 139, 144,
    165, 170, 171–2
  effect of garlic 137
  effect of inheritance 169–70,
    171–2
  effect of soluble fibre 132–3
  high levels increase risk of heart
    disease 164–5, 253
  measurement 166–9
blood clots *see* emboli &
  embolisms; thrombosis
blood clotting factors 132, 148, 281
blood flow 15–17, 149, 178, 310,
  316
blood potassium, effect of
  diuretics 88–9, 180, 308–9
blood pressure
  arterial 11–12, 16, 279
  borderline between 'normal' &
    high pressures 1, 19–20, 230,
    240–1
  capillary 11, 16

Index

blood pressure *(continued)*
  diastolic 13–14, 55, 73, 282
  effect of aging 20, 44–5, 142–3, 222
  effect of altitude 210
  effect of contraceptive pill 219, 220
  effect of pregnancy 228–30
  high *see* high blood pressure
  low 17–18, 86, 87, 117, 183
  reasons for short-term rises 4–5, 16, 24, 38, 47, 61–3, 75, 149, 197, 207, 217–18
  systolic 13–14, 55, 72–3, 81–2, 286
  target 80, 117
  variations in average levels around the world 26–8, 45, 142–3
  variations in individuals 5, 11–13, 14–16, 61
  venous 11–12, 242, 287
  why blood is under pressure 2, 10–11
blood pressure measurements
  accuracy 59–64, 65–6, 75
  in children 35, 64
  home measurements 66–75
  knowing your own 7, 14, 116
  made by doctors & nurses 55, 65–6
  made with a catheter in the arm 14
  made over brachial artery 12, 13–14, 55
  numbers needed before taking decisions on treatment 3, 46, 59, 63–4, 82, 92, 98–9, 105–6, 113–14, 207
  numbers needed for follow-up 8, 114

blood pressure measurements *(continued)*
  in pregnancy 228, 231, 233–4, 237, 240, 245
  reasons for inaccurate measurements 59–61, 70, 77, 78, 121, 181
  reasons for unexpectedly high measurements 47, 61–3, 75, 207
  sounds heard 13–14, 55, 72–4
  technique 55, 69–75
  timing of measurements 61, 69–70
  training requirements 65–6, 68, 73
  units 13
  use in diagnosis 3, 46
  what the figures mean 13–14
  when taking oral contraceptives 219
  see also sphygmomanometers
blood tests 48–9, 115, 166–7, 317
blood vessels 11, 12
  see also by type, eg arteries
blood viscosity 12–13, 184, 210, 264
blood volume 12–13, 13, 85, 229, 280
BMI 124–5, 280
body fat 121–2, 123–4, 127
body mass index 124–5, 280
books & publications 325–8
BP-lowering drugs
  accidental overdoses 110, 113
  affecting body's responses to extreme conditions 204, 214
  aims of treatment 22, 76, 80, 117
  altering dosage or drug types 76, 96, 110–11
  and asthma 8, 188–9, 192, 311

BP-lowering drugs *(continued)*
  BP level reduction obtained 86
  brand & generic names 84, 85, 106, 206, 282, 289
  brand name order listing 291–301
  choice of drug 93–4
  combining different BP-lowering drugs 86, 95–6, 103, 308
  combining with drugs for other health problems 108, 111–12, 175 *and see also those other problems or the drugs for them by name, eg* arthritis; corticosteroids
  costs 85, 288
  decisions about starting treatment 90, 92–3
  dose frequency & timing 107, 307, 317
  drug resistance 116–17, 132, 201
  effect of non-drug treatments on doses needed 6, 82, 93, 109, 121, 144
  effectiveness 89–90, 96–7
  failure to respond to them 116–17, 132, 201
  future changes in treatment 277–8
  generic name order listing 302–5
  in hospitals 112
  how they work 85–6
  identifying your drugs 96, 106–7, 163
  individual variations in response 94–5, 96
  injections unnecessary 91
  and kidney failure 197–8, 313
  obtaining abroad 206, 210–11
  overtreatment 86, 87, 117, 207

BP-lowering drugs *(continued)*
  in pregnancy 231–4, 244–5, 308, 311, 313, 316
  remembering to take them 8, 109–10, 116
  safety 89–90, 110, 113, 232–3
  sedatives & tranquillisers unsuitable alternatives 83, 97
  side-effects *see* side-effects of BP-lowering drugs
  SR preparations 90–1, 113, 260–1, 316, 317
  stopping treatment 97–9, 105–6, 112–13
  stress reduction unsuitable alternative 5, 83
  treatment for particular age groups *see* children; elderly people; younger adults
  types available 84–5, 289–318
  when they are needed 6–7, 82, 90
  see also individual groups of drugs by name, eg beta-blockers *(complete list of groups on pages 290–291)*
brachial artery 12, 13–14, 55, 68–9, 73–4, 280
brain
  aneurysms 251–2
  effect of uncontrolled high BP 249–50, 251–2
brainstem 280, 316
brand names 84–5, 106, 280, 289
  BP-lowering drugs listed in brand name order 291–301
  in other countries 206, 210–11
bread 128–9, 135, 143, 145, 146
breathing problems 191–2
  see also asthma
breathlessness 32

British Hypertension Society
  guidelines 81, 94, 290, 328
bronchitis 191–2
bursting effects 247–8, 250–2, 253
butter 133, 136, 138, 139, 140–1

CABGs 261–3
caesarean section 244, 280
calcium-channel blockers 315–16
  for angina 113, 178, 260–1, 315
  BP level reduction obtained 86
  combined with anti-ulcer drugs
    196
  combined with other BP-
    lowering drugs 179, 310, 315,
    316
  compared to other BP-lowering
    drugs 85
  ethnic variations in response 95
  first introduced 93, 315
  not recommended in pregnancy
    234, 316
  side-effects 179, 316
  SR preparations preferred 91,
    260–1, 316
calories, definition 122, 280
cancer 133, 152
capillaries 11, 16, 242, 248, 280
capillary blood pressure 11, 16
capillary network 16, 248, 280
carbon monoxide 154, 155
carotid arteries 249–50, 265, 266
causes of high BP
  angina 249, 257–8, 259
  heart attacks 205, 249
  pre-eclampsia 236–7
  primary high blood pressure
    3–4, 21–2, 35–45, 94, 142–3,
    204–5, 277
  searching for causes during
    diagnosis of high BP 47–51

causes *(continued)*
  secondary high blood pressure
    21, 35–6, 44
  stroke 250, 253, 264
  TIAs 249–50, 265
CCUs 255–6
cheese 133, 138, 139, 143, 145
chemicals, possible cause of high
  BP 204–5
chicken 134, 139
children 22–3, 34–5, 42–3, 64, 113,
  191
cholesterol 133, 164, 165, 166,
  280
  in blood *see* blood cholesterol
  in plaque *see* plaque
cholesterol-lowering drugs 170,
  173–7
circulation & circulatory system
  11, 178, 310, 316
claudication 114–15, 178, 179, 249,
  280
clinical trials 269–70, 272–6, 280
clinics, for treatment & follow-up
  29–30, 117–18, 276–7
clonidine
  causing depression 105, 199,
    200, 317
  combined with alcohol 109
  for elderly people 104–5
  popularity 316
  and rebound high BP 99, 112–13,
    317
  SR preparations preferred 91,
    113, 317
clothing, affecting BP
  measurement 70
clots, blood *see* emboli &
  embolisms; thrombosis
clotting factors 132, 148, 281
co-A inhibitors 177

coarctation of the aorta 21, 35–6, 281
coenzyme-A reductase inhibitors 177
cold hands & feet, side-effect of beta-blockers 178, 310, 316
cold weather, effect on BP 75
combined oral contraceptives 218–19, 220
complementary therapies 155–61, 281
  see also individually by name, eg acupuncture
complications see consequences of uncontrolled high blood pressure
consequences of uncontrolled high blood pressure 2, 19, 22, 79–80
  blocking effects 247–50, 253
  bursting effects 247–8, 250–2, 253
  risk prediction 81–2
  risks increased by smoking 6, 80, 102, 152, 165, 253
  risks reduced by treatment for high BP 19–20, 79–80, 90, 101, 247–9, 253
  risks rising with age 20, 45
  why you need to know about them 246–7
  see also individually by name, eg stroke
constipation 197
contraception 218–22
contraceptive pill 8, 218–21
controlled trials 269–70, 272–5, 281
convenience foods 138, 143
coronary angiograms 259, 262
coronary arteries 101, 164, 166, 257, 281

coronary artery bypass grafts 261–3
coronary care units 255–6
coronary heart disease 281
  and cholesterol-lowering drugs 173, 174
  effect of alcohol intake 132
  effect of exercise 149, 261
  effect of fat in diet 138, 141, 144, 256
  effect of HRT 224
  risk increased by being overweight 121, 123
  risk increased by diabetes 192
  risk increased by high blood cholesterol 164–5, 167–8, 253
  risk increased by high BP 2, 19, 20, 22, 101
  risk increased by smoking 152, 165, 256
  risk reduction 132, 256
coronary thrombosis see heart attacks
corticosteroids 40, 108, 185–6, 189–92, 281
costs
  BP-lowering drugs 85, 288
  complementary therapies 158
cough 104, 251, 263, 312
cuffs 13, 53, 55, 70, 281
  for children 35, 64
  correct sizing 60–1, 77–8, 121
  speed of deflation 60, 72, 74–5

dairy foods 133, 138, 139, 145
  see also individually by name, eg milk
decongestants, nasal 39
deep vein thrombosis 209–10, 242–3
dehydration 212–13, 312

Index

depression 116, 198–200, 281
  during menopause 224
  effect of drugs acting mainly on the brainstem 105, 199, 200, 317
  in elderly people 105, 106
diabetes 281–2
  and ACE-inhibitors 193
  control 76, 192
  effect of beta-blockers on hypo warning signs 193
  indicates that BP-lowering drugs may be needed 90, 92, 98
  links with high BP 121, 192
  retina examinations 115–16, 195, 252
  and sugar in diet 136
  and thiazide diuretics 104, 193–5, 308
  and weight control 121, 192
diagnosis
  angina 259
  artery damage 49
  high blood pressure 46–51
  minor strokes 51
  pre-eclampsia 240–3
diarrhoea 212, 312
diastolic pressure 13–14, 55, 73, 282
diet
  books & publications 325–6
  cholesterol-lowering 171–3
  during pregnancy 240, 243–4
  healthy eating 131–7
  national variations affecting BP levels 26, 45, 142–3
  recommended changes for people with high BP 131, 137
  reducing fat intake 6, 128, 135–6, 138–9, 140–2, 143–4

diet *(continued)*
  reducing sodium intake 5–6, 133, 143–7
  vegetarian 132–4
  see also alcohol; food; weight control
dietary fibre 128–9, 132–3, 134–5
dietitians 129, 131, 144, 243, 282
digestive system problems 197–8, 211–13
diuretics 306–9
  BP level reduction obtained 86
  combined with other BP-lowering drugs 87, 96, 108
  compared to other BP-lowering drugs 85
  effect on blood potassium 88–9, 180, 201, 308–9
  first introduced 306
  for heart failure 180, 181, 264, 309
  how they work 85, 306
  not recommended in pregnancy 234, 308
  with potassium supplements 84, 88–9, 308–9
  sodium restriction advised 109, 306
  types 84, 306
  see also by type, eg thiazide diuretics
doctors
  accuracy in measuring blood cholesterol 169
  accuracy in measuring BP 65–6
  antenatal care 230–1
  attitude to complementary therapies 155–7, 158
  changing your GP 224–5
  consulting when abroad 205–7, 211

doctors *(continued)*
  declining to operate on smokers 262–3
  discussing your health problems with them 162–3
  fear of *see* white coat hypertension
  follow-up by 117–18, 119
  future roles in treating high BP 276–7
  general practice BP clinics 29–30, 276–7
  helping you stop smoking 153–4
  holistic approach to treatment 157
  measuring your blood potassium 180
  measuring your sodium intake 147–8
  opinions on home BP measurements 67
  treating heart attacks 255–6
  treating terminal illness 267
  treatment guidelines for 81, 94, 174, 290, 328
double-blind trials 272, 273, 282
dreams 310–11, 317
driving 204, 226
dropsy *see* oedema
drowsiness 109, 204, 317
drug trials 89–90, 269, 282
drugs
  of addiction & abuse 40–1
  causing rises in BP 38–41, 62, 182–3, 185–6
  combining drugs for different health problems 108, 111–12, 175 *and see also those health problems or the drugs for them by name, eg* arthritis; corticosteroids

drugs *(continued)*
  drug names *see* brand names; generic names
  identifying 96, 106–7, 163
  for nausea & vomiting 111–12, 211–12
  for treating high blood pressure *see* BP-lowering drugs
  see also individual groups of drugs by name, eg tranquillisers
drugs acting mainly on the brainstem (BP-lowering drug group) 316–17
  BP level reduction obtained 86
  for elderly people 104, 316–17
  first introduced 93, 316
  side-effects 199, 216, 317
  see also clonidine; methyldopa
duodenal ulcers 88, 184, 195–6
dynamic exercise 38, 150

ECGs 50, 256, 259
eclampsia
  chances of developing it 239–40
  effect of diet 240
  inheritance 239
  magnesium 236
  what it is 234–5, 282
economics of treating high blood pressure 28–30
ECT 199
eggs 133, 145, 165
elderly people
  ACE-inhibitors 104, 312
  alpha-blockers 87, 315
  beta-blockers 104
  choice of BP-lowering drugs 104–5

Index

elderly people *(continued)*
  depression 105, 106
  drugs acting mainly on the brainstem (BP-lowering drug group) 104–5, 316–17
  effect of age on BP 20, 44–5, 81, 209
  effectiveness of treatment 20, 45, 103–4, 201
  impaired glucose tolerance 193–5
  stopping BP-lowering drugs 97–8, 105–6
  thiazide diuretics 104, 193–5
  thrombosis prevention when travelling 209–10
electrocardiograms 50, 256, 259
electroconvulsive therapy 199
electronic sphygmomanometers 54, 55, 61
  accuracy 55–6, 60, 77, 78
  home use 68, 74–5
  purchasing considerations 77–8
emboli & embolisms 248, 249, 250, 282
  micro-emboli 249–50, 265
emergency contraception 221
emotions
  effect on BP 4–5, 16, 38, 47, 61–2, 75
  effect on sex life 215
  fear of doctors *see* white coat hypertension
  fear of knowing about complications of high BP 246–7
  see also anxiety; stress
employment 202–7
energy balance 4, 121, 122, 136
energy throughput 122

essential hypertension 21–2, 282
ethnic variations
  blood cholesterol 166, 171–2
  numbers of people with high BP 26, 28, 45, 142–3
  response to BP-lowering drugs 95, 310, 312
exercise 148–51
  books & publications 327
  effect on blood flow 15–16, 149
  effect on BP 38, 47, 102, 148–9, 214
  role in weight control 122, 127, 129, 148
  sports 38, 213–14
eyes
  effect of uncontrolled high BP 250, 252, 253
  retinal examinations 25, 35, 50, 116, 195, 252

facial paralysis 266–7
fainting
  during pregnancy 229–30
  effect of low blood pressure 17–18, 87, 117
  side-effect of adrenergic neurone blockers 317–18
  side-effect of alpha-blockers 86–7, 104, 315
  side-effect of BP-lowering drugs 87
  side-effect of ganglion-blockers 318
  temporary blackouts & giddiness 250
family history *see* inheritance
fat
  on body *see* body fat
  in diet *see* fats & oils

fats & oils
  amounts in food 133, 135–6, 138–9, 140–1
  effect on blood cholesterol 138, 139, 144, 165, 170, 171–2
  reducing intake 6, 128, 135–6, 138–9, 140–2, 143–4
  types 139–40
fear of doctors *see* white coat hypertension
fibrates 176
fibre, dietary 128–9, 132–3, 134–5
fibrillation 66, 180–1, 279, 282
fibrinogen 38, 148, 282
finger sphygmomanometers 58–9
fish 134, 145
fits, eclamptic 234, 236, 239
flushing 176–7, 316, 318
  hot flushes 33, 222, 223
flying 209–10
foetus 232–3, 282
folic acid 232
follow-up 8, 113–19
  economic & health advantages of GP follow-up clinics 29–30
  home BP measurements usually unnecessary 67–8
  when working abroad 206
food
  cholesterol content 133, 165
  fat content 133, 135–6, 138–9, 140–1
  fibre content 128–9, 132–3, 135
  potassium content 88, 132
  sodium content 133, 142–7, 172
  spicy foods 132
  see also diet *and individual foods by name, eg* meat
fruit 128–9, 132, 135, 144, 264
fulminating, definition 236, 282
fulminating pre-eclampsia 236

ganglion-blockers 318
gangrene 249
garlic 137
gastric ulcers 88, 184, 195–6
generic names 84–5, 106, 282, 289
  BP-lowering drugs listed in generic name order 302–5
  in other countries 206, 210–11
genes 41, 94, 170, 282
gestosis *see* pre-eclampsia
glucose drinks 136
glucose intolerance 193–5
glyceryl trinitrate *see* nitroglycerin
'good' cholesterol *see* HDL cholesterol
gout 187–8, 283, 308
GPs *see* doctors
groups
  self-help & support groups 227
  weight-reduction groups 130–1
GTN *see* nitroglycerin

haemorrhages
  in brain arteries 251–2
  subconjunctival 33, 286
half-life 91
HDL cholesterol 148, 166, 167, 170, 175–7, 283
HDP *see* pre-eclampsia
headaches 25, 32, 33, 34–5, 316
healthy eating 131–7, 138–9
heart, pumping action 11, 12, 13–14, 55
heart attacks 283
  affecting choice of BP-lowering drugs 179
  aspirin 184, 255, 256–7
  beta-blockers 310
  causes 205, 249
  indicates that BP-lowering drugs may be needed 93

Index

heart attacks *(continued)*
  prevention 165, 256–7
  risk increased by calcium-channel blockers 316
  risk increased by high BP 2, 19, 45, 80
  risk increased by rebound high BP 105
  risk increased by smoking 152, 253, 256
  risk reduced by angina treatments 260–1
  risk reduced by reducing blood cholesterol 165
  risk reduced by treatment for high BP 90, 101, 253
  and sex 218
  symptoms 254–5
  treatment 255–6
heart disease *see* coronary heart disease
heart failure 179–81, 263–4, 283
  ACE-inhibitors 181, 264, 312
  beta-blockers 179–80, 311
  diuretics 180, 181, 264, 309
  and exercise 149, 261
  indicates that BP-lowering drugs may be needed 93
  risk increased by high BP 2, 22, 80, 250–1, 263
  risk reduced by treatment for high BP 90, 253
  thrombosis prevention when travelling 209–10
heart output, effect of BP-lowering drugs 85, 310, 311, 313
heart rhythm
  effect of asthma relievers 190
  effect of beta-blockers 179, 310, 311

heart rhythm *(continued)*
  effect of blood potassium 88
  effect of calcium-channel blockers 179, 315
  fibrillation 66, 180–1, 279, 282
heartbeats
  irregular 34, 223, 263–4
  palpitations 33–4, 222–3, 284
  slowed by beta-blockers 311
heartburn 196–7
herbal medicines 40, 160
heredity *see* inheritance
high blood potassium, and diuretics 88–9, 309
high blood pressure
  borderline between 'normal' & high pressures 1, 19–20, 230, 240–1
  malignant 16, 24–5, 277, 284
  in particular age groups *see* children; elderly people; younger adults
  in pregnancy *see* eclampsia; pre-eclampsia; pregnancy
  primary *see* primary high blood pressure
  secondary *see* secondary high blood pressure
  types 21–2
high density lipoprotein cholesterol *see* HDL cholesterol
holistic treatment 156, 157, 283
home remedies bought over the counter 39
  see also by type, eg aspirin
homeopathy 161, 283
HOP *see* pre-eclampsia
hormonal contraceptives 218–22
hormone replacement therapy 223–4
hormones 229, 283

hospitals
  follow-up clinics 117–18
  future role in treating high BP 276–7
  what to do with your drugs when in hospital 142
hot flushes 33, 222, 223
HRT 223–4
hyperkalaemia 88–9, 309
hypertension
  definition & origin of the term 18, 283
  essential 21–2, 282
  'high blood pressure' as preferred term 5, 36–7
  malignant 16, 24–5, 277, 284
  primary *see* primary high blood pressure
  secondary *see* secondary high blood pressure
  white coat 23–4, 57–8, 61–2, 287
hypertension-oedema-proteinurea syndrome *see* pre-eclampsia
hypertensive disease of pregnancy *see* pre-eclampsia
hypoglycaemia 193
hypokalaemia 88–9, 283, 308–9

ibuprofen *see* NSAIDs
impaired glucose tolerance 193–5
impotence 87, 215–17, 283, 307–8, 310, 317
indigestion 196–7
induction 231, 239, 244, 283–4
inflammatory arthritis 182–7
inhalers, asthma 189–92
inheritance
  ankylosing spondylitis 186
  high blood cholesterol 169–70, 171–2

inheritance *(continued)*
  high blood pressure 4, 41–2, 47, 191
  indicates that BP-lowering drugs may be needed 93, 220
  pre-eclampsia & eclampsia 236–7, 239
  and response to BP-lowering drugs 94
inherited familial hypercholesterolaemia 167, 170
insurance 46, 207–8, 211

joules, definition 122, 284

kidney damage
  assessing 49, 240, 241, 242
  effect of malignant hypertension 24, 25
  effect of pre-eclampsia 241–2
  effect of uncontrolled high BP 2, 80, 197, 252
  risk increased by diabetes 192, 195, 197
  risk reduced by treatment for high BP 90, 253
kidney failure
  BP-lowering drugs 197–8, 313
  effect of eclampsia 240
  effect of high blood potassium 89
  effect of uncontrolled high BP 2, 197, 252
  risk increased by diabetes 192
kilocalories, definition 122
kilojoules, definition 122

LDL cholesterol
  effect of cholesterol-lowering drugs 175–7

Index

effect of exercise 148
effect of fat in diet 144
levels in familial
   hypercholesterolaemia 170
measurement 167
what it is 166, 284
leg pain *see* claudication
legs, swollen *see* oedema
lifestyle modification 82–3
   see also individual topics, eg
   weight control
lipids 167, 284
lithium 199
liver damage 201, 317
long-term consequences *see*
   consequences of uncontrolled
   high blood pressure
loop diuretics 309
low blood potassium, and diuretics
   88–9, 180, 308–9
low blood pressure 17–18, 86, 87,
   117, 183
low density lipoprotein cholesterol
   see LDL cholesterol
'low fat' foods & spreads 139,
   140–1, 145
lupus erythematosus 314

magnesium, for eclampsia 236
malignant hypertension 16, 24–5,
   277, 284
margarine 135–6, 139, 140–1, 145
massage 159
measurements
   blood cholesterol 166–9
   blood potassium 180
   blood pressure *see* blood
     pressure measurements;
     sphygmomanometers
   peak flow 76, 154, 189
   sodium intake 147–8

meat 132–3, 134, 145, 165
mechanisms of action
   ACE-inhibitors 312
   alpha-blockers 314
   beta-blockers 309–10
   BP-lowering drugs 85–6
   calcium-channel blockers 315
   cholesterol-lowering drugs
     175–7
   diuretics 85, 306
   drugs acting mainly on the
     brainstem 316
   ganglion-blockers 318
   vasodilators 313
medicals, for work or insurance
   46, 202–3, 207–8
medication *see* drugs
meditation 159
menopause 33, 222–4
menstruation 33, 62
mercury sphygmomanometers 13,
   53
   accuracy 55–6, 77–8
   home use 68, 70–3
   purchasing considerations 77–8
methyldopa
   BP level reduction obtained 86
   combined with alcohol 109
   combined with drugs for other
     problems 111–12, 199, 200,
     211–12
   for elderly people 104, 316–17
   and liver damage 201, 317
   and rebound high blood
     pressure 99, 113
   side-effects 104, 199, 200,
     211–12, 317
   use in pregnancy 244, 316
micro-emboli 249–50, 265
midstream urine specimen 241
migraine 35

milk 133, 138, 139, 143
mmHg, definition 13, 284
mmol, definition 142, 166
monitoring treatment *see* follow-up
monosodium glutamate 5, 142
monounsaturated fats 139–41
morphine-related painkillers 184–5
mortgages 208–9
muscle, replacing body fat by muscle 121–2, 127
muscles surrounding arteries
  effect of BP-lowering drugs 85, 310, 315, 318
  role in altering BP 3, 12, 16
myocardial infarction *see* heart attacks

nasal decongestants 39
national variations
  blood cholesterol 166, 171–2
  numbers of people with high BP 26, 28, 45, 142–3
  treatment for high BP 205–7
nausea & vomiting 111–12, 211–13, 312
nicotine & nicotine substitutes 154, 155, 262
nicotinic acid 176–7
night sweats 33, 222, 223
nitroglycerin 178, 255
noise, possible cause of high BP 204
non-inflammatory arthritis 182–5
non-steroidal anti-inflammatory drugs 39–40, 62, 108, 182–3, 186–7, 284
nosebleeds 33
NSAIDs 39–40, 62, 108, 182–3, 186–7, 284

numbers of people
  with high blood pressure 1, 25–6, 28
  with pre-eclampsia 237–9
nurses
  accuracy in measuring BP 65–6
  discussing your health problems with them 162–3
  follow-up by 118–19
  holistic approach to treatment 157
  running weight-control groups 131
  training you to measure your own BP 68, 73, 77

obesity *see* overweight
obstetricians 230–1, 238, 239
oedema 241, 242–3, 284
oils
  olive 137, 140, 141
  vegetable 140, 141
  see also fats & oils
oily fish 134
olive oil 137, 140, 141
ophthalmoscopes 25, 35, 50, 116, 195, 284
oral contraceptives 8, 218–21
organ damage
  from untreated high BP *see* consequences of uncontrolled high blood pressure
  indicates that BP-lowering drugs may be needed 93
osteoarthritis 182–5
osteoporosis 223–4, 284, 307
outsize cuffs 60–1, 77–8, 121
over-the-counter drugs 39
  see also by type, eg aspirin
overbreathing 33
overtreatment 86, 87, 117, 207

Index

overweight
  associated health problems 121, 197
  BMI 124–5
  cause of high BP 4, 22, 36, 47, 120–1
  children 42–3
  and inaccurate BP measurements 60–1, 121
  reasons for weight gain 122, 138
  thrombosis prevention when travelling 209–10
  see also body fat; weight control

pain
  arthritis & joint pain 8, 182–8
  in back *see* spondylitis
  in chest *see* angina; heart attacks
  in legs *see* claudication
painkillers 39–40, 182–5
  see also by type, eg NSAIDs
palpitations 33–4, 222–3, 284
paracetamol 111, 183–4, 185
Parkinson's disease 199–200
peak flow measurements 76, 154, 189
periods, menstrual 33, 62
personality types 5, 37
PET *see* pre-eclampsia
phenothiazine drugs 200
PIH *see* pre-eclampsia
pill, contraceptive 8, 218–21
placebo effect 156, 271, 272, 284–5
placebos 270–2, 284
placenta 229, 237, 285
plaque 285
  effect on arteries 12–13, 81, 101, 164, 166, 237, 248
polyunsaturated fats 139–41

potassium
  effect of diuretics on blood potassium 88–9, 180, 308–9
  effect of intake on BP levels 36, 132
  foods high in potassium 88, 132
  in rehydration solutions 212–13
  supplements 88–9, 309
potassium sparing diuretics 88–9, 308–9
poultry 134, 139, 145
pre-eclampsia
  causes 236–7
  chances of developing it 237–9
  diagnosis 240–3
  effect on baby 239
  effect of diet 240
  fulminating 236
  inheritance 236–7, 239
  other names for 235–6
  symptoms 240–3
  treatment 244–5
  what it is 235, 285
pre-eclamptic toxaemia *see* pre-eclampsia
prednisolone *see* corticosteroids
pregnancy
  ACE-inhibitors not recommended 234, 313
  antenatal care providers 230–1, 238
  beta-blockers 234, 244, 311
  borderline between 'normal' & high BP 230, 240–1
  BP-lowering drugs 231–4
  BP measurements 228, 231, 233–4, 237, 240, 245
  calcium-channel blockers not recommended 234, 316
  causing fall in blood pressure 228–9

pregnancy *(continued)*
  diet 240, 243–4
  fainting 229–30
  methyldopa 244, 316
  'new' v. 'established' high BP 230–1
  oedema 241, 242–3
  protein in urine 232, 235–6, 240, 241–2
  thiazide diuretics not recommended 234, 308
  trimesters 229
  see also eclampsia; pre-eclampsia
pregnancy-induced hypertension *see* pre-eclampsia
pregnancy-related hypertension *see* pre-eclampsia
premature babies 229, 231, 239, 244
prescriptions
  prescription charges 96, 225–6, 308
  private 226, 288
  repeat 96, 111, 162–3, 219
preventers, asthma 189–91
prevention
  heart attacks 165, 256–7
  stroke 184, 265–6
  thrombosis when travelling 209–10
PRH *see* pre-eclampsia
prices *see* costs
primary high blood pressure 21–2, 277–8, 285
  causes 3–4, 21–2, 35–45, 94, 142–3, 204–5, 277
  in children 23
primary hypertension *see* primary high blood pressure
private prescriptions 226, 288

progestogen-only pill 219, 220
prostate, enlarged 63, 75, 198, 314–15
protein (type of food) 133, 243
protein in urine 49, 115, 195, 197
  in pregnancy 232, 235–6, 240, 241–2
publications & books 325–8
pulmonary circulation 11, 285
pulse
  brachial artery 68–9
  in groin, feet & ankles 47, 49
  wrist 34, 65, 66, 68–9, 71–3
pulses (type of food) 132–3, 135
pyelography 50

racial differences
  effect on BP levels 28
  response to BP-lowering drugs 95, 310, 312
randomised controlled trials 272–3, 285
rebound high blood pressure 99, 105, 112–13, 317
reflux oesophagitis 196–7
rehydration solutions 212–13, 312
relaxation 5, 83, 158–9
relievers, asthma 189–90, 192
repeat prescriptions 96, 111, 162–3, 219
research
  angina & CABGs 262
  cholesterol-lowering diets 171–2
  complementary therapies 156–7, 161
  high BP plus other health problems 163–4
  high BP in younger adults 99–100
  pre-eclampsia & eclampsia 239–40, 243–4, 245

research *(continued)*
  safety & effectiveness of BP-lowering drugs 89–90, 232–3
  taking part 273–6
  using animals 232, 268–9
  why it is needed 274
  see also trials
retina 285
  effect of malignant hypertension 24, 25
  effect of uncontrolled high BP 2, 50, 80, 195, 250, 252
  examining with ophthalmoscope 25, 35, 50, 116, 195, 252
  risk of damage increased by uncontrolled diabetes 195, 252
rheumatoid arthritis 182, 183, 185–6
risks from untreated high BP *see* consequences of uncontrolled high blood pressure
roughage *see* dietary fibre

saccharin 129, 142, 145
safety, BP-lowering drugs 89–90, 110, 113, 232–3
salads 135, 136–7
salt *see* sodium
salt substitutes 146
saturated fats 139–41
scales, accuracy 126–7
schizophrenia 97, 200
screening
  for high blood cholesterol 167–8, 174
  for high BP 29, 43, 99–100
'season ticket' 225–6
secondary high blood pressure 21–2, 285–6

secondary high blood pressure *(continued)*
  causes 21, 35–6, 44, 277
  in children 23, 34–5, 43
  diagnosis 48, 49, 50
  in younger adults 44
secondary hypertension *see* secondary high blood pressure
sedatives 83, 97
self-help & support groups 227
sex 214–18
shopping, carrying 226
side-effects 286
  aspirin 184
  asthma drugs 189–91
  BP-lowering drugs *see* side effects of BP-lowering drugs
  cholesterol-lowering drugs 173, 175–7
  corticosteroids 185–6
  morphine-related painkillers 185
  NSAIDs 182–3
side-effects of BP-lowering drugs 7–8, 87, 95, 204, 290
  in elderly people 103–5
  impotence 87, 215–16
  reporting them to your doctor 95, 114
  unexpected long-term side-effects 89–90, 101
  when using more than one drug 96, 308
  see also individual groups of drugs by name, eg beta-blockers *(complete list of groups on pages 290–291)*
sinus arrhythmia 34
sleep 5, 14, 16, 226
slow release drugs 90–1, 113, 260–1, 286, 316, 317

smoking
  and chest problems 152, 192
  effect on treatment for high BP 152–3
  increases risks associated with high BP 6, 80, 102, 152, 165, 253, 256, 264
  stopping 152–5, 158, 262–3, 265, 326–7
snacks 128, 138, 139, 143, 145
social class, effect on BP levels 27, 28
sodium
  and ACE-inhibitors 103, 109, 116, 312
  amounts found in food 5–6, 133, 142–7, 172
  in antacids 196
  connection with salt 142, 143, 146
  and diuretics 109, 306
  high intake as cause of high BP 5, 26, 36, 45, 142–3
  intake during pregnancy 243–4
  intake in national diets around the world 26, 45, 142–3, 172
  measuring your intake 147–8
  reducing intake 5–6, 133, 143–7
  in rehydration solutions 212–13
  in saccharin 129, 142, 145
sodium bicarbonate 135, 142, 147
sodium chloride 142
sodium glutamate 5, 142
sodium nitrate 142
soluble fibre 132–3
sounds heard when measuring blood pressure 13–14, 55, 72–4
sphygmomanometers 13, 52–4, 286
  accuracy 55–6, 60, 77–8
  fingertip models 58–9

sphygmomanometers *(continued)*
  home use 67–75
  purchasing considerations 76–8
  quality standards 56, 78
  suitability for use on children 64
  24–hour blood pressure monitors 56–8
  see also cuffs
spicy foods 132
spiral muscles surrounding arteries
  effect of BP-lowering drugs 85, 310, 315, 318
  role in altering BP 3, 12, 16
spondylitis 186–7
sports 38, 213–14
SR drugs 90–1, 113, 260–1, 286, 316, 317
standards, for sphygmomanometers 56, 78
static exercise 38, 151, 209, 213
statistics
  chances of developing pre-eclampsia or eclampsia 237–40
  numbers of people with high BP 1, 25–6, 28
  used by mortgage & insurance companies 208–9
steroids *see* corticosteroids
stethoscopes 55, 70
stress
  during pregnancy 243
  possible cause of high BP 5, 18, 36–8
  stress reduction 5, 83, 158–9
stroke 286
  aspirin 184, 265
  causes 250, 253, 264
  death rates 26, 28

Index

stroke *(continued)*
  declining treatment 267
  distinguishing from Bell's palsy 266–7
  indicates that BP-lowering drugs may be needed 93, 98
  minor strokes 51, 265
  prevention 184, 265–6
  risk from high alcohol intake 132, 264
  risk increased by diabetes 192, 264
  risk increased by high BP 2, 19, 20, 22, 45, 80
  risk increased by rebound high BP 105
  risk reduction 90, 101, 121, 138, 149, 253
  and sex 218
  warning signs 264–5
subconjunctival haemorrhages 33, 286
sugar 128, 129–30, 136, 140–1
support & self-help groups 227
sustained release drugs 90–1, 113, 260–1, 286, 316, 317
sweeteners, artificial 129–30, 142
swollen legs *see* oedema
symptoms
  of consequences of high blood pressure 114–15
  heart attacks 254–5
  heart failure 179, 263
  high blood pressure *see* symptoms of high blood pressure
  low blood pressure 17–18, 117
  menopause 33, 222–3
  pre-eclampsia 240–3
symptoms of high blood pressure 31–5

symptoms of high blood pressure *(continued)*
  absence of symptoms 3, 18–19, 31–2
  in children 34–5
  malignant hypertension 25
systemic circulation 11, 286
systolic pressure 13–14, 55, 72–3, 81–2, 286

target blood pressure after treatment 80, 114, 116–17
target weight 126
tension
  in artery walls 18, 36
  in the mind *see* stress
terminal illness, declining treatment during 267
tests
  blood tests 48–9, 115, 166–7, 317
  for causes & effects of high blood pressure 48–51, 115–16
  eye tests 25, 35, 50, 116, 195
  urine tests 48–9, 115, 195, 197, 232, 240–2
thiazide diuretics 306–8
  combined with ACE-inhibitors 87, 103, 108, 116, 312–13
  combined with other BP-lowering drugs 96, 308
  effect on blood potassium 88–9, 308
  effect on diabetes 104, 193–5, 308
  effect on gout 186–7
  effect on osteoporosis 223–4, 307
  for elderly people 104, 193–5
  ethnic variations in response 95
  first introduced 93
  low doses most effective 307

thiazide diuretics *(continued)*
   not recommended in kidney failure 198
   not recommended with lithium treatment 199
   not recommended in pregnancy 234, 308
   with potassium supplements 84, 88–9, 308–9
   side-effects 104, 216, 307–8
   for younger adults 102–3
thrombosis 209–10, 242–3, 286
   coronary *see* heart attacks
TIAs 90, 93, 184, 249–50, 265, 286–7
tiredness 95, 117, 310, 317
total blood cholesterol 167, 170, 286
toxaemia 286
trade names *see* brand names
tranquillisers 83, 97
transient ischaemic attacks 90, 93, 184, 249–50, 265, 286–7
travel
   holidays 209–13
   insurance 208, 211
   travel sickness & diarrhoea 211–13
   working abroad 205–7
treatment
   angina 177–8, 259–63
   ankylosing spondylitis 186–7
   arthritis 182–6
   asthma & other breathing problems 188–92
   claudication 178
   declining when terminally ill 267
   depression 198–9
   eclampsia 236
   fibrillation 180–1
   fulminating pre-eclampsia 236

treatment *(continued)*
   gout 187–8
   heart attacks 255–6
   heart failure 180–1, 264
   heartburn 196–7
   high blood pressure *see* treatment for high blood pressure
   impotence 216–17
   Parkinson's disease 200
   pre-eclampsia 236, 244–5
   schizophrenia 200
   ulcers 195–6
treatment for high blood pressure
   affected by other health problems 162–4 *and see also those other problems by name, eg* heart failure
   aims of treatment 22, 76, 80
   BP measurements needed before taking decisions on treatment 3, 46, 59, 63–4, 82, 92, 98–9, 105–6, 113–14, 207
   with drugs *see* BP-lowering drugs
   economic factors 28–30
   failure to respond to treatment 116–17, 132
   future changes 277–8
   guidelines for doctors 81, 94, 290, 328
   holistic approach 156, 157
   monitoring *see* follow-up
   national variations 205–7
   obtaining when abroad 205–7
   options 80–1
   for particular age groups *see* children; elderly people; younger adults
   reasons for 19–20, 79–80, 90, 101, 247–9, 253

Index

treatment for high blood pressure *(continued)*
  for smokers 152–3
  taking responsibility for your own treatment 1–2, 8
  without drugs 82–3, 92, 99–100, 102 *and see also individual topics, eg* weight control
trials
  clinical 269–70, 272–6, 280
  controlled 269–70, 272–5, 281
  double-blind 272, 273, 282
  drug 89–90, 269, 282
  randomised controlled 272–3, 285
  taking part 273–6
  uncontrolled 270
triglyceride 134, 167, 176, 287
trimesters 229
24–hour blood pressure monitors 56–8

ulcers 88, 184, 195–6
uncontrolled trials 270
units
  blood cholesterol 166
  blood pressure measurements 13
  energy measurements 122
  sodium intake 142
unsaturated fats 139–41
uric acid 187
urine collection
  kidney function check 240, 241
  sodium intake measurement 147–8
urine output, effect of diuretics 306, 309
urine tests 48–9, 115, 195, 197, 232, 240–2
uterus 237, 242, 287

vaginal dryness 223
vasodilators 93, 245, 313–14
vegans 133
vegetable oils 140, 141
vegetables 128–9, 132, 135, 136–7, 145, 147, 264
vegetarian diet 132–4
veins 242, 287
venous blood pressure 11–12, 242, 287
venules 287
vertebrobasilar insufficiency 250
very low density lipoprotein cholesterol *see* VLDL cholesterol
viscosity, blood 13
VLDL cholesterol 148, 166, 167, 170, 175–7, 287
vomiting & nausea 111–12, 211–13, 312

water tablets *see* diuretics
wealth, effect on BP levels 27, 28
weight control
  BMI 124–5
  books & publications 129, 325–6
  combining diet & exercise 121–2, 127, 129, 148
  crash diets not recommended 127
  and diabetes 121, 192
  effect on BP 4, 102, 120–2, 277
  and healthy eating 131–7, 138–9
  for heartburn 197
  recommended diet 4, 127–9, 138
  recommended weight loss rate 126–7
  role of artificial sweeteners 129–30
  target weight 126

weight control *(continued)*
  weighing yourself 126–7, 129
  weight-reduction groups 130–1
  younger adults 102, 120–1, 277
weight gain, reasons for 122, 138
white coat hypertension 23–4, 57–8, 61–2, 287
work 202–7
wrist pulse 34, 65, 66, 68–9, 71–3

X-rays 50

yoga 159

younger adults
  causes of high BP 22, 43–4, 277
  effect of weight control on control of BP 102, 120–1, 277
  high alcohol intake as cause of high BP 4, 22, 62, 131–2, 200–1, 277
  irregular pulse 34
  obtaining mortgages 208–9
  overweight as cause of high BP 4, 22, 120–1, 138, 277
  treatment 20–1, 80, 99–103, 132, 277